Superhighway Robbery

Crime Science Series

Series editor: Gloria Laycock (Jill Dando Institute of Crime Science, University College London)

The Crime Science Series is the first to be devoted to international research and practice on crime reduction. By this we mean not only the prevention of crime using the now standard approaches offered by situational crime prevention, but also the study of detection and the development of scientific strategies and tactics aimed at increasing the repertoire available to the police and their partners – and all within an ethical framework.

There are huge gaps in our knowledge that this series aims to fill. It should prove relevant to scholars and students with an interest in crime prevention but also to the police and their criminal justice and community partners. One of the greatest challenges facing us today is to continue with the development of new goods and services, which provide yet more criminal opportunities, but to do so in ways that do not lead to inexorable increases in crime.

Titles in the series

Superhighway Robbery: preventing e-commerce crime, by Graeme R. Newman and Ronald V. Clarke

Crime Reduction and Problem-oriented Policing, edited by Karen Bullock and Nick Tilley

Superhighway Robbery
Preventing e-commerce crime

Graeme R. Newman

and

Ronald V. Clarke

WILLAN
PUBLISHING

Published by

Willan Publishing
Culmcott House
Mill Street, Uffculme
Cullompton, Devon
EX15 3AT, UK
Tel: +44(0)1884 840337
Fax: +44(0)1844 840251
e-mail: info@willanpublishing.co.uk
Website: @www.willanpublishing.co.uk

Published simultaneously in the USA and Canada by

Willan Publishing
c/o ISBS, 5824 N.E. Hassalo St,
Portland, Oregon 97213-3644, USA
Tel: +001(0)503 287 3093
Fax: +001(0)503 280 8832
Website: www.isbs.com

First published 2003

ISBN 1-84392-018-2

British Library Cataloguing-in-Publication Data
A catalogue record of this book is available from the British Library

Typeset by Pantek Arts Ltd, Maidstone, Kent
Printed and Bound by T.J. International, Padstow, Cornwall

Contents

Foreword
by Gloria Laycock

Notwithstanding the crime falls of the late twentieth century, crime levels in advanced western democracies remain unacceptably high. The response of many governments to this has effectively been 'more of the same': more police, bigger prisons, a streamlined court system, faster 'justice'. If immediate reductions in crime are needed, the best on offer seem to be community penalties or restorative justice. And there are a plethora of studies and reports suggesting that if these responses work at all, they do so only to a limited extent. Something else is needed.

In this book, Newman and Clarke show the way. They provide a systematic analysis of the burgeoning crime opportunities offered by the Internet and e-commerce. Situational crime prevention retains elements of social constructionist views of behaviour and also recognizes the importance of dispositions, but focuses on the ways in which this knowledge can be applied to prevent crime. Prevention of crime is its key concern. The causes of crime or the liberation of deviants are not.

The beginning assumption is simple. Information technology has brought tremendous efficiencies into the marketplace, spawning what we now call 'e-commerce'. Business has been quick to take advantage of the new opportunities it provides: online payment systems, retailing web sites, databases to track customer preferences and interests, tracking of product and many more. The new opportunities offered by e-commerce have also provided new opportunities for those who would commit crime. These opportunities are vast. The electronic nature of the marketplace means that the link of crime to specific geographic location has been severed. Crime can be committed internationally and may create simultaneously millions of victims. The situational approach says: 'What practically and specifically can be done to prevent or reduce this victimization?'

Newman and Clarke proceed to review the current scene of crime in the e-commerce environment, and analyse systematically the delivery systems of e-commerce that bring products and services to customers, and identify the points of risk and opportunities provided for crime that these systems offer offenders. In doing so they draw on a wide range of literature, including business management and marketing, security management, information technology, and the extant research on situational crime prevention that also incorporates relevant literature of psychology, sociology and economics analysis. Crimes – both new and old – are identified in the information society: extortion, terrorism, fraud, theft, and computer crime are surveyed and their uniquely new applications in the e-commerce environment outlined.

The identification of the opportunities for crime in the e-commerce environment is followed by an account of the specific steps that can be taken to prevent e-commerce crime at particular points of risk. The authors here show how two different aspects of situational crime prevention can be brought to bear to prevent crime: to use a narrow approach to analyse specific situations where opportunity presents itself to the offender, and to use a broad approach to garner the necessary resources and partnerships needed to introduce the changes and modifications to situations that are necessary to reduce or remove criminal opportunity.

In the narrow approach, the authors apply the widely used 'sixteen techniques of situational crime prevention' to the points of vulnerability to crime of e-commerce revealed in the book. In doing so, they demonstrate the power of the situational approach to adapt to a rapidly changing environment of criminal opportunity. The broad approach of situational crime prevention leads to an assessment of the role of control in society, the identification of active and passive control and the ways in which various kinds of control can be applied. The major organizations and institutions that function to implement control in society are considered in the light of how they may provide partnerships or cooperate in modifying crime provoking situations in the informational technology environment.

This account of control confronts the most difficult choice facing modern democracies in the twenty-first century: how to hold individuals accountable for their actions (both criminal and non-criminal) without demanding that they give up too much of their privacy or freedom.

The question of what is 'too much' hinges not so much on rules of principle, but upon the ultimate price to be paid if we do not act preventively. Technology makes it possible to exercise massive degrees of control through the use of advanced tracking technology. But technology also makes it possible for motivated individuals to bring terror to people on a massive scale, including the use of weapons of mass destruction. Since the tragedy of 9/11 we understand that we cannot wait for such crimes to occur. Rather, prevention is in this case the only cure. The authors therefore conclude with a challenge to criminology of the twentieth century: give prevention a central place, or become irrelevant.

Gloria Laycock
Jill Dando Institute of Crime Science
University College London
June 2003

Preface

This book grew out of papers prepared for the Foresight Panel on Crime Prevention, Department of Trade and Industry.[1] That panel, composed of leading executives from business, the Civil Service and academia, was concerned to address the new opportunities for crime that will emerge in the twenty-first century. The chairman of the panel succinctly summed up the mission of the panel in his foreword to the publication *Turning the Corner on Crime*:

> The future may offer increased opportunities for crime unless we prepare now…we need to ensure that a crime is made harder to commit but when it happens detection is assisted by the best technology available…
> (Lord Sharman of Redlynch, Chairman, Foresight Crime Prevention Panel)

To attempt to predict the future is a well-known folly, but in the realm of e-commerce, the future is already here. The speed of technological innovation has moved forward dramatically in the past ten years. It is not so much that we need to prepare for the new opportunities for future crime as it is that we need to catch up with those that have already presented themselves.

The request we received from the Foresight panel was to examine specifically the crime risks in the delivery system of products to e-commerce consumers, but we expanded our approach to deal with e-commerce crime generally. In turn this required us to deal with general and specific characteristics of the information technology environment in order to give context to our situational analysis. Although situational crime prevention has enjoyed wide application to many different crime problems, we have been surprised at just how well the approach fitted with the information technology environment. The idea

of information as a 'hot product' virtually wrote itself, and it was aston-
ishing to find the vast numbers of crime opportunities in the e-commerce
environment.

We write this book in a period of economic turbulence and fear of terrorism
in the USA and elsewhere. These concerns have accentuated and perhaps
exaggerated basic issues that preoccupy many political scientists and other
students of society. There is an increased demand by both people and governments for more and better security – especially prevention of crime rather than
trying to cope afterwards with the damage it has done. There is also a clamour
for more transparency in the keeping of corporate accounts, given the debacles
of the collapse of Enron and the deceptive accounting of WorldCom. At a minimum, these debacles reflect the failure to apply classic auditing techniques
that are specifically designed to prevent the kinds of massive frauds that have
allegedly been committed by these and other companies in recent times. These
techniques resemble quite closely the approach of situational crime prevention, particularly the more recent innovations in CAATT (Computer Assisted
Audit Tools and Techniques), which applies pattern analysis and analytical
reviews to company electronic records. That these techniques were not
applied, even by those charged with the responsibility of applying them, has
been well publicised in the media. Why they were not applied is a question
that regrettably reaches beyond the subject of this book. For it is a question
that can be answered only by a careful analysis of corporate organisation and
the structure and politics of the business world, issues that are examined by
many texts concerning business practices and white-collar crime.

This is not to say that situational crime prevention is irrelevant to wider
political and business issues. In fact, in Chapter 7, we do address some
issues about how to implement situational crime prevention techniques that
depend on marshalling cooperative relationships among business, government, trade associations and citizen groups. We also address what we
consider to be the few essential issues of the future of situational crime prevention in the e-commerce environment in the concluding chapter, where
we are led to a discussion of the broader philosophical and political issues of
surveillance, privacy and identity in the information age, and to a consideration of the place of situational crime prevention in modern criminology.

In Chapters 2, 5 and 6 we draw heavily on a paper by Alan McKinnon
and Deepak Tallam (Logistics Research Centre, Heriot-Watt University,
Edinburgh), work also commissioned by the Foresight Panel on Crime, for
an assessment of the risks involved in changes in home delivery systems
as a result of the rise in home shopping and retailing on the Internet. Their
detailed knowledge of the business practices and delivery systems in
retailing, plus the information they collected from interviewing individuals in the field, demonstrate the considerable complexities in moving
products from manufacturer to customer. Hopefully, their work helps to

link our more theoretical approach to the everyday problems presented by the delivery of goods to the home that have been drastically expanded as a result of the increase in home shopping spawned by the facilities of e-commerce.

Many individuals and organisations have assisted our work. We operated under the auspices of the Jill Dando Institute of Crime Science, University College London and we are grateful to Gloria Laycock, the Institute's Director, and her colleague, Nick Tilley, for their many helpful suggestions. Phyllis Schultze of the Rutgers/NCCD Library of Criminal Justice at Rutgers University helped us very much with the acquisition of source materials. Without her help, we could not have completed this book.

Graeme R. Newman and Ronald V. Clarke
May 2003

Note

1   These papers were: 'Etailing: new opportunities for crime, new opportunities for prevention', by Graeme R. Newman and Ronald V. Clarke (April, 2002: http://www.foresight.gov.uk/default1024.htm) and 'New crime threats from etailing: theft in the home delivery channel', by Alan McKinnon and Deepak Tallam (April 2002: http://www.foresight.gov.uk/default1024.htm).

Chapter 1

Situational crime prevention in the information society

'He that will not apply new remedies must expect new evils, for time is the greatest innovator.'

Sir Francis Bacon (Nader, 1966: viii)

In this book we move situational crime prevention to the apex of societal change, the prime feature of that change being the revolution in information technology. We argue that, although many of the security principles of situational crime prevention have been around for many centuries, its unique feature is that it can be adapted to changing conditions and environments. If we are successful in convincing the reader of this thesis, then we will have fulfilled the promise of situational crime prevention described – somewhat ambivalently – by David Garland (2001) in his book *Culture of Control*. Garland characterised situational crime prevention as an approach of criminology that emerged as a result of certain changing conditions of 'late modern' society. He identified those conditions as changes in the structure of the family and household, changes in social ecology and demography, the democratisation of social life, and the electronic mass media. He does not, however, single out information technology as an unremitting force that has changed and continues to change the basic fabric of society[1]. This book ascribes to information technology a much heavier role in regard to the new opportunities for crime that it has spawned, and also accentuates the close link that exists – and has always existed – between situational crime prevention and technology.

Garland also argued that situational crime prevention emerged as a conservative reaction against the 'penal welfare' theories advanced in the post Second World War UK and USA, theories that favoured researching the social and psychological causes of crime, and recommending such solutions to crime as eradicating poverty, redistribution of wealth through taxation, welfare for the poor, and an emphasis on rehabilitation in corrections. During this period the police were also 'professionalised'. They became the prime keepers of law and order, but they also became more distant from the community as patrols were motorised. The research of the

1

1970s, which claimed that 'nothing works', spawned the conservative reaction against the solutions to crime offered by the society of penal welfare, and it was situational crime prevention that emerged as a beneficiary of the 'nothing works' conclusions that resulted from that research. Whether or not these conclusions were overdrawn, situational crime prevention has a convincing record that *it* works. In this book, we go further and show that it will work in new settings and conditions. By 'work' of course, we mean reduce or prevent crime, and in this book, this means specific sorts of crime that occur in the e-commerce environment.

To advance this claim we argue that the information revolution forms the vast backdrop of late modern society. While changes in lifestyle, family structure and authority, and all the rest of the sociological and cultural changes identified by scholars such as Garland, are no doubt significant and have in themselves created conditions for new patterns of crime to emerge, we think that technology lies behind all these factors. It would, of course, take another book to prove any kind of causal ordering of such an arrangement. This we do not claim. However, we do want to argue that information technology lies both in the background and foreground of societal change. Information technology is part of the background of modern society because it is part of its ancient history. The 'revolution' (hardly the correct word for a process that has continued unremittingly since the birth of civilisations everywhere) in information technology began when writing was first invented. Whether first chiselled on stone or painted on tablets or papyrus, this was the first crucial step of the information revolution. It transformed deeds and ideas into written symbols and it separated words and ideas from their owners (that is to say, those who remembered them and communicated them orally to others). It created a way to store information that existed apart from the brains of individuals. Without it, civilisation as we know it could not exist.

Changes in the technology of information storage and transmission have also had enormous effects on the direction and growth of civilisations. The invention of the printing press in Europe, coupled later with significant advances in transportation, began the steady movement towards the democratisation of knowledge (the precursor to the democratisation of social life to which Garland refers), making information of all kinds available to all who could read. We would hesitate to argue which came first: widespread literacy or the availability of texts for people to read, but our guess is that technology makes things possible and behaviour follows unremittingly. In our own time, it is surely clear that computers came on the scene well before most people could use them. It was not until computers became easy to use – in contrast to the large mainframes whose operations were jealously guarded by specialists – that computing became ubiquitous. And the 'final' step in the last decade of the twentieth century was the Internet that made the sharing, transmission and storage of information virtually infinite, and most importantly accessible to everyone. This is the point at which information technology has inserted itself into the foreground of our lives – very much the foreground if one includes as part of the information revolution the pervasive presence of the mass media of television, radio and mass circulation newspapers. Not only is information technology in the foreground, it is *in our faces* constantly. The interesting late modern twist is that the onset of cable and satellite TV and the news distribution via the Internet has provided to individuals the option of choosing what they will listen to, watch or read. Furthermore, the Internet makes it possible even for individuals with little capital to publish their own information to millions of potential readers. Thus technology continues its unrelenting march towards the creation of wonderful opportunities for expansion of knowledge. It also creates opportunities for commerce by introducing new ways to track products and customers, and new efficiencies in servicing customers and moving product.

We are not alone in painting this picture of the benefits of information technology to society. The economist Peter Drucker (2001) has convincingly argued that the twenty-first century will be the century in which knowledge and knowledge professionals dominate the economy and society.[2] It will be (if it is not already) a society that will be driven by information and knowledge. At the heart of this revolution is the breathtaking speed at which information is transmitted and bears down on society, constantly providing new ways of communicating, of preserving and accessing knowledge, and of tracking persons and objects. These changes bring with them tremendous opportunities to enhance older ways of doing business, such as robotic and distributed manufacturing[3] (Bharat, 1999) and the sale of goods and services through the Internet – e-commerce.

There is a downside of course. While these changes are revolutionising commerce, they have also brought with them new opportunities to commit crime. From a situational crime prevention perspective this is to be expected. In the twentieth century the mass production of the automobile helped spawn the crime sprees of such criminal 'heroes' as Bonnie and Clyde. While one may say that a bank robbery is still a bank robbery regardless of the getaway vehicle, the robbers' use of a car has considerable implications for prevention and enforcement. In fact, the automobile was ubiquitous in much of organised crime of the early 1900s, and it greatly expanded crime opportunities for many ordinary criminals. Today, the computer, as we will see, is a much more efficient means of escape from the scene of the crime. A comparison between crime patterns that emerged as a result of two rather different (though ultimately closely connected) technologies – the invention of the automobile and the invention of the Internet – helps identify how technology itself actually makes new crimes possible.

3

Figure 1.1 Motoring offences (UK) and hacking (USA) incidents reported in their first years of life.

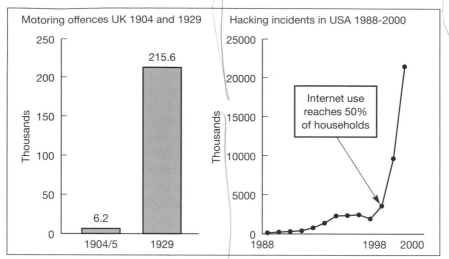

Sources: Motoring offences: Plowden, William (1971) *The Motor Car and Politics 1896–1970*. London: Bodley Head, Appendix A, p. 454. Hacking incidents: CERT/CC, Carnegie Mellon.

Figure 1.1 portrays the total volume of reported motoring offences and computer hacking incidents for which data are available for the first years after the new technologies became accessible to the public. There are some clear difficulties in interpreting these data, not the least of which is that they come from different countries, and they report actual volume, not rates, so it is difficult to know for sure exactly what it is that is measured[4]. However, the considerable increase in the incidents for each cannot be interpreted in any other way than by the obvious fact that the opportunities for such crimes were made possible by technology: the creation of the automobile and the networked computer[5]. The data on hacking offers persuasive evidence that the dramatic rise in hacking incidents coincides with Internet usage reaching 50 per cent of households. This chart furthermore considerably underestimates Internet access since many individuals access the computer either at school, home or at public places such as libraries and Internet cafes. As we shall see, the opportunities for hacking are considerably enhanced by the Internet. Before the Internet, hacking into corporate or government computers was confined to persons with specialised knowledge or insider information, or both.

Another point we would emphasise concerns the origin of these data. In the case of motoring offences it was, and continues to be, the Home Office. In the case of hacking, it is an entirely private, university-based organisation called CERT/CC. This difference points up one important way in which control of crime has changed in late modern society, and supports Garland's (2001) claim that control is spreading horizontally throughout society. That is, more and more of crime control is becoming part of the normal activities of groups and organisations whose traditional responsibility has not been the control of crime. Or to put it another way, responsibility for crime control is being shed by central governments on to private or quasi-private organisations. From the point of view of the history of information technology, we could say that control of crime is itself going through a democratising process. It could be argued of course that we have here compared apples and oranges. Motoring offences are, after all, *offences* with the status of having been reported to government policing authorities and eventually recounted by the Home Office. In contrast, the hacking incidents result from reports that people or organisations make to a private organisation. So, strictly speaking – even legally speaking – they aren't crimes at all. However, the damage that these hacking incidents wreak is considerable, potentially far worse than many motoring offences. Furthermore, we think it reasonable to argue that a legalistic approach does not help solve the problems created by hacking and other computer-related crimes. Calling these acts crimes merely attaches a label that immediately narrows the possible response to one of punishment. Nor does it even help to think of hacking incidents as at the early stage of becoming defined as a crime by some kind of criminal justice processing. Such a process certainly operates in regard to motoring offences, where offences are detected or reported by police, offenders charged and, depending on the offences, sent to trial or dealt summarily with a fine. The situational crime prevention approach, however, makes no essential distinction in regard to such problems of definition. Incidents that produce harm, loss or damage are the focus of situational crime prevention. For many years they have also been the concern of security managers in large and small corporations. And there has been a slowly growing trend on the part of business to see criminal justice agencies as not well equipped or prepared to solve corporate and even public security problems. The approach of problem oriented policing that focuses on problems rather than crimes is heavily influenced by this perspective advanced by situational crime prevention. All of these observations fit neatly into Garland's argument that control in late modern society is becoming increasingly amorphous, steadily moving away from the idea that a centrally organised government should solve or even take responsibility for crime control or prevention. It is with this mindset that we apply in this book the principles of situational crime prevention to the e-commerce environment.

E-commerce is generally taken to mean the conduct of buying and selling – mostly retailing, though increasingly including business-to-business sales – in the new environment of information technology. The situational crime prevention approach directs us to focus on the specific situations in which opportunities for crime occur. It is a challenge to apply this approach to the information technology environment because of the obvious difficulties in defining what situations are in cyberspace. There is also some difficulty in defining what is and is not computer crime. Many crimes have been identified over the past ten years as 'typical' of the computing environment. Yet some of these are simply old crimes given a new face (Law Commission, 1988; Nimmer, 1985). Some computer crimes directly threaten the e-commerce environment, while others do so indirectly. However, all such crimes affect the e-commerce environment in the same way that crime affects any neighbourhood. There is extensive evidence that if crimes of any kind are allowed to proliferate, their effect on the neighbourhood is to provide an attractive setting for more crimes of a different sort, usually more serious crimes (Wilson and Kelling, 1982). So too on the Internet. If investment or medical frauds, for example, are allowed to proliferate, they provide a climate for other kinds of crime, and they also affect the public perception that in turn may affect consumer confidence in buying products on the Internet.

Much of a highly technical nature has been written over the past decade on 'computer security' in response to the losses that have resulted from computer crimes of various kinds (mostly hacking). However, there has been little systematic attention given to the specific situations and settings in which computer crime occurs in the e-commerce environment. Hacking by outsiders is only one of many sources of loss to the e-commerce enterprise. While the information age provides the general backdrop for crime, situational prevention helps to identify specific vulnerabilities of e-commerce and to provide a range of appropriate remedies. This book identifies the 'broken windows' of the e-commerce 'neighbourhood' and proposes a range of remedies by adapting the widely used 16 techniques of situational crime prevention to the e-commerce environment (Clarke, 1997). In the past, situational crime prevention has been mostly applied to particular types of theft, and to a limited degree to specific kinds of assaults. Some of these studies have focused on settings that might be defined as those produced by the 'information society' such as the use of caller ID and the theft of cell phones, but most have focused on what may be loosely called 'traditional settings'.

In order to apply situational crime prevention to the e-commerce environment, it is obviously important to have a clear idea of what that approach entails. There is now a considerable body of both theoretical and empirical research supporting the situational crime prevention approach. The following general outline describes situational crime prevention as it is applied in this book. It has become apparent in recent years that there is some confusion as to what the situational crime prevention approach encompasses. Clarke has pointed out, for example, that there is a narrow and a broad conception of situational crime prevention (Clarke, 2000). The narrow conception tends to stay closely rooted to analysis of specific situations of crime. The broad conception is more aligned to issues of developing public policy and general inferences concerning crime control. Both approaches are relevant to the e-commerce environment. In general, we use the narrow approach when analysing specific situations, particularly the transactions that occur in the course of e-commerce buying and selling. However, we use the broad approach when we discuss ways of modifying situations, largely because modifying situations in the e-commerce environment leads to factors that lie beyond one specific situation.

Situational crime prevention

Much has been written on what encompasses the situational approach to the understanding, prevention or reduction of crime. We may characterise the *approach* as involving the following four elements:

1. It primarily seeks to solve crime problems in an action setting. Its approach is very similar to that of 'operations research' (Wilkins, 1997) in which the researcher works closely with those persons who are actually on the job (e.g. police, victims and others who are involved in situations in which specific crimes occur). The problem or problems are pinpointed, data are collected (sometimes in reverse order if it is difficult to identify the specific problem[6] without first having collected the data) and solutions adopted. Then data are collected to find out whether the solution was successful.

2. Its methodology is to analyse and break down an identified crime problem into its specific parts, using whatever scientific techniques will do the job. Situational crime prevention is uncomfortable with general crime categories such as 'theft', preferring instead much more specificity (e.g. 'theft from shopping bags in marketplaces', or 'theft from cars in parking lots').[7]

3. Situations in which crimes occur are the focus of study for they demand specificity: they provide concrete clues to both the behaviour of the criminals and how the environment (both social and physical) – as seen through the prism of the situation – may be changed to affect criminal behaviour.

4. As an explanatory theory of crime it is unique in that it assumes the explicit value of preventing or reducing the identified crime problem. The approach, therefore, is unabashedly value-driven (Newman, 1997a).

We may characterise the *theory* about criminal behaviour as involving the following four assumptions:

1. Criminals carry out their crimes according to a limited rationality. That is, given their commitment to achieving the particular goal of their crime (e.g. robbery of a bank) they follow a rational course of action that will lead them to completion of that task. Of course their goal (robbing a particular bank) may or may not be a rational choice of action in itself, depending on their life circumstances (Cornish and Clarke, 1986; Opp, 1997).

2. Modifying a situation to make it more difficult to complete a criminal project is the logical response to criminal behaviour.

3. Personal predispositions and other causes of crime (e.g. family history, race, heredity, social class) are relegated to a place of secondary importance in understanding crime. This is because they are viewed as (a) variables that are too abstract and non-specific (Newman, 1997b) and (b) factors that are not generally accessible to direct change, as are situations (Clarke, 1995).

4. The extent to which criminals can be prevented from carrying out their 'mission' depends on the strength of commitment that they have to completing their crime. Introducing barriers at bank counters may thwart those specific kinds of robberies. If the criminal is committed, another way will be found. In various forms, this is called displacement (Clarke, 1995).

All the above points have been thoroughly discussed in the literature, so it is not necessary to repeat that discussion here. Instead, we identify a few salient issues that seem to be especially relevant to a discussion of situational crime prevention applied to the e-commerce environment, beginning with the nature of situations.

Virtual situations?

Recent work on situational crime prevention theory has expanded the parameters of the situation considerably. In its initial conception, the idea was confined to a physical setting, derived from the work of environmental criminologists who developed the concept of CPTED (or crime prevention through environmental design). The arrangement of public space, such as the design and layout of public housing, shopping malls and parking lots, were the focus of study (Jeffery, 1971; Newman, 1972). However, it is clear that thinking of situations as confined to one particular place is very limiting. Today, situational crime prevention has imported ideas from cognitive psychology into the situational analysis. Individuals' perceptions of the situations have been included in a substantial revision of the original table of twelve features of situational crime prevention, resulting from criticisms that the idea of 'limited rationality' depended on how the individual actor perceived the situation (Wortley, 1996). Changing situations without knowledge of how they were perceived, it was argued, ran the risk of the researcher assuming that the situations (even if physical settings) were perceived in one way by all participants, when in fact they may be perceived in a different way by the criminals. It is apparent, though, that once the argument is conceded that different individuals perceive situations differently, the question of what is a real situation becomes a problem. Situations may indeed exist inside people's heads, as Katz has eloquently argued: '…the causes of crime are constructed by the offenders themselves, but the causes they construct are lures and pressures that they experience as independently moving them toward crime' (Katz, 1988: 216). Offenders actually construct situations internally, he claims, and then react to these constructions as though they were real (physical).

While this is an obviously important issue, in defence of the original more narrow conception of the situation, one would expect that, as researchers worked in the action setting with those 'on the job', they would necessarily discover how the situations were perceived by all actors involved. That is to say, while individuals may vary widely as to how they perceive the same situation, there may yet be sufficient commonality in their perceptions to allow general inferences to be drawn. These general inferences are also made by Katz who might be considered the most extreme proponent of the situation-as-perception. The assumption also forms the basis of the entire approach of Erving Goffman's classic analyses of everyday social interactions.

An example of how situational prevention assesses a situation in both physical and 'virtual' terms is that of obscene phone calls. Obscene phone calls are made from a physical place, but the elements of this place may vary considerably, and do not include the physical place of the recipient. In fact to describe the 'situation' in physical terms is seriously to misconstrue it. The situation in this case is constructed of two people who may be miles apart, a minimum of two telephones also distant from each other, plus the means of connection between the two, which may be via a complex of wires and cables, or via various kinds of microwaves, or a combination of all these. The physical settings of each telephone may also vary. The obscene caller may call from a public pay phone, or from a stolen cell phone, and so on. However, the most significant feature that made obscene phone calling possible is the fact that the two individuals (the caller and the victim) are strangers to each other, and the obscene caller could remain completely anonymous (until changes in information technology occurred in the 1980s allowing caller ID). Anonymity in committing a crime is an obviously desirable element to the offender. It is the major defining element of the situation of obscene phone calling, along with the physical elements just described. And anonymity is not a purely physical feature of a situation. In fact it is essentially an element of *information*. And in the twenty-first century, where does one find information? Traditionally we have found it in books, but today we find it more and more in and between computers, fleeting through space on beams of light or waves of sound. We call this cyberspace. And throughout this book we will demonstrate that the prime ingredient of cyberspace is information that both defines and constructs situations in which crime occurs. It is, we argue, a 'hot product' that resides in the 'hot context' of cyberspace, providing many new opportunities to commit crimes of many different kinds. Opportunity is the second important feature of situational crime prevention.

Opportunity structure and social structure

Examining situations in which crimes occur leads us to look for the opportunities that situations provide for the offender or intending offender to commit crimes of specific kinds. This approach is commonly referred to as analysing the opportunity structure of crimes (Clarke, 1995). Analysts begin with the situation or situations in which the crime occurs, and almost always find that these general settings can be broken down into increasingly small component parts. The ways in which this is accomplished may depend on the facilities or access to information available. It may require the collection of information from participants in the situations in which the crime occurs, such as offenders, victims and law enforcement personnel. Information collected, however, is always focused on how the crime is committed, what facilitates its commission, what barriers are avoided or overcome by the offender, and so on. This focus leads to a mapping of the opportunity structure of the crime, and hopefully the points at which the course of action taken by the offender can be thwarted. In sum, the conceptual approach is on 'how' not 'why' – although the answers to 'little whys' may be sought along the way, such as why did the burglar choose this house to enter rather than another. But the big sociological why, the why of 'the causes of crime', is not addressed.

There is an important reason for this. As noted above, situational crime prevention demands specificity, and where possible treats situations as concrete settings (this does not of course mean that they are physical settings, as we have already shown). Thus questions of the relationship between social class and crime – a perennial topic of study in the sociological approach to crime – are seen as too abstract. Furthermore, they do not lead easily to prevention. It is the highly abstract nature of the concept of social class, for example, that makes it almost impossible to discern from the literature whether or not there is a correlation between social class and crime. This is also exacerbated by the vagueness of the word 'crime' which situational crime prevention also insists on breaking down to the most specific category of action possible. Take the example of the classic 'broken windows' paper by Wilson and Kelling (1982). They noted that neighbourhoods (usually specific areas of the city) that were neglected and allowed to deteriorate, where vandalism and other minor crimes were tolerated, led offenders to perceive that social control was weak and that they could safely commit more serious crimes. Many inferences for changes to reduce or prevent crime in that and similar neighbourhoods were made from these seemingly simple, perhaps even common-sense, observations (Garland, 2000: 2). Had Wilson and Kelling applied the traditional sociological approach, they would have taken the run-down neighbourhoods as symptoms of lower social class, which would have led to completely different policies. Furthermore, the inference is suspect that run-down neighbourhoods are symptoms of low social class, since there are many well-kept streets and houses in poorer areas. Jumping to the abstraction of social class therefore introduces not only an element of vagueness, but also of bias. Worse, it leads to policies that cannot, without massive and even revolutionary social upheaval, ever be achieved. Thus, the contrast between opportunity structure and social structure is great. Opportunity structure is grounded in a concrete analysis of the opportunities that situations throw up to would-be criminals. They make specific crimes by specific individuals possible. Social structure is grounded in vague generalities and inferences about income, employment, 'class consciousness' and so on, with a highly tenuous link between those abstractions and the equally abstract notion of 'crime'.

It might be argued, though, that focusing so closely on the opportunity structure of crimes in such narrowly defined situations ignores significant and important aspects even of specific crimes. Certain types of organised crime in which criminals adhere to a particular set of values and ways of doing business may be examples of such crimes. Here, the offenders bring with them a level of commitment to a situation, and it is this level of commitment that has to be recognised as part of the situation to be assessed. Similarly, certain Internet crimes are commonly believed to be the result of the 'hacker's ethic' which, it is often claimed, derives from a 'culture' or 'subculture' to which computer buffs adhere. This raises the interesting question of the relationship between situations and culture. For is not culture a highly abstract term of the same kind, bringing with it the same problems as 'social class'? We would say not.

Situational culture

It is perhaps typical of the abstract nature of much of sociology that there should be a long and difficult controversy surrounding the concepts of culture and class. The work of Kornhauser (1978) epitomises this controversy, where it is argued that culture does not exist, or at least that it is subsumed within social class. Most criminology textbooks therefore compare and contrast cultural versus class explanations of crime. Situational crime prevention does not need to address this issue, since it is concerned with applying techniques of prevention to specific situations. Whether or not a particular value is class based or culturally based is largely irrelevant. All that is needed is that the particular value or set of values be identifiable empirically, and that these values can be exploited in order to modify decision-making in a specific situation. The work of Cavallo and Drummond (1994) on drink-driving in Australia applied a number of situational techniques to reduce the level of drink-driving, not the least of which were random breath tests. One of the techniques used an intensive advertising campaign that targeted the beer drinking culture. 'Good mates don't let mates drink and drive' was the slogan. This approach acknowledges the existence of (in this case) a strong subcultural attitude that valued heavy drinking in any setting, and refused to acknowledge that individuals who drove while drunk were either impaired or responsible for the accidents they may have caused. It also targeted a positive aspect of Australian subculture, the strong value of 'mateship'. This was an example of targeting an advertising campaign at a specific situation – one in which a mate is urged to stop another mate from making an 'idiot' of himself. This is a situational view of culture, recognising that a situation that is bound up with deep and broad cultural values can be modified using known techniques that intervene in an individual's decision-making at just the right time. Heavy assumptions of psychology are embedded in this approach (guilt, shame and peer pressure[8]). But the techniques of advertising which are essentially designed to affect directly an individual's decisions and choices at a specific moment – usually to buy a particular product brand – are well established. Other simpler culturally based techniques are applied. The simple 'No smoking' sign is an example, as is the common 'Shoplifting is stealing'. We shall see in Chapter 3 that the hacker subculture as exemplified by the 'hacker's ethic' promotes values that rationalise and justify committing computer crime of various kinds.[9]

Do these techniques and others described in Chapter 6 'work'? There is now a substantial body of research that shows that they do (Clarke, 1997). There are, of course, many issues to resolve. There is some question as to the long-term success of specifically focused crime reduction programmes.[10]

The extent to which one can generalise from the results of one successful case study to another situational problem has yet also to be studied. That is to say, the generalisability of findings based on narrowly focused crime reduction studies is yet to be determined. However, while all situations are different, actors bring with them common traits that are conditioned by the actors' past histories, which are in turn conditioned by a common culture. This view of situations allows for the notion of enduring values and a common psychology that makes them modifiable (i.e. guilt and shame), a view that comes close to recognising the importance of *dispositions* in the commission of crimes. Since situational crime prevention is commonly thought of as antagonistic to dispositions (i.e. the dispositional approach confounds the problem of crime with the problem of the criminal), this requires a brief clarification.

Enduring qualities of situations

We have suggested in the above section that individuals – all individuals – bring with them to a situation a common psychology. That is, their behaviour is rationally goal oriented, they make decisions, their decisions are affected by values of various kinds, they feel guilt and shame, and so on. That is to say, the diverse situations in which crimes occur are bound by a common thread: *human nature*. Without common assumptions about human behaviour, situational crime prevention could not operate. It depends on individuals behaving in more or less predictable ways. It assumes certain common and enduring traits, values and psychological mechanisms. Does this common psychology mean that we could all potentially become criminals? Possibly, but it also means that we could all potentially *not* become criminals, unless one assumes that there is a bias towards criminality built in to human nature. We cannot resolve this issue since it has been the stuff of drama and high tragedy for centuries. What we can say is that when it comes to analysing situations it may not matter, although we do think that the common ways in which situations in both their physical and social aspects have evolved through the ages indicate that societies are organised on the assumption of security against intrusion. Houses are built everywhere with the design of secluding the residents behind walls, to be able to see out, but not see in. And in buildings composed of apartments, there have been sentries or doormen controlling access since at least ancient Roman times. Thus situational crime prevention recognises certain enduring aspects of crime. It recognises the ancient crimes of theft and assault, for example. It simply accepts that as times change, so also do the situations in which these ancient crimes are committed. Thus we find it commonly observed that, with the revolution of the Internet, many old crimes (e.g. con games, fraud, theft and harassment) have found new opportunities for implementation. Situational crime prevention does not hope to eradicate these old crimes – an unrealistic ambition given their long history – but rather to reduce or eliminate the new opportunities that arise in new situations. The ambitions of situational crime prevention are therefore very modest. It does not claim to eradicate or even reduce crime (or sin), but merely to have a concrete effect in a definable and manageable setting. Unlike sociology, which pursues grand aims such as the eradication of social class and promotes the nebulous idea of 'equality', situational crime prevention promises only what it can deliver.

There is, however, one enduring human frailty that constantly manifests itself in situations, indeed that requires situations in order to transform it into folly: susceptibility to temptation. This trait has been identified as such by many religions, and studied by psychologists under various names and various schools including learning theory, motivational theory and psychoanalytical theory to cite but a few. Clearly, it is specific situations where individuals are subject to temptation.

Situations as precipitators of crime

The relevance of temptation to situational crime prevention was identified by Newman and Marongiu (1997) in their review of the link between utilitarian theories of action and situational crime prevention. Wortley (1997) extended this idea by identifying additional ways in which tempting situations may directly contribute to the commission of crime:

1. *Situations that prompt or provoke* an offender to action by providing cues that may elicit criminal behaviour. Loud music with sexually explicit lyrics in pubs may contribute to sexual assaults committed against female patrons. Or on the Internet, provocative language used in chat rooms may result in a stalker tracking down a woman to her home address.

2. *Situations that permit* individuals to engage in offensive behaviour that is normally proscribed. The most common examples are disinhibition (commonly induced by drugs such as alcohol[11]) or deindividuation that can arise as a result of crowd membership. The latter occurs on the Internet constantly, since, as we shall see throughout this book, the anonymity afforded to individuals on the Internet feeds directly into the capacity to commit a variety of crimes – from theft and fraud to harassment – and get away with them.

3. *Situations that exert pressure* are commonly those in which individuals feel forced to conform to the pressure of a group, or live up to expectations. For example, the computer labs on college campus where many

students use computers in group settings may engender individuals to indulge in hacking, when others are 'also doing it' especially if the hackers' ethic is dominant. Of course, on the Internet, a 'group' may exist in cyberspace, so that being a part of a group (either anonymously or deceptively) is made much more possible.

In all of these examples, we see that the situational determinant of offender behaviour is defined by the perceptions of the individuals who contribute to that situation. The situation provides the opportunity for individuals to commit crime. To use ordinary language, according to whether individuals are 'weak' or 'strong', they will give in to the situational opportunities afforded them. Furthermore, many situations are well known for their attributes and may be sought out by offenders. For example, paedophiles may hang around schoolyards, or in online chat rooms. Potential fraudsters may place their misleading advertisements and cons on the Internet. Or thieves will go 'where the money is'. The techniques for prevention therefore require an understanding of how situations that provoke, exert pressure or offer anonymity may be minimised. Since almost all situations involve these elements to some degree, hard choices have to be made in terms of control, and this is all the more reason to focus on a very specific form of criminal behaviour to prevent.

So even where situations do not cause crime they make specific kinds of crime possible. As we have noted above, enduring psychological conditions of individuals contribute to how a situation is perceived and whether that situation will invoke offensive behaviour or not. These psychological conditions transcend situations since individuals bring with them their psychological capacities that were formed throughout their lives from birth to the present. This is why common crimes such as theft, fraud, assault, robbery, homicide exist in the vocabulary of all known human societies. However, the specific attributes of these crimes – how they are committed in time and space (i.e. time of the day, the physical and social settings) – vary considerably. Thus, as we will see in Chapter 3, experts claim that cybercrime (computer crime, e-commerce crime) is largely made up of old crimes given a new face. One can rob a bank without physically going to that bank. This is because the Internet affords new opportunities to offenders. What these opportunities are and how they may be eliminated or avoided form much of the subject matter of this book. Because situational prevention demands that we analyse these opportunities as situations, which must then be examined often in minute detail, we recognise that some of the material, especially in Chapter 4, may be too detailed for the general reader. So we provide below a brief overview of the general argument and major insights that the book provides into e-commerce crime prevention.

Overview of the book

As we have noted earlier in this chapter, situational crime prevention is a highly adaptable approach to crime prevention. It is an approach that has been applied to many diverse settings. This is the first time that the approach has been applied wholesale to e-commerce, and by implication certain aspects of cybercrime. We have so far argued that situational crime prevention has a close affinity with technology because of the new opportunities that technology unveils for individuals and groups to experience new things, 'things' (such as, for example, television, computers) which in turn may affect their everyday lives and lifestyles, and patterns of living (in the case of the latter, for example, the automobile). Technology lies behind even social structural factors such as family arrangements and organisation (for example, labour-saving appliances that make it possible for all adult members of the household to work in jobs outside the home). The latter observation has been made convincingly by Marcus Felson (2002) in his *Crime and Everyday Life*. It is a simple step to claim that with new opportunities to do things differently, also come new opportunities to commit crime differently. And so, we argue, the new ways of doing business on the Internet (mostly retailing), which we loosely term e-commerce, have introduced great benefits of efficiency for businesses and enhanced service to customers, along with concomitant increased opportunities for doing crime differently.

Information technology has transformed the structure of commerce dramatically over the past three decades. It has impacted on how products are brought to market, the ways in which customers pay for them, how transactions are processed, how customers make decisions to buy, and many other factors. The major innovation has been the efficiencies made possible by the processing and collection of information. E-commerce enterprises are able to track people and products to a degree never before possible. Products can be tagged and followed through their life cycle, even from owner to owner. Customer preferences and activities on Internet websites can be tracked and information about them stored and retrieved in many useful ways. The application of these information technologies thus enables businesses to improve and target their marketing strategies, speed up the delivery of their products to customers and dynamically maintain their inventories in accordance with market needs. In sum, information technology has given them much greater control over the movement of products and the behaviour of their customers.

One would have thought that with so much more control over their products and customers (and one should also add over their employees) the opportunities for crime would be considerably reduced, because much of what we have just conveyed adds up to greater surveillance of people and products – a well-established method of crime prevention. Unfortunately, the e-commerce environment, especially the online environment that uses the Internet, is nothing short of criminogenic. The crime-prone features of the e-commerce environment are generally of three kinds. The first is the popular view of the Internet as wild frontier, where there is little order, no law, and all are (or ought to be) free to do and say what they want. The values promoted by such a culture are those that cherish an antagonism to any authority (the Internet has a highly decentralised organisation, 'no one controls the Internet', 'everyone owns everything on the Internet'). The lawlessness of the Internet derives from the globalisation that has occurred either because of, or in coincidence with, the Internet. Goods, ideas and communication cross international borders effortlessly. Thus laws governing such activities change from one country to the other, creating opportunities for criminals to exploit these gaps in law and control.

The second is that the information systems that are the oil of the e-commerce environment are themselves criminogenic. We sum up these criminogenic features of information systems by the acronym SCAREM. Information systems provide the opportunities for *stealth*, where criminals may sneak into the databases of, say, a bank, completely invisible, take what they want, and even leave no or little trace of their entry. Computer hackers, motivated by the 'hacker's ethic' of the Internet frontier, respond, sometimes obsessively, to the *challenge* to 'beat' the system, which means that their motivations may not be the simple one of theft, but rather of being able to brag that they brought down or broke into the system. *Anonymity*, a traditionally valued prized in e-commerce, provides individuals on the Internet a degree of privacy in their communications and purchases. But it also provides criminals a means of exploiting the system by enabling them to carry out crimes, especially those such as bank transfer fraud that require intrusions into a system over a long period of time. Particularly convenient to criminals is the possibility to conduct *reconnaissance* in order to identify suitable targets. Computer programs, easily available for download on the web, can be employed to scan the web for individual computers that are vulnerable to attack. *Escape* is virtually guaranteed if the criminal exploits the characteristics of the Internet to the fullest. By using the Internet addresses of other users, using another person's or organisation's computer or computing environment (universities are a favourite target) criminals may cover up their trails, making escape all but inevitable. Finally, perhaps the greatest attraction of the information systems is that a single crime is readily *multiplied* into many additional crimes, eventually into more cash or other benefits. For example, hacking into corporate or government databases opens up the possibility to commit more crimes, from terrorism and blackmail to credit card fraud, by exploiting the value that is embedded in those databases.

The third criminogenic element of the e-commerce environment is the prime target of e-commerce crime: information itself. Although the recognition that one particular crime may lead to many additional crimes raises the question of what exactly are the targets of criminal behaviour in cyberspace, there is little doubt that the ultimate target of crime in cyberspace is information. We suggest that there are four kinds of information which criminals target in different ways. The kinds of information are: intellectual property, intelligence, information systems and services of various kinds (banking, purchasing, etc.). The kinds of targets are: operational targets, transitional targets, proximate targets, convertible targets, attractive targets and incidental targets. These categories of information and targets are described in detail in Chapter 3. For the moment, we wish to show that, if we think of information generally as the prime target of e-commerce crime, we can easily apply the principles of situational crime prevention to uncover its criminogenic attributes. Clarke (1999) used the acronym CRAVED to describe the elements of consumer products that made them vulnerable to theft. These 'hot products' are Concealable, Removable, Available, Valuable, Enjoyable and Disposable. Using these characteristics, it is a simple matter to demonstrate that information is perhaps *the* hot product. Information is a product that is eminently *concealable*. It is, after all, just files that can be moved around at lightning speed, and hidden in nooks and crannies almost anywhere on the Internet, even on an unsuspecting individual user's computer without the user's knowledge. Similarly, information is easily *removable*. A few commands entered into a computer, and files can be copied, leaving the original copy in place. And the copies are identical to the originals, thus rendering the act concealable. Information is supremely *available*, in fact it is the platform of advocates of the frontier culture of the Internet that *all* information is potentially available. Much information is *valuable*. Massive databases of personal information of customers have become extremely valuable to merchants; music and videos (information in a different form) are of course valued consumer products that are also *enjoyable*. Finally, information and products of the Internet are easily *disposable* because of the wonderful facilities offered by online auctions where just about anything can be sold.

The identification of the criminogenic attributes of information systems and information itself, however, only tells part of the story of e-commerce crime. Situational crime prevention requires that we also study the situations in which these attributes are exploited for the criminal's gain. Thus in Chapter 5 we examine closely the specific transactions that occur in a typical online purchase, unravelling the actors and interactions involved in the transactions, the points at which these transactions occur along the value chain (that is, the location of a product along its journey from manufacturer or service provider to consumer or customer). Vulnerabilities to crime vary in amount and in kind depending on where in the value chain the threat occurs. Here we identify four elements of e-commerce purchasing transactions: (a) the method of payment; (b) the parties involved in the sale or transaction; (c) the delivery of the product to the buyer; and (d) the type of product or service purchased. This risk analysis is necessarily detailed, covering many aspects of buying and selling (both benefits and risks) as well as actual home delivery of an item, which is the main way that products bought online are delivered to the customer. Our excursion into the risks entailed in home delivery is assisted by the work of Allan McKinnon and Deepak Tallam (2002), who conducted a study of the vulnerabilities of the delivery systems that have emerged in on-line shopping in the UK. The risks of home delivery take us into the area of tracking of products and the vehicles used to deliver them, so we see an interesting connection between two technologies of different eras: technology of vehicle design of the twentieth century, and the addition of anti-theft features to vehicles made possible by the technology of the twenty-first century, those of tracking and mapping technology. It goes without saying, of course, that if one can track products and the vehicles in which those products are transported, one can also track the individuals who drive or attend those vehicles. It is at this point that we move away from the analysis of the opportunity structure of e-commerce crime to the techniques that can be used to prevent or reduce it.

While technological solutions are undoubtedly important in preventing crime in the computing environment, the situational prevention approach provides many other techniques that can be used to reduce criminal opportunities. These methods seek to (a) increase the effort that the criminal must make in order to carry out crime; (b) increase the perceived risk of the crime; (c) reduce the anticipated rewards of the crime; and (d) remove excuses for the criminal. Adapting the widely used 16 opportunity-reducing techniques that are based on these four categories to the e-commerce environment provides a number of solutions that go beyond technological fixes, although these always remain very important.

The categories of increasing effort and increasing the risk for the offender depend heavily on technological know-how. The major categories of reducing rewards and removing excuses tend to depend more (though not entirely) on other techniques that do not depend on being ahead of the criminal in technology, but upon the modification of social, psychological, cultural and procedural factors that impinge on the situation. These techniques are discussed in detail in Chapter 6. Their application to the e-commerce environment leads to one significant conclusion: in order to carry out many of the techniques described, it takes many individuals and organisations to work together. This is where the broad approach of situational crime prevention becomes important, both in terms of getting the job done and in terms of its impact on policy, both private and public. It is also where the idea of policing the e-commerce environment enters the scene.

So far, the problem of crime in the e-commerce environment resembles a kind of arms race (Ekblom, 2000). We try to identify the vulnerabilities of e-commerce to crime, isolate the situations that can be modified in order to make it more difficult for the offender to exploit these vulnerabilities, and make changes to those situations which either transform them into something else, or eliminate the opportunities altogether. Offenders are assumed to do likewise: they scan the information and delivery systems for vulnerabilities and find means of exploiting them. Each time we introduce a new technique or use a new technology (tracking software and hardware for example) the criminal tries to go one better. It often seems the criminal has the upper hand, mainly because of the incredible new opportunities for crime that information technology has made possible. Computer users, whoever they are, go on a kind of 'moral holiday' in a lawless, frontier land of cyberspace. In this book we emphasise the advantages that the Internet offers the criminal computer users: anonymity, deception, stealth, invisibility, excitement of the challenge and even social approval of the Internet culture. In such a crime-prone culture, where does one turn for help? Is cyberspace so crime-prone because there are no police?

This is a difficult case to make because the source of crime seems to reside in the criminogenic nature of cyberspace itself. Besides, there are few criminal laws specifically directed at the Internet that police could be called upon to enforce. And even though there are traditional crimes, such as fraud, pornography, stalking, theft, terrorism or vandalism, that one could call the police about, when they happen in cyberspace, what police force is equipped to deal with them? Because of the global (dis)organisation of cyberspace, it is unrealistic to expect a national or even a global police force to enforce such laws, when so many cyber-crimes are committed across national boundaries. So, when we speak of 'policing' e-commerce, we mean something other than the traditional idea of policing, when a victim or citizen calls the police to report a crime or a problem. What situational crime prevention means by 'policing' is the mobilisation of individuals and organisations to work together in order to change the situations identified as producing opportunities for crime. It means that significant participants or contributors to the situations that are deemed at risk must form effective working partnerships in order to change them.

There are two features of this kind of 'policing' that are of considerable interest to situational crime prevention. First, we find that the coordination of a wide variety of organisations is often necessary in order to modify a criminogenic situation. In Chapter 7 we present the case study of the successful reduction in credit card fraud to illustrate this contention. Going beyond a case study, however, it is difficult to identify exactly what groups will need to be involved in the 'policing' of specific crime-reducing situations. In the case of e-commerce, we suggest that the main participants of interest are likely to include: regular police (i.e. uniformed, beat cops and detectives) whose function in the world of e-commerce is still emerging; merchants; trade associations; consumer groups; corporate security staff and private policing organisations; human relations and management staff; Internet service providers (ISPs) such as AOL and MSN; accounting organisations and staff; managers and designers of public spaces; designers of products and services; and collectors and guardians of records.

Second, the extent to which this 'policing' is in the foreground (active control) or in the background (passive control) may have significant policy implications for accomplishing the coordinated intervention necessary for the reduction of criminal opportunity. By active control we mean policing that intrudes forcefully into the private lives of individuals, some would say invading their privacy. It tends to be oriented to identifying rule breakers. The objects of this control may or may not be aware of the intrusion. Passive control is achieved largely by arranging the environment (whether physical, informational or systemic) so that it becomes a part of the everyday lives of individuals, accepted mostly without question.

The design of highways, whether for automobiles or for information are good examples. Much of this control is accepted happily by most individuals because of the obvious benefits of order and convenience that it brings to everyday life. Viewed from this perspective, there are plenty of sources of control in the e-commerce environment. In fact, one could almost go so far as to say that the idea that the Internet is a place without order (though it may be lawless) is a myth. In Chapter 7, we show that there are many sources of governance and control in cyberspace, some easily classifiable as active or passive controls, and others as hybrids of these.

We identify active controllers as:

- the Internet users themselves who 'spy' on each other just as did inhabitants of the New England village of Puritan times depicted in Hawthorne's *The Scarlet Letter*;

- corporate security organisations;

- state-funded public/private policing organisations;

- law and regulation, though much of this is directed towards protecting consumer privacy.

We identify passive controllers as:

- the Internet service providers (ISPs, e.g. AOL, MSN, college campuses) that provide access to the Internet;

- decentralised or 'distributed' command and control on the Internet. There are authorities that set standards and protocols (e.g. web addresses) for the exchange of information across the Internet. Without them, the Internet would grind to a halt. However, they are not centralised authorities.

We identify hybrids of active and passive controllers as:

- bureaucracies, government and corporate, who are the keepers and collectors of records;

- the marketplace, where trust and self-interest combine to create order out of buying and selling.

The picture that emerges from this broad approach of situational crime prevention when applied to e-commerce is one that must marshal all the means and sources of control necessary to do the job. When one examines the means of control described above, and the extensive list of those organisations whose function it is to do the controlling, it is apparent that, taken together, the potential of control in late modern society is certainly vast. This realisation constitutes the dark picture painted for us by various French philosophers concerning postmodern society – a panoptic society, where big brother watches all individuals, where surveillance is the order of the day. Indeed, this book reviews the new technologies that make it possible to track the lives of people and products in ways that were once the stuff of science fiction. Situational crime prevention embraces such technologies with enthusiasm. And why not?

Situational crime prevention has already been criticised for employing or advocating mechanisms of control that raise privacy issues, such as CCTV on street corners (von Hirsch, 2000). But in the world of e-commerce the unavoidable necessity of employing a wide range of controls becomes starkly apparent. Because of its global reach, cyberspace controls cannot be managed at a local, small-town level. The reach of 'policing' is spreading away from a centralised welfare government and becoming embedded in the fabric of everyday lives. The line between law enforcement and intelligence (that is spying) is becoming increasingly blurred, particularly as a result of September 11, though this trend had begun well before. The New York City Police Department, for example, has established its own international terrorism squad, complete with foreign operatives. The introduction of mapping technology into policing has also demanded the collection of a vast amount of information concerning cities and their inhabitants that goes far beyond the needs to solve a specific crime. This information, used wisely, will help police prevent many crimes. Is situational crime prevention the cause or beneficiary of these shifts in policing and control in society? In the final chapter we examine this issue, especially in the light of ideological criticism levelled against situational crime prevention that it is a reactionary, conservative criminology, that does not give a hoot about privacy rights, and is deeply antagonistic towards the rehabilitative ideal of penology, so popular in the middle of the twentieth century during the giddy heights of the welfare state.

A note on method

There is by now a substantial body of research on the effectiveness of various techniques of situational crime prevention. In the field of e-commerce there are very few formal studies that have been conducted with the specific intent to demonstrate or evaluate the effectiveness of techniques advocated by situational crime prevention.[12] Fixes to plug design errors in software are also widely reported, but actual evaluations of whether or not these corrections have thwarted hacking are rarely conducted. This is because no sooner are these security corrections reported than they are followed by the discovery of other security holes. Of course, the announcements of the discovery and correction of security holes in software are read carefully by hackers as well as security managers. The literature on private security and loss prevention also reports many cases of reduction of crime as a result of particular techniques, but again these are rarely conducted as evaluative studies, and are usually after-the-fact reckoning of before and after designs. Other studies, such as the case of credit card fraud reduction, adopt a combination of data collection and historical description of interventions and their supposed effects over several years. These are particularly effective accounts, providing much descriptive detail needed to assess the role of various partnerships and agents of change involved in modifying criminogenic situations.

In the realm of cybercrime, however, there is but a handful of studies conducted that collect anything like first-hand information.[13] The majority of articles on computer crime or cybercrime are descriptive attempts to develop classifications of cybercrime, and equally descriptive attempts to demonstrate its extent and cost to society. The device used in many of these articles is to retell apocryphal stories of famous hacking incidents, and to report from various sources (usually from the popular or 'respectable' press) the monetary costs of various cyber crimes. We report such numbers with some hesitation, and with the warning that they should be treated with deserving scepticism. There are both public and private interests in seeing that such numbers and events are recounted as dramatically as possible. Private software companies stand to gain considerably if they are in the business of selling anti-virus and firewall software. Governments must be convinced, and convince their constituents, that there really are serious problems that are only solvable by government intervention, or at least by government/private partnerships. We should add, however, that statistics reported by reputable private organisations, such as those reported in Figure 1.1, should be treated with no more scepticism than those reported by governments. The only essential difference between the two is that criminology has produced extensive research on how governments collect crime data. Unfortunately, criminologists have paid very little attention to the statistics collected by private organisations concerning crime and its prevention. In any case, the numbers and stories of cybercrime are part of the fabric of the information society, and it is in this vein that we present them, especially in Chapter 3. Even there, though, we have condensed them into a series of tables, and avoided lengthy recounting of details. We have used them as analytical tools rather than as evidence.

Finally, many of the articles and sources we have relied upon have come out of disciplines or fields of study that have little seemingly to do with criminology. Obviously, since this book is about e-commerce, we have relied heavily on the established literature and modes of expression of business and marketing, as well as economics, sociology, psychology, and even anthropology. We emphasise here that situational crime prevention is an approach and a theory that is not bound by disciplines. It focuses on situations, which, depending on where they arise, are best understood from many different perspectives.

Notes

1   Garland (2001) makes four brief references to technology, which are placed together with a list of other social, cultural and economic factors, the comparative weight of which Garland makes no assessment.
2   By now, this is not an especially new observation. It reflects the idea of the 'post-industrial society' described by Daniel Bell (1976). The idea has been developed by many economists and political scientists of various persuasions to describe these irreversible changes: '...just as machines are the tools of the industrial economy, computing and telecommunications technologies are the tools of a new "information economy"' (Williams, 1988: 15).
3   Distributed manufacturing is a model of manufacturing that uses information technology to coordinate the different stages or processes in manufacturing an item that may occur in disparate locations, and to ensure that the manufacturing process responds directly to fluctuations in demand.

4 If we consider the rates computed per vehicle and per computer, we find an interesting difference between the two types of technology. For motoring offences per vehicle the rate for 1904 was 39 per thousand vehicles, whereas for 1929 it was 9. With regard to hacking in the US, the rates per computer (per household) were 0.01 per 1,000 households owning a computer in 1989 and 0.41 in 2000. The effects of the Internet can be roughly gauged. Data are only available for Internet usage for 1997 on. The rates computed according to Internet access per household are 0.11 per 1,000 households in 1997 and 0.5 in 2,000. (Data on computer usage obtained from US Bureau of Census: http://www.census.gov/population/www/socdemo/computer.html). The difference between the crime patterns of the two forms of technology is most likely because there was a flurry of legislative activity in the UK at the beginning of the twentieth century that multiplied the number of motoring offences drastically, and also created conditions that contributed to the likelihood that more offences would be committed, by legislating unrealistically restrictive speed limits. Speed traps were widespread during this period. Legislation liberalising motoring offences occurred in 1929–30. See Plowden (1971).

5 It is unfortunate that we do not have data for the intervening years from 1906 to 1928. The Home Office did not begin the routine collection of such statistics until 1929. The data for 1904/5 were collected as a result of a special Royal Commission into motor vehicles. See Plowden (1971).

6 Identifying the problem is as much conceptual as it is methodological. The difficulties in identifying the 'right' problem are considerable (Gilling, 1996).

7 For a range of examples see Clarke (1997).

8 The earlier table of 12 techniques of situational crime prevention was expanded to 16 as a result of the observations made by psychologists that guilt and shame should be included as an important part of situational intervention. See Clarke (1997); Wortley (1996).

9 We make this observation without passing judgment on whether there are positive or redeeming qualities to the hacker's ethic, or estimating how 'cohesive' are the various strains of hacker cultures, particularly to the point of collaborative hacker activism and political protest. Taylor argues that the media has demonised hackers as a group, which may or may not be so. Our concern is to identify the situations in which hackers are provided opportunities to commit crimes. See Taylor (2001).

10 Homel *et al.* (1997) have raised a question as to whether introducing 'responsible drinking' through enlightened pub management in a tourist resort would be effective in the long term.

11 The lack of regulatory feedback in communications in cyberspace contributes to disinhibition of online stalkers (Ellison, 2001).

12 A few exceptions with before-and-after comparisons include studies of electronic article surveillance (EAS) (e.g. DiLonardo, 1996), phone cloning (Clarke *et al.*, 2001) and credit card security (see Chapter 7).

13 Outstanding exceptions are Mann and Sutton (1998); Jerin and Dolinsky (2001).

Chapter 2

The e-commerce environment

The trust that binds

All commerce depends on trust between strangers (Fukuyama, 1995). Trust is an abstract idea that has evolved over hundreds or perhaps thousands of years, its role in market economies clearly identified by Adam Smith, the first to truly understand market economies: 'Mankind brought together in a mutual Intercourse of good Offices' (Smith, 1996: xliv). By 'trust' we mean that, in any commercial exchange, each party to the exchange will reciprocate. In a typical retailing situation the problem of trust is theoretically reinforced by a face-to-face exchange between the buyer and seller. There are many assumptions of trust in this simple exchange. For example, there are assumptions that the product purchased does or is what the seller says it is, that it is 'safe', that the seller in fact is a genuine representative of the retailer or manufacturer, and so on. The buyer guarantees that the money he or she hands over is not counterfeit. These and many other assumptions are familiar aspects of retailing. Retailers and manufacturers try their best to overcome the problem of being strangers to their customers by advertising their products and services so that they become 'household names', offering trusted products so that buyers will enter a store they can trust. There are also many ways in which the assumption of trust is abused. Shoplifters will try to acquire an item without paying, often taking advantage of the inviting displays of items shopkeepers use to entice customers. Retailers and manufacturers may use deceptive advertising to create a false sense of familiarity with the product. There is, therefore, a constant tension between the maintenance of trust on the part of both buyers and sellers, and the attempts by each party to come out the 'winner' from the exchange: the buyer wants to pay as little as possible for a high quality article, and the seller wants to sell as much product at the highest price that the market will sustain. This tension provides the situational context within which crime prevention analysts have traditionally focused their efforts: surveillance to prevent shoplifting, tamper-proof packaging, careful arrangement of product displays, tagging or marking of products, monitoring of inventory, attention to lighting and other architectural aspects of the retail floor.

E-commerce also depends on trust between strangers, though these are strangers of a different kind who never or rarely meet 'face to face'. The exchanges themselves, however, are more complex and are of greater variety. In the field of online retailing, some of the traditional crime prevention techniques that focus on location-based situations or product displays are obviously not relevant. However, as we noted in the previous chapter, situational crime prevention, although it has its early roots in location-based situations, now essentially focuses on the participants in situations which give rise to crimes. In the online world shoplifting of specific articles cannot occur in quite the same way as on the retail floor, but as we will see, situations present themselves in the online environment where items can be 'shoplifted'. Similarly, typical crime prevention techniques of monitoring people and products on the retail floor cannot be applied in quite the same way, but as we will see, surveillance of people and products takes on a whole new meaning in retailing that occurs in the e-commerce environment. There are elements of the old and the new in e-commerce, which is only to be expected, given its origins in the history of retailing generally and the history of electronic communication and storage of information.

Precursors to e-commerce

The great advantage of a retail store is that the customer can pay for the item and receive it immediately. This arrangement requires that the retailer buy up a lot of inventory to keep in stock so that the buyer can obtain the item immediately upon paying for it. Other forms of retailing have tried to match this great advantage by offering the convenience of shopping from home. Early in the twentieth century, mail-order catalogues emerged, often in conjunction with large retail chains (for example, Sears Roebuck, whose first catalogue, including only watches and jewellery, appeared in 1888). Large retail stores then began to allow customers to pay for an item over a period of time using 'lay-away' or 'lay-buy' plans, in which the customer chose an item in the store, and it was put away for the customer who paid it off over a period of time.

When it was recognised that the mail-order catalogue was an effective means of presenting products to customers, televised shopping channels emerged to exploit this medium to convey details of the products to customers. Ordering by mail and ordering by phone became part of the ordinary retailing marketplace. The advent of credit cards made this process of payment even easier. It made it possible for the customer to pay for an item, even though the customer did not, at the specific time of the sale, actually have the money in hand to pay for it. Using a credit card over the phone to pay for an item was a first and very big step towards the online environment.

However, the credit card could not have emerged as a method of payment without the introduction in the early 1970s of electronic funds transfer (EFT) between banks. This was made available over private networks which revolutionised financial markets. By the end of the decade computers were well established behind the scenes transmitting payments and storing the remittance information. By today's standards the computers were slow. They were lodged in one place and not very accessible or movable. Their inaccessibility proved to be a great defence against crime, but with the onset of the Internet in the 1990s, private networks became enmeshed with 'public' networks making them far more accessible. In any event, as far as e-commerce is concerned, even by the 1980s, the seemingly simple exchange of money for a product was becoming more complex. Individuals using a credit card could now purchase an item with someone else's money (the bank's or the merchant's) and pay for the item later (at a higher price, of course, if the customer did not pay off the amount owing on the credit card within a specific period of time). These events laid the groundwork for online retailing. Furthermore, the introduction of the Internet and other electronic advances made it possible for vendors to develop much more sophisticated ways of monitoring and tracking both their products and their customers.

Basic features of e-commerce

The defining features of e-commerce can be described from three basic perspectives (Kalakota and Whinston, 1997):

1. *Communications* technology enhances the delivery, accessibility and storage of information concerning products, services and customers, and oils the process of payments by telephone or computer networks.

2. Technology increases the *efficiency* of the business process by automating business transactions and workflows, such as tracking inventory and customers, streamlining business-to-business ordering and receiving, allowing management to cut costs while improving quality of the product and speed of service.

3. *Online storefronts* offer the capability of buying and selling products, information and services on the Internet.

The overall motivation driving e-commerce is, of course, that which drives all commerce, whether electronic or not: to do more with less, to increase productivity, to maximise value. However, although it is obvious that e-commerce operates upon time-honoured precepts of regular commerce, it is instructive to examine more closely the differences between the old and the new in e-commerce. This is because, according to the situational crime prevention perspective discussed in the previous chapter, the new situations thrown up by the electronic ways of doing business should provide new opportunities for crime. Table 2.1 summarises the distinguishing features that contrast e-commerce with traditional commerce, pointing out the advantages and disadvantages of each. We should emphasise that this contrast is overdrawn. It is likely that any specific business transaction will reflect both the old and the new. In addition, there are many businesses that do not primarily offer goods for sale online, but that do benefit greatly from electronic tracking of product and customers.

Table 2.1 Comparison between traditional commerce and e-commerce.

Feature	Traditional commerce	E-commerce (online and offline)
Retailing storefront	*Localised storefront.* Business will choose a neighbourhood where there are other successful businesses, a 'good neighbourhood' which conveys integrity, lighting and signage that advertises its trusted brand name.	*Globalised storefront.* The Internet is a global enterprise. Opening a storefront (i.e. a website) risks operating in the neighbourhood of all kinds: gambling sites, pornography sites and even fraudulent sites. Choosing a 'good neighbourhood' is especially difficult. Thus design and presentation of the website assumes major importance in conveying integrity and trust. Privacy policies and guarantees of security must be immediately visible.
Tracking of products	*Time and location-bound.* Periodic counting of inventory, made costly by labour needed to make accounting, sometimes necessary to close store for a period while inventory taken. Location-bound: each retail store must do its own count, unrelated to counting when shipped from factory.	*Dynamic.* Inventory can be maintained constantly by the use of bar codes and other electronic tagging methods; linked to supplier so that inventory can automate ordering; linked to customer so that products can be tracked via customer use.

Table 2.1 Comparison between traditional commerce and e-commerce

Tracking of customers	*By debt*. Small stores traditionally allowed trustworthy customers to buy on account and pay the account periodically. Enormous amount of labour is needed to accomplish this in large stores where customers are not known personally.	*Customer monitoring*. Customers can be monitored in many ways: records of their key strokes at the website are collected and processed for preferences and buying habits; product tracking via customer ownership provides additional information on customers; credit card and other personal information collected and used to identify customers demographically, creditworthiness, etc.
Product assessment	*Try before you buy*. The greatest advantage of the traditional retail store is that the customer can touch, feel, smell and otherwise view the product. This works well with clothing, shoes, small and large appliances. However, unless salespersons are especially knowledgeable and well trained, it may be difficult to get accurate or extensive information concerning appliances, especially electronic products. Of course, physical access to the product, especially if it is small in size, makes shoplifting possible.	*Try before you buy* is literally possible with much software that can be downloaded on a 'shareware' basis. To purchase the product, the customer purchases a 'key' to unlock the software. Online shopping for clothing is difficult (even though some sites have provided creative ways to 'try on' apparel online), unless the business is prepared to accept a high percentage of product returns. However, websites can provide extensive information about products, in great detail, especially of electronic products, tools and appliances.
Price assessment	*Comparison shopping* is time consuming and requires considerable travel to many stores in order to identify like items and their prices.	*Comparison shopping* is perhaps the greatest boon (for the customer) of online retailing. Price competition is at its greatest, websites even specialise in providing electronic surveys of prices in many product categories and specific items.
Customer assessment	*Face-to-face assessment* is possible upon which judgments of 'honesty' may be made (whether justified or not). 'Have a nice day' transactions promote store	*Face-to-face assessment* is as yet not possible, so other means are used such as maintenance of massive credit and other information about the customer, utilisation of

	goodwill and establish a 'close relationship' with the customer. However, identification of customer is cursory so customer retains anonymity.	third-party assessment such as companies providing electronic cash. Relationship with the customer must be established through the design of the website and its 'user friendliness'. Customer gives up anonymity.
Seller assessment	*National (or international) chains* have the upper hand because of their instant recognition. False storefronts are expensive to establish and maintain.	*National (or international) chains* have the advantage, but the web provides a relatively inexpensive facility for constructing a false storefront and even to make it look like that of a national brand. Deception is easier.
Customer dependence	Customers are *dependent* on large national chains for a variety of product, information about pricing and product quality.	*Customer independence* is 'empowered' by the availability of a huge range of product and detailed pricing and product information. Savvy customers check out items in a local store, then shop for lowest price on the web.
Delivery of product	Delivery is immediate *if* the product is in stock. Dynamic inventory of course should help maintain stock of popular items.	Delivery is necessarily delayed, because product must be shipped directly from merchant to consumer. This can be costly, and extends the time taken for completion of the transaction by up to several days.

Online and offline

E-commerce is composed of both online and offline technology. For reasons of clarity, we choose to define *online e-commerce* as that which occurs on the Internet, where computers are networked globally and in theory are accessible to all who have a computer connected to the Internet. Of course there are many ways to deny access to users and many ways for users to gain access to restricted sites, and these are discussed later in the book. By *offline e-commerce* we mean that technology may be used extensively for communication and monitoring business practices, but that these networks are privately constructed, not directly connected to the Internet, so in theory are less accessible to the public (though these became the targets of hackers before the wide use of the Internet, as we will see in the following chapter). As we noted earlier in this chapter, banks were the first users of these internal networks in the 1970s. There are, of course, many technical ways in which private networks may be connected through firewalls and other devices to the Internet, so the distinction between offline and online is not always clear. Finally, offline networks may collect, transmit and store information concerning product movement and inventory via bar coding and various wireless tagging technologies. The majority of businesses today are hybrids of online buying and selling and offline monitoring and movement of goods and services.

While Table 2.1 serves to briefly summarise the differences between traditional commerce and e-commerce some of these differences have more significance than others in terms of crime prevention issues. These are discussed further in sections which follow.

Customer identity

Customer assessment, part of which includes establishing the identity of the customer, is an issue of major importance. It has practical implications for crime prevention and far-reaching policy and philosophical implications for the role of crime prevention in the information age. We will consider here the practical significance and save discussion of the broader implications until after we have surveyed the criminal opportunities in the information age and the crime prevention techniques applied to counter them in later chapters.

In the traditional commercial transaction the customer establishes authenticity by one simple act: handing over cash for the item to be purchased. The seller accepts the cash (assuming it is not counterfeit) as a sufficient authentication of the buyer. Nothing else is needed. In this case the customer is able to preserve anonymity. Although the two participants in the situation, the buyer and the seller, may exchange pleasantries, they are essentially strangers to each other. The exception, of course, is the frequent customer to the local diner, bar, pub or corner shop, where the customer happily gives up identity in return for recognition as a 'regular'. However, although businesses seek to establish a productive relationship with their customers, there is a significant downside to having too close a relationship with the customer. Banks routinely rotate their tellers through different branches to avoid their becoming too close to the customers. The first principle in any security textbook, based on military procedures, is never to grant entry or access to an individual based on personal familiarity. Individuals must provide proof of identity that transcends personal familiarity. In the online environment, while the Internet offers many ways of hiding one's 'true' identity, as we will note in the next and subsequent chapters, nevertheless activity on the Internet leaves an electronic record or trail which can in most cases – with considerable effort – be tracked.

And, because the major form of payment on the Internet is with a credit card, the individual must be prepared to give up anonymity for the convenience of purchasing with a plastic card. The simple, convenient transaction with a credit card (whether online purchase or offline purchase) immediately activates a whole range of procedures the sum total of which is to produce massive databases of personal and credit information about customers. These databases may be used both to verify authenticity of the customer's creditworthiness and to provide demographic and other marketing information. Here then is a very new situation, one that immediately invites the interests of criminal activity, for it creates a new target for crime (the database) that may turn out to be very valuable in several ways. How valuable will be this target, and the kinds of criminal attack that it may invite, depends on the panorama of criminal activity in the information age which we will discuss in the following chapter. For the moment, it is sufficient to observe that the new situations thrown up by e-commerce provide new opportunities both for improving productivity but also new situations that are opportunities for would-be offenders.

Monitoring, tracking and surveillance

We have implied so far that any use of technology whether online or offline is subsumed under e-commerce, and what's left is traditional commerce. However, surveillance occurs in both settings, and it is not clear how we should categorise it. For example, on the traditional retailing sales floor, security personnel and sales associates are typically charged with the responsibility of maintaining surveillance of customers in order to prevent shoplifting.[1] Surveillance may also be enhanced by careful arrangement of product displays, width of aisles, height of displays, line of sight from the checkout location and so on. Many stores may also use surveillance cameras (banks and drug stores are typical). We are inclined not to categorise such a store as one using the new approach of 'e-commerce', unless the information collected is transformed into a database that is then used to enhance customer identification, and identify customer patterns of behaviour and shopping. Typically, however, surveillance tapes are not stored for long periods and offer limited identification possibilities.[2] We are inclined therefore, to think of such electronic aids as just that: small extensions of the human senses of vision and hearing that help in the process of surveillance. They do not in and of themselves typically produce databases that may be used as ways to enhance the value of products (enhance the value chain as we will discuss further below).

In contrast, products that are electronically monitored with the latest RFIDs (Radio Frequency ID tags: see Chapter 7) provide a much more powerful value enhancement. Not only do they create the possibility to check that an item has been paid for when the person leaves the store, but also the tags provide extensive, sometimes interactive, information concerning the product itself, automatic inventory and ordering information, and even tracking of the product after it leaves the store or is even transferred from one owner to another. The monitoring and tracking devices, when combined with the databases of personal information collected in the e-commerce environment, offer powerful opportunities for the control and prevention of many kinds of crime, although they do offer new opportunities for offenders, such as the misuse of personal information, the theft of individuals' identities through hacking into the databases of e-commerce business, and many other risks to be discussed in the following chapter.

Globalisation

There are additional implications of the globalisation features of e-commerce not mentioned in Table 2.1. National and international businesses are able as never before to sell more easily across national and state borders, thereby avoiding various kinds of taxes including sales taxes and customs duties. This new opportunity alone provides the opportunity for tax avoidance and black market commerce. Customers have been quick to recognise the advantages of cross-border shopping. In the United States, where every state and region may have a different rate of sales tax, it is common for customers to drive across a state line in order to purchase items at a lower sales tax rate. In Europe, the same may apply by crossing national borders to purchase items such as alcohol, cigarettes or perfume where tax or duty is lower: customers enjoy 'tax-free' shopping. The US Congress even passed a moratorium on taxation of online transactions. As well as tax avoidance, businesses may also exploit conflicting and vague laws of different states and nations concerning the legality or illegality of selling certain products such as gambling, pornography and prescription drugs. In fact, there exists a kind of 'frontier' culture on the Internet where the applicability of conflicting laws is highly complex and in many cases unenforceable, a culture that can be exploited both by sellers and customers alike. The disadvantage, however, from a business point of view is that this grey area of international law and applicability of national law has provoked considerable activity from international organisations to regulate and legislate many aspects of e-commerce, as we outline in Chapter 8 when we review policing on the Internet.

Trust, again

The globalised storefront and the transfer of economic activity to a website rather than personal transactions between seller and buyer (even if they are strangers) as in traditional commerce obviously impinge on the question of whether each participant in the transaction can trust one another. Actually, in the typical traditional sale the question of trust is resolved by cash and immediate receipt of the product, as we noted above. However, the trust involved also rests on other general factors such as the reputation of the national store, its brand name, the physical condition and location of the store and so on. Trust in the online retailing environment is much more dependent on the transaction experience itself. The sale or purchasing experience, that is the actual transaction, is much more drawn out. There are two reasons for this. The first is that the complexities that lie behind the acceptance of a credit card or other form of online payment must be processed seamlessly. They are not as simple as merely ringing up the amount and taking cash from the customer. Second, web retailers want to take the time to capture as much information from the customer as possible so that it may be used for future marketing and security purposes. The latter tends to militate against trust, unless used in sparing and careful ways. That Amazon.com keeps a record of the tastes one has in books may be an effective marketing ploy, but it also reveals to the customer that he is being watched.

In fact, trust is the major issue that concerns online retailing. In 1998 a survey by Commercenet (Lombardi, 1998) revealed that the top reasons for consumers not buying on the web were lack of trust and the concerns about the payment mechanism. E-commerce retailers have spent much money in establishing reasons to be trusted (encrypted online payment certificates) and in making the payment mechanism as smooth as possible (one-click purchase via credit card or digital cash). The driving force in e-commerce web design has been to make selling faster, to reach customers more quickly and efficiently, to make buying more efficient and easy, and to allay customer concern for security (perhaps the most direct measure of 'trust'). Thus 'one-click' technology as pioneered by Amazon.com to 'assist' customer decisions to buy has dominated web design. At the same time, the ultimate measure of trust from the customer's point of view is whether he receives value for money: that is delivery of the product. Thus the major disadvantage of online shopping – having to wait for delivery of the item purchased – still dogs the e-commerce trade. And a great deal of pressure has been put on delivery services such as UPS and FedEx (both of which existed well before the computing environment emerged) to provide efficient and quick delivery systems, and systems that allow for tracking of purchased goods. Delivery systems are usually seen as part of the 'value chain' of commerce.

The e-commerce value chain

The value chain is a term used to identify the points at which value is either added to or subtracted from a product as it moves from manufacturer to customer. The various value chain models essentially lay out the organisational structure of buying and selling. They also coincidentally serve to identify the points (and thus the situations) at which products and businesses may be vulnerable to criminal activity, since they identify points of value. The value chain in e-commerce differs markedly from that of the traditional commerce value chain as demonstrated in Figures 2.1 and 2.2, largely because of the onset of the information age. There are several important differences between the old and new models of the value chain:[3]

- In e-commerce, value lies almost entirely in the customer. The old adage 'the customer is always right' seems to reflect this view, but it is given new meaning in the e-commerce environment. We can see from Figure 2.2 that a large amount of e-commerce activity centres on the POS (point-of-sale), which is used as a vehicle to collect extensive information on the customer's preferences, credit background including credit card information, and buying habits.

- Thus e-commerce websites are driven by the four traditional values of retailing, and then some: speed of service (it can never be too fast), convenience (one-stop shopping, one-click shopping, ease and transparency of order entry and fulfilment), personalisation (ability to provide customers with precisely the products they are looking for), and price ('nothing can be too affordable').

- Large databases of customer information are therefore collected, stored and analysed. They are the first and obvious targets for criminals, as they represent valuable information both for the business that owns the data (and thus could be damaged by any criminal attack on the data base) and for competitors.

- POS is also used as the point for adjusting inventory on the retail site (if it is even kept any more) and for automatically sending an order to the maker to replace the item just sold. The reduction of inventory reduces the amount of goods that are capable of being stolen by stock room employees, one of the most common forms of theft in retail establishments. Dynamic ordering also reduces the necessity to order a large number of particular items for any one shipment, again reducing the chances of theft out of back-door operations (i.e. at the loading dock), since items stolen from a small number are more likely to be noticed than items stolen from a very large number.

- Final delivery of the product is made by third-party delivery companies that now allow close electronic monitoring and tracking of every item. This extra link in the purchasing process adds opportunity for crime. While delivery companies have well-established procedures to maintain security of deliveries, common crimes are those related to traditional credit card fraud such as false delivery addresses and false claims of not having received or ordered the item.[4]

- Return of merchandise is an important point of information collection from the customer, but it also allows for criminal opportunities, especially in the disposal of stolen goods in conjunction with credit card fraud (goods purchased with a stolen credit card may be returned for cash).

- In contrast, the manufacturing end has been considerably simplified. Large inventories of product are mostly not needed. In fact with distributed manufacturing, inventories of the final product are kept to a minimum because the product is constructed according to requested customer configuration, and the parts are received from the distributed parts makers as the orders are received from the retailer. Alternatively, the manufacturer forms a close partnership with the retailer and provides product only for that outlet. Sears appliances or Marks and Spencer labels are examples of close partnerships between retailing and manufacturing. Of course, these partnerships existed before the online world, but it is apparent that the new information systems environments considerably enhance these partnerships. In fact there are many cases in which the partner company is barely distinguishable from the retailer. For example, Federal Express has transformed itself into a full-service company for selected companies with whom it has a close partnership. It receives orders, fulfils the orders and maintains inventory control. In one instance it managed to cut the customer delivery cycle from four weeks to seven days for one of its clients, National Semiconductor.[5] Companies that specialise in order fulfilment also provide modern technology in 'picking and packing' which reduces the amount of human involvement with inventory and therefore reduces the opportunity for employee theft of inventory.

These changes have considerable implications for resource allocation on the part of e-commerce retailers, manufacturers and suppliers, and ever increasing demands of consumers. These are McKinnon and Tallam (2002:5):

provision of home delivery on a much greater scale, requiring investment in new, larger depots, handling systems and vehicle fleets;

expansion of the range of products purchased from the home, particularly to include groceries;

emergence of a new generation of 'e-tailers' and 'e-fulfilment' companies with little or no previous experience of providing home delivery;

socio-demographic trends leading to an increase in the proportion of single-person households and people spending more time away from home. This reduces the likelihood of someone being at home to receive deliveries;

Figure 2.1 The traditional retail value chain.

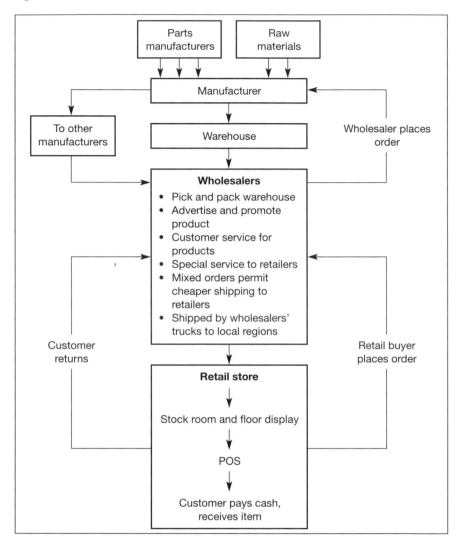

consumers demanding more rapid delivery, putting retailers and their carriers under intense time pressures;

development of new forms of 'unattended' delivery involving the use of 'reception' boxes and databases containing information on consumers' delivery preferences;

construction of a new logistical infrastructure to support a large increase in home shopping, comprising e-fulfilment centres (i.e. local depots purpose-

Figure 2.2. The e-commerce retail value chain.

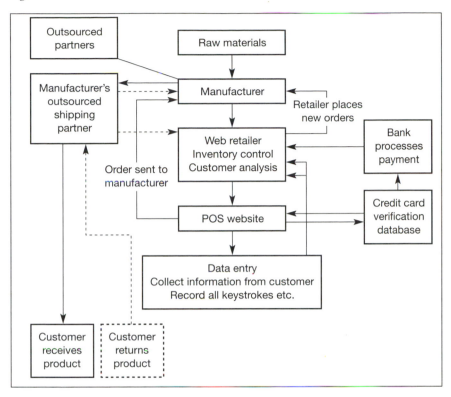

built for home delivery operations) and community collection points (or 'e-stops') where consumers can go to collect home-ordered products;

introduction of new technology that can help to secure home delivery channels against theft.

Figures 2.1 and 2.2 provide a schematic contrast between the old and new value chains. More detailed analyses are possible, as we show in Chapter 4 when we analyse specific situations at particular points in the value chain. Tools are available such as supply chain mapping for analysing the distribution of inventory, order cycle times and transport efficiency. This tool has seldom been used to investigate patterns of criminal activity. A recent study by the Universities of Leicester and Cranfield (in McKinnon and Tallam, 2002) employed this approach to measure the level of 'shrinkage' in the fast-moving consumer goods supply chain across Europe, estimating the value of stock losses and attributing these losses to different causes at differing transactional points in the value chain. A similar framework can be applied to the analysis of theft in home delivery chains extending from the main supply point to the home. This reveals that home-ordered products can follow markedly different routes to the home and be exposed to varying degrees of risk at particular points on these routes. Using this approach we can classify these routes and indicate the theft risks at different nodes and links. Chapter 5 discusses in greater detail the nature of these risks and the points at which opportunity for crime occurs. Yet even in the face of these known risks, the sphere of e-commerce continues to expand.

The growth of e-commerce

Given the challenges of establishing trust in the online marketplace described so far, it is remarkable that the rates of online revenues have increased so greatly in the past decade in the UK, Germany and the USA. This would suggest that the problem of trust is gradually being overcome. According to McKinnon and Tallam (2000:16–22):

> Despite the collapse of the dot.com share bubble, the volume of online sales to the home has continued to grow at a healthy rate. In addition to the new entrants to the home retail market (the so called 'pure players'), many catalogue mail-order and 'bricks and mortar' retailers have successfully diversified into online shopping and are expanding their volume of sales direct to the home. In 2000, the UK home shopping market was worth roughly £15 billion, two and half times its value in 1994 (£6.5 billion). It is growing at around 20 per cent per annum and has been forecast to reach £24 billion by 2004 (Figure 2.3).

Figure 2.3 Past and projected growth of the UK home shopping market.

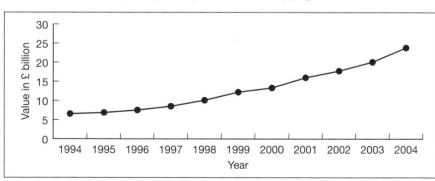

Source: Keynote (2001).

There are several types of home shopping, some of it online, some of it not so online. The varieties serve to remind us of the difficulty in distinguishing between online and offline in the e-commerce environment. The varieties are as follows:

- *General mail order* is defined as the purchase of goods through catalogue sales, either directly or via an agent. If the customer places the order by mail, then we may conclude that the catalogue sale is 'offline'. If made by telephone, chances are that the telephone service is networked into a vast computer system of switches and relays. Whether or not it is accessible via the Internet will depend on the configuration of the service by the service provider. If the order is placed on a cell phone, of course, the chances of the order being placed 'online' – that is on a publicly accessible network – are much higher. If the order is paid for by a credit card, then the transaction is necessarily electronic, though may be offline. The orders are delivered to the customer by parcel delivery service, post or via a network of local agents. The parcel may or may not be tracked, and it may or may not be tracked via the Internet. In the US the US Postal Service provides a limited tracking of articles; UPS and FedEx provide extensive tracking on the web of all articles shipped. The main marketing tool is the catalogue. The UK catalogue mail-order sector is dominated by companies that control over 90 per cent of the market.

- *Direct marketing* employs techniques such as off-the-page advertising/ selling and direct mail shots and inserts to generate sales, the vast majority of which are distributed directly to the home. Ordering and delivery follow similar procedures as for catalogue sales.

- *Direct selling* involves the use of independent agents who visit consumers at their homes and try to sell them goods or services. The agent can deliver the goods directly or arrange for their distribution through a separate distribution network. Cash sales are more common, especially if sales are pressured. In this case, the 'hard sell' undermines the trust with the result that many US states have enacted laws that require cooling off periods before a sale is declared final. However, credit cards are also common, and, as above, once credit cards enter the picture, the sale is an e-commerce sale (though offline).

- *Electronic (or 'online') home shopping* uses the Internet, accessed by computer, other digital device or cable, digital or satellite TV, to market products, receive customer orders and arrange payment. Ordering is electronic whether by phone or on the web, and credit cards are the most common form of payment. Articles are delivered as for catalogue sales.

There are many examples of business models that are hybrids of all these types. Table 2.2 shows the Keynote forecasts of the growth of each of these forms of home shopping over the period 1998–2003 in the UK. Similar though faster growth is demonstrated in the US. However, even though the market share of electronic shopping has increased considerably, it still struggles to account for the 10 per cent of all retail sales that was predicted during the dot.com boom (Underhill, 2000: 16–22).

Table 2.2 The UK home shopping market by sector £ bn (%).

	1998	*2003*
General mail order	5.8 (56.9%)	9.9 (48.7%)
Direct marketing	1.8 (17.6%)	2.7 (13.3%)
Direct selling	1.9 (18.6%)	3.6 (17.7%)
Electronic home shopping	0.7 (6.9%)	4.1 (20.2%)
Total	10.2 (100%)	20.3 (100%)

Source: Keynote (1999).

Conclusion: it's information

We have described the organisational features of e-commerce and contrasted them to those of traditional commerce, with an emphasis on retailing. We have depicted e-commerce as a highly complex process that aims to streamline the day-to-day handling of goods, services and customer relations. Throughout, we have hinted at some of the opportunities both for committing crime (ease of deception on websites, hacking into valuable databases) and for controlling crime (ease of surveillance using databases of personal information) that have been created by the revolution in information technology. However, the approach of situational crime prevention demands that we ask what exactly is at risk? What specifically is the target of criminals? This knowledge is necessary in order to modify the opportunities that arise in the e-commerce process of buying and selling. For example, we noted in Table 2.1 that specific, physical products could not be shoplifted in the online storefront or website. However, we noted that these same products could nevertheless be stolen using the unique resources of the Internet. A thief could hack into the database of the merchant, acquire the identity or credit card information of another customer and thereby purchase the item. The key word here is 'information'. While technology has provided all kinds of devices to move, scan, transmit, store and transform information into many different forms (video, light streams, audio, bar codes to numbers, and many more) it is the input and output of these devices that is crucial to e-commerce. In fact we have seen throughout this chapter that the stuff of e-commerce is really about information: identifying and authenticating persons, counting and tracking products, collecting and storing customer data. All of these activities have taken centre stage in e-commerce simply because e-commerce has emerged in response to the opportunities and innovations provided by the information technology revolution.

It follows, therefore, that if we are to identify the vulnerabilities of e-commerce to crime, we should understand what opportunities information technology provides to those who would commit crimes that target information. In the next chapter we examine the idea of information as a target of criminals of the information age. Identifying a target, however, is not so simple, since the target is often a fast-moving one in the world of information technology. And to determine exactly how value is attached to information that makes it an attractive target to criminals is also a challenging task. As we shall find, the waters are further muddied when one considers that, in a global society, all information is connected to all other information.

Notes

1 A well-run sales floor will also have sales associates observing customer behaviour in order to improve displays of goods, refine approaches to customers and so on (Underhill, 2000).
2 This may change with new technology, such as face pattern recognition and other biometric recognition techniques. See http://www.biometricsinstitute.org/bi/types.htm.
3 Information from a variety of reports and texts has been used to construct these figures. However, by far the most detailed and incisive is the UNCTAD e-commerce and development report in 2001. For example, UNCTAD summarises succinctly the challenges facing e-commerce as follows:

- larger number of small parcels or packages due to a larger number of buyers making direct orders and a larger number of sellers than in traditional trade;
- large numbers of online customers, mostly unknown to the sellers;
- demand for shipments is more unpredictable and unstable as it originates from many more customers;
- origins and destinations of shipments are more widely dispersed, given that more buyers place direct orders with producers and distributors and more sellers access buyers globally;

- accountability for shipments extends through the entire supply chain, compared with traditional logistics in which accountability is limited to single links of the supply chain;
- customers have high expectations about the quality of services and demand fast delivery of shipments;
- higher incidence of cargoes returned to the supplier than in traditional trade;
- greater demand for and availability of information covering transactions over entire supply chain, thus allowing online shipment tracking and other supply chain management functions;
- more focus on one-to-one marketing, creating demand for customised delivery and post-transaction services;
- greater complexity in fulfilling international orders than in traditional trade, thus preventing some retailers and service providers from being involved in international e-commerce;
- the emergence of demand for online processing of shipments, including cargo booking, bills of lading/airway bills, freight payment, landed price calculations and tariff management;
- substantial increase in the volume of small shipments, leading to growth of demand for warehousing, transport and other logistics infrastructure that can handle many more small shipments.
- greater scope for customer self-service.

4 The reduction of credit card fraud is presented as a case study in Chapter 7. See also Levi (2000).
5 Many of these modern partnerships began as outsourcing, especially in the realm of information technology, which made it possible to 'get big' quick (Kalakota and Robinson, 1999).

Chapter 3

E-commerce as the target of crime

On 22 April 2000 a McDonald's employee was killed by a bomb that had allegedly been placed in a Brittany, France store by a terrorist group. This bomb was one in a series of bombings directed against the encroachment on France by McDonald's, yet its effects did not close down McDonald's stores all over France (except for a day of mourning for those killed). Nor did it affect the operation of any McDonald's outlets in the United States or elsewhere.

Consider another case. Soon after September 11, an unknown individual, utilising the anonymity provided by the US Postal Service, sent anthrax-laced letters through the mail to prominent politicians and public figures. The effects of these few letters were enormous and far-reaching. The terrorist had made use of a network – perhaps the oldest network in existence – that connects all people and businesses to each other. All persons and entities that have a postal address – and that is just about everyone – may be reached using that network. Because of their connectedness, networks of any kind provide opportunities to criminals, depending on their motivations. The fact that people and organisations are connected to that network makes them vulnerable to attack.

Now let us return to the McDonald's example. Suppose instead that the terrorist targeted not random individuals frequenting the McDonald's restaurant, but rather hacked into the electronic network of McDonald's that automates and monitors the inventory, ordering and distribution of products throughout the McDonald's worldwide chain. Introducing a worm or other information-destructive program into the McDonald's network would have the capability of bringing much of McDonald's operations to a standstill. No innocent lives would be lost, of course, but the impact of the crime would in dollar terms and in terms of harm to McDonald's operations be enormous. But even in these three examples, other businesses, with the exception of those who are directly connected to McDonald's (suppliers for example), can feel relatively safe from such attacks. The attacks are confined to particular victims and particular locations, or in the case of the US Postal

Service, to a definable and slow network. But now take the case of the 'I Love You' virus that was released in the Philippines in May of 2000. In no time it had caused the shutdown of the House of Commons e-mail facility and brought to a halt many businesses throughout the world. Any business, no matter what its product or service, that was connected to the Internet was vulnerable and felt the effects within hours of release of the virus. The lesson here is that at least as far as the Internet is concerned, any business that is connected to it is at risk of criminal attack, even if that business is not directly or even specially the target of the criminal. Since information has become the key ingredient of e-commerce as we saw in the previous chapter, all of e-commerce becomes a target. In fact, the interconnected world of the information age substantially changes the idea of targets in situational crime prevention. If information is the target, we need to examine more closely what exactly information is in the e-commerce environment and how it may be targeted.

Where is the money?

The e-commerce environment has been created by the age of information technology. Electronic ways of collecting, storing and transmitting vast amounts of information have made it possible for e-commerce businesses to develop in new directions, to offer new services to customers, to enhance marketing, and to control the distribution and fulfilment of products. Information and its efficient processing creates value in the e-commerce world. And where there is value, there is the opportunity for crime. The old saying that a thief robs banks because that is where the money is certainly applies here. Except that – where is the money in the e-commerce environment of the information age? In fact, money exists mostly in the form of information, as transmissions of electric current, sound waves or light waves. How do we identify exactly where the value lies in the information of the e-commerce environment? Is all information, no matter where or what it is, subject to criminal attack? Does all information have value, or is some information useless and thus has no value at all? We would suggest that all information potentially has value to criminals, but its value depends on what kind of information it is, who owns it and the motivation of the criminal. Where information resides and where it travels is also an important element in determining the value of information, but these factors have more to do with how or where the information is targeted for attack, an issue that will be discussed later in this chapter.

Types of information in the e-commerce environment

In the e-commerce environment, four main categories of information can be found, as follows:

- *Intellectual property.* The value of intellectual property is readily convertible into cash, items of consumption or items that will generate cash. In this case, information is encased in objects mostly physical though increasingly electronic that are consumer items. Examples are books, CDs, DVDs, software, recipes and maps. The information is therefore subject to criminal threat as are any consumer products.

- *Intelligence.* The databases constructed by e-commerce retailers concerning their customers' personal and credit information are of considerable value in at least three ways: they are obviously very valuable to the business that built the database, so if stolen may be used to extort money; the credit information, if stolen, may be used to steal the identities of customers and thereby steal products using their credit cards; and finally, because such databases are so central to doing e-commerce business, they have value to terrorists as targets of attack in order to disrupt commerce. It is true that these databases are sometimes bought and sold by businesses to other businesses, but generally they are not consumer products.

- *Systems.* Electronic information is not static like the printed page of a book that resides on a shelf in a library. The true value of electronic information lies in its movability. Huge amounts of information can today be transported around the world in seconds. This dynamic form of information is essential for the efficient use of databases and the monitoring and collection of such information. Since information systems are built upon complex interconnected computer networks that make up the Internet, it follows that the Internet contains considerable value, and as more consumers and businesses connect to the Internet, its value as an information resource (i.e. as a market) necessarily increases. The Internet therefore becomes a natural target for predators, depending on their motivation. The system itself – the backbone that turns static information into dynamic information that can be used in business processes (not to mention intellectual and educational uses) – becomes a prime target of value. The vulnerability to particular types of criminal attack lies in the ease with which the transmission of information may be disrupted, and the information system brought to a halt.

- *Services.* The electronic age provides services of all kinds, many that we take for granted. Telephone services are the obvious and visible form of this type of information. Many physical appliances such as cell phones, wireless PDAs (personal digital assistants) with web access, web radios, cable and satellite TV, provide access to electronic services of various kinds. And of course, the home computer provides access to all the services (old and new) now marketed on the web: online banking, online purchasing of prescription drugs, online medical advice, online stock purchasing and much more. The existence of such services online immediately places them in the computing environment, and therefore subject to all the risks of that environment. As we will see shortly, the risks are considerable. Suffice it to say that theft of services, a crime that existed long before the information age, is now made more possible in the online world because it has made them more accessible.

Ownership of information and criminal motivation

Businesses are rich, are they not? If they own information the information ought to be worth money to them. So criminals may be motivated to steal or otherwise threaten to damage databases owned by business in order to extort protection money. We will recount examples of these kinds of crimes later in this chapter. However, we have so far considered value in purely monetary terms. Depending on the interests and/or motivations of the potential offender, any kind of information may become important. This insight became clear after the September 11 tragedy. Terrorists and would-be terrorists were found to have collected all kinds of information ranging from plans of nuclear and other energy producing sites, plans depicting railroads and energy grids, but also photographs of major tourist sites. One could argue that tourist photographs of, say, the Eiffel Tower have barely any monetary value. One can buy postcards of the Eiffel Tower and its surroundings for just a few pence. But when one thinks of such photographs as providing information that could be used in planning an approach to blowing up the Eiffel Tower, the value of those photographs changes immediately. There may be little monetary value in such information, but there may be considerable political and terrorist value (that is creating fear, causing chaos, instability, provoking violent response, etc). In sum, the ownership of information certainly contributes to its value, but so also does the intent of the criminal. Lessons of September 11 have taught that owners of information may be unaware that their information has the kind of value it does to potential criminals. The revelation that a suspected terrorist harboured photographs of Disney World must surely have been a shock to Disney, a company with an impressive record of social control within the confines of its leisure parks (Shearing and Stenning, 1987).

In sum, we can see that, because of the unique attributes of the information age – the connectedness of information, the dynamic communication of information – identifying what or whether particular kinds of information will become the target of crime in the e-commerce environment is especially difficult.

Where's the target?

One of the central features of situational crime prevention is the idea of 'target hardening'. This idea has a long history in security practice and derives theoretical support from the classic paper by Cohen and Felson (1979), who argued that direct-contact predatory crime resulted from the confluence of three minimal elements: a likely offender, a suitable target and the absence of a capable guardian against crime. This formula has served researchers and practitioners of situational crime prevention well for many years. However, in the light of the interconnectedness of most e-businesses, and especially those directly doing business on the Internet, it is now obvious that the question of what exactly is a target deserves further elucidation. If information itself actually is a prime target, as we have suggested so far in this chapter, we need to refine this proposition a little more. We have already done this minimally by identifying the different kinds of information and how value is attached to them. But now we need to consider the rational course of action that an offender may take in carrying out a crime in the e-commerce environment. Is the very first step that the offender takes the identification of a suitable target? There may, in fact, be more than one target, and these targets may differ in terms of their utility in completing the crime. Targets can be characterised in at least seven different (though overlapping) ways:

1. *Prime targets.* In regard to theft, we can say that the prime target of the thief is the item or items to be stolen. In the information age, information or information systems often become the prime targets because they either represent the objects to be stolen (e.g. money in the form of data in a bank's computing system) or provide the route or access to the coveted objects of theft (e.g. a password to use with a stolen ATM card).

2. *Transitional targets.* A burglar may plan to steal jewellery (his prime target) but in order to carry out his crime he must target a house in order to gain access to that target. Or, in the information age, a thief may plan to steal money from an online bank, so may target a particular computer or network in order to gain access to bank accounts.

3. *Proximate targets.* Thieves will follow a rational course of action in order to reach their goal. While their target may be a particular house or car, if they are confronted with barriers – locks or security alarms – they may be diverted to a different target. A thief will not steal a locked car if an equivalent car is nearby and is unlocked. Similarly, hackers will scan computer networks to find a computer that has no lock or security control.

4. *Convertible targets.* A criminal may steal a car in order to carry out a bank robbery. Or, in the information age, a thief may steal a cell phone in order to use the telephone services, or steal a credit card in order to purchase goods.

5. *Attractive targets.* Objects, persons or locations may 'invite' criminal attack because of their intrinsic attractiveness, depending both upon the motivations of the criminal but also the features of the object. For example, railway cars are an attractive object for graffiti artists because of their visibility to large numbers of people. Houses with broken windows are attractive targets for more vandalism. Official government or high-profile business websites are attractive targets to hackers who want to embarrass those in authority and demonstrate their computing prowess.

6. *Incidental targets.* Bystanders to a bank robbery may be injured. However, in the information age everyone and every organisation is a bystander to computer-related crime. A hacker may release a virus or worm in order to bring down a major website, but the effects of such worms, because of the connectedness of networks such as the Internet, means that even if one particular website is targeted, others in distant locations will also be affected. Furthermore, unlike a simple shoplifting in a retail store, in the e-commerce environment, every act of theft undermines trust, the core of e-commerce, and this affects the whole of the e-commerce environment. Thus the entire e-commerce environment is the incidental target of every tiny online theft. The fact that the number of people now online has increased tremendously in the last decade, and the number of websites has increased enormously as well, means that there are obviously more targets of opportunity for criminals. The number of people online increased from about half a million in 1995 to more than 50 million in 2000. One estimate suggests that the average worldwide loss per online person due to Internet fraud rose from $427 in 2000 to $636 in 2001[1].

7. *Undifferentiated targets.* These may be the most common targets resulting from the release of computer viruses, and are similar to incidental targets. Offenders may release viruses simply to disrupt the entire network, usually the Internet. In this case the target is undifferentiated in the sense that no specific object or person is targeted for attack.

Finally, there is one attribute of the information age that contributes to the identification of targets of crime, and that is the capacity for surveillance. The literature on stranger serial killers and child molesters reveals that these criminals typically stake out places looking for their victims. In order to find a suitable victim, child molesters will hang around schools and playgrounds, while serial killers or rapists may stake out shopping malls or car parks. On the Internet, however, it is possible to conduct large-scale, computerised searches for suitable targets. Hackers can download software that will automate the process of surveying large numbers of computers that are connected to the Internet, looking for security holes, thus identifying potential targets that can be either used to commit other crimes or attacked as prime targets. A computer system that is well secured may therefore have the effect of displacing crime to other computers that are not so well protected. While this example bears a close similarity to proximate targets described above, the difference is that in the case of car theft, for example, the selection of an unlocked car may be more or less random, or at least depends on an unlocked car being proximate to the locked car. In the case of computing systems, physical proximity is completely unnecessary. The hacker can simply conduct surveillance over large sections of the Internet in order to find a suitable target. There are no restrictions of either space or time, since the speed of surveillance is conducted at the speed of the Internet, which gets faster every year.

This last point concerns the special capacities of the computing environment that we have alluded to throughout this and the previous chapter, revealing that computers are both targets and tools of crime (Department of Trade and Industry, 2001).[2] As we have seen, computers and computer systems are targets for crime because they perform two major functions: (a) they store large masses of information that have value to their users and thus to potential criminals; and (b) they are able to transmit large masses of information of many different kinds to other computers and devices at increasingly rapid speed. Criminals may steal or corrupt valuable information by either gaining unauthorised access to the computer that stores the information or by intercepting any transmission.

Computers may be used as a tool for crime much as automobiles were used to enhance getaways in bank robberies. Drug runners benefit by the enhanced communications provided by cell phones (essentially computers); pornographers use computers for storage and exchange of paedophilic images; money launderers may channel illegal drug proceeds through hidden bank accounts and web store fronts that are easily constructed using the modern tools of electronic and online banking and other services of the Internet.

A wide range of crimes is made possible by, or enhanced by, the computing environment. We have already suggested that many such crimes may not be directly related to e-commerce, but depending on the circumstances, they in fact can have a serious impact on the marketplace. As we noted, the deliberate infection of the Internet with a virus or worm can wreak havoc with the e-mail systems of companies on the other side of the globe. Companies that depend on e-mail as a means of communication with their customers or business partners will be directly affected, even though the initial release of the virus may not have been intended to infect that particular business. Because of the vast interrelatedness of computers, computer networks and telecommunications, a seemingly small act of hacking may become a massive act of sabotage, with severe effects on e-commerce itself. Thus, in order to provide some understanding of the vulnerability of e-commerce to crimes of the information age, we provide in Tables 3.1 to 3.3 a survey of crimes of the information age and indicate the targets involved.

Crimes of the information age

In Tables 3.1–3.3 we classify crimes committed on the Internet or against computer systems according to the extent that they have direct or indirect effects on e-commerce businesses. The line between each category is of necessity arbitrary. There are obviously many crimes that fit more than one category.

- *Table 3.1* lists those crimes that have *direct* effects on e-commerce, usually victimising a specific business (though inevitably this damage trickles down to customers through higher prices). There are two types of crimes included in this category: those that impact directly on specific e-commerce product types (intellectual property and services) and those whose impact affects all e-commerce enterprises (information systems and intelligence). Crimes included in the specific product type are telecommunications theft, cloning of cellular phones, video piracy, software piracy and copyright infringement. Those whose impact applies to all e-commerce are terrorism, electronic funds transfer fraud, hacking, industrial espionage, denial of service, cross-border crime, extortion and blackmail, and credit card fraud. In this group of crimes, specific businesses are usually the prime target, but obviously in the second group of crimes that involve terrorism, there are many incidental targets to these crimes.

- *Table 3.2* lists those crimes that mostly have an *indirect* effect on e-commerce (although depending on the circumstances their impact can sometimes be direct). These crimes generally create an ambience of fraud and distrust on the Internet such that they contribute to the customer's lack of confidence to do business. Just as one would not go shopping for an important item of quality in a run-down neighbourhood that is ridden with prostitution, drug dealing and pornography, one is also distrustful of shopping at an e-commerce site if the crimes of this category are widespread on the Internet. These crimes undermine the central ingredient of e-commerce, which is trust (Gambetta,

1988). They include stalking, harassment, money laundering, investment fraud, telemarketing fraud, sale of stolen or illegal goods, and identity theft.

- *Table 3.3* lists another group of crimes that create a 'frontier climate' by exploiting grey areas of the law. Crimes included here are gambling, pornography, tax evasion, criminal conspiracy and aiding and abetting of crime. Their overall effect is similar to those of Table 3.2: to undermine the climate of trust of the e-commerce neighbourhood.[3] Their prime targets are often specific customers or groups of customers, and are not usually directed towards business targets.

The crime types in Tables 3.1–3.3 do not necessarily conform to legal categories (Ingraham, 1980), nor are they discrete crimes in themselves as Wasik (1991) shows in an excellent analysis of what is and is not computer crime according to English common law. In fact, many criminal events committed within the computing environment probably contain more than one crime type. We have adopted the common descriptors of crime types in order to provide the context of the crime threats that predominate in the computing environment – the environment within which e-commerce resides. The seriousness of the crime threats is summarised in the column concerning the extent of the type of crime, if known, and the estimated costs to e-commerce of those crimes. Although estimates of such costs are always speculative and open to criticism, the chances are that they are underestimates because they represent only those incidents that have been detected. Some additional general estimates (Keeling, 2001) of the costs of computer-related crime are:

- $6.7 billion – the cost worldwide of the first five days of the 'I Love You' bug of spring 2000;

- $125,000 per hour is the estimated cost worldwide to businesses for web outages;

- $142,000 was the average cost in the USA of network security breaches in 1999 according to the FBI;

- 55 per cent of US companies in 1999 experienced at least one breach of computer security in 1999, according to the FBI;

- on average, 41 per cent of security-related losses in the USA is the direct result of employees stealing information, and the average cost per incident was $1.8 million.

Table 3.1: Crimes of the computing environment having direct effects on e-commerce.

Crime type or incident	Examples	Estimates of extent or cost
Theft of telephone services	*Convertible target*: obtained **employee's access code** and software from Internet. *Transitional target*: hacked into telephone company **computer system**, and assumed systems operator status. See also cell phone cloning, below.[4] *Prime target*: telephone **services.**	In the UK, £290 million one incident in 1990 (Grabosky, 2001) and 5 per cent of total industry turnover (Grabosky, 2001; Schiek, 1995). 'Phreaking' for fun in the 1980s, small amounts of between £500 and £1,000 in the UK (Clough and Mungo, 1992).
Video piracy	*Prime target*: **intellectual property**. Counterfeit copies of movies and video games downloadable from the Internet. Hacker posted on a well-known hacker website (http://www.2600.org) a program to decode DVDs (DeCSS) and convert them into downloadable files.[5] Video game makers sue Yahoo! for selling pirated games at auction.[6]	Ten per cent of all movies can be downloaded from the Internet illegally, and for free.[7] Piracy drives down prices, occurs in over 65 countries.[8] Industry cost estimated $3.2 billion worldwide from piracy in 1998.[9] Some 270,000 Dutch web addresses offer a movie or TV show illegally for sale or most often free.[10]
Software piracy	*Prime target*: **intellectual property**. Easy copying from disks and CDs, obtain protection-free copies from the Internet.	$7.4 billion worldwide lost in 1993 according to Software Publishers Association.[11]
Copyright infringement	*Prime target*: **intellectual property**. Reproduction of copyrighted material on the Internet. Trading in copyrighted songs and recordings via peer-to-peer. Most famous case: Napster music site, used by millions, shut down because of copyright infringement.[12]	Worldwide annual costs to industry approx. $15–17 billion annually.[13]

Vandalism	*Incidental or undifferentiated targets*: **everyone** connected to the Internet. Most infamous example of the 'worm' virus released into the Internet causing untold damage within hours infecting 10 per cent of Internet hosts, many out of business for up to two weeks.[14]	Trillions of dollars. See hacking and terrorism below.
Spying, industrial espionage	*Prime target*: **information system**. Most famous example: intruder into Lawrence Berkeley Lab computer tracked down and caught (Stoll, 1989).	More recently, intruders found 'sniffing' in Rome USA Lab, Griffiss Air Force Base. Cost: $211,000 plus cost of investigation.[15]
Terrorism	*Prime target*: **information system and intelligence**. The US Defense Department receives some 60–80 hacker attacks a week to its computers. In February 1998, 11 Dept of Defense computers were broken into. In 1998, a 'cracker' cyber terrorist disabled a Chinese satellite to protest western investment in China.[16]	It is estimated that there are upwards of 30,000 hacker sites on the Internet that provide tutorials on how to write viruses, choke networks and announce meeting points for hackers all over the world.[17]
Electronic funds transfer fraud	*Convertible target*: **information system and intelligence database** of banks. Irrevocable transfer of funds, usually offshore, extremely difficult to prevent, especially when perpetrators typically use fictitious identities (Chapman and Smith, 2001).	Over 50 per cent of banks surveyed report having been victimised by fraud (Chapman and Smith, 2001). See also below, cross-border crime.
Hacking	*Prime target*: **specific information system or intelligence**. This is the most well known computer crime. Hackers have broken into banks in Los Angeles, the Los Alamos National Research Center, the LA Police Department, Scotland Yard, Pacific	In 1995 estimated that hackers cost business $800 million.[20] In 2000 the estimate is $1.6 trillion worldwide.[21]

Table 3.1: Crimes of the computing environment having direct effects on e-commerce (continued).

Crime type or incident	Examples	Estimates of extent or cost
	Telephone[18] and many more. The most infamous hacker Kevin Mitnick cost hi-tech companies at least $291.8 million.[19] In contrast to virus releases which aim at *undifferentiated targets*, hackers usually target specific organisations. To hackers, these systems are also commonly *attractive targets*.	
Denial of service	*Prime target*: **specific information system or intelligence.** The most sophisticated version is distributed denial of service, in which an individual exploits bugs or loopholes in operating systems (usually Windows) to cause a flood of messages to be sent via hundreds of computers to one website which effectively closes it down.[22]	It is predicted because of the rapidly increased availability of bandwidth (fast connection to the Internet) to users, and the more powerful personal computers (especially running Windows XP), that distributed denial of service will increase drastically in coming years. All major e-commerce sites have been victimised.[23]
Cross-border crime	*Prime target*: **trusting customer.** Boy buys a DVD player on Amazon auction site. Wires money to seller in Moldova. Never receives item. Finds out that many others have been victimised as well. Amazon partially reimburses victim.[24] See also credit card fraud below. The auction web site is a *transitional target* for the fraudster.	Russian in St Petersburg accesses Citibank's funds transfer system and deflects payments of $10.7 million to his own account in Russia (Smith, 2001). Internet ideally suited to cross-border crime since the Internet exists beyond national boundaries.
Extortion and blackmail	*Transitional target*: **bulletin board** used to convey threat to kill Microsoft president Bill Gates. Offender	Banks have begun to appease online extortionists by paying them off. Gangs have amassed up to £400

	used encrypted messages and images posted on AOL Netgirl Bulletin Board, demanding transfer of $5,246,827.62 to a Luxembourg bank account. Offender caught, tracked to Long Grove, Illinois.[25]	million worldwide by issuing threats to destroy computer systems by using information warfare techniques.[26]
Cloning of cellular phones, phone cards	*Convertible target*: buy cell phones in bulk, **clone to other numbers and discard after use**. The US DEA numbers were cloned by the Colombia Drug cartel (Denning and Baugh Jr, 2000).	Estimated in 1996 $1 million to $2 million worth of illegal phone use per day in the United States and Canada.[27]
Credit card fraud	*Convertible target*: in an example of cross-border crime, two British men in Wales hacked into e-commerce websites in the USA, UK, Canada, Thailand and Japan and stole **credit card information for 26,000 accounts**. Stolen numbers sold in cybermarkets of former Soviet Union.[28]	Losses for this crime alone exceeded $3 million. Visa estimates that online credit card fraud accounts for 25–28 cents of every $100 spent, about four times worse than the offline rate of 7 cents per $100.[29] Recent estimates of losses globally are in the billions.[30]
Accounting fraud	*Convertible targets*: these include intervening in the **information systems** underlying the automation of buying and selling; purchasing and payment fraud, circumvention of payment authorisation controls, and many other techniques that utilise opportunities afforded by the lack of paper trails in computerised record-keeping. The scandals of Enron and WorldCom accounting are recent hi-tech examples of these essentially old crimes (Crowder, 1997).	Circumvention of auditing controls (e.g. WorldCom, estimated costs close to $3 billion) and manipulation of electronic markets, e.g. insider trading and false purchasing (e.g. Enron, estimated costs in hundreds of millions).[31]

Table 3.2 Crimes of the computing environment having indirect effects on e-commerce.

Crime type or incident	Examples	Estimates of extent or cost
Stalking	*Prime target*: **women who register with online dating** websites are tracked down by would-be suitors (Jerin and Dolinsky, 2001). *Incidental targets*: all of **e-commerce**. Crimes like stalking cannot be compartmentalised or localised in the Internet. They affect the entire 'global neighbourhood' of the Internet.	In 2000, estimated that of worldwide population of users there are 3,000 Internet stalkers.[32]
Harassment	A man, spurned by a woman, posted on an online bulletin board an invitation to her home for a 'gang rape fantasy', giving her address, phone number, and how to bypass her burglar alarm. Eight men showed up.[33] *Prime target*: an **individual's personal information**. *Transitional target*: the **bulletin board**.	Typical targets are inexperienced users of the Internet, and women (US DOJ, 1999).
Money laundering	*Prime and convertible target*: infiltration of **banking system** by organised crime, use of electronic non-bank transfers and cyber-banking, and many other sophisticated techniques (Financial Action Task Force, 2001).	Estimated that one trillion dollars is laundered every year (Williams, 1997: 239).
Investment fraud	*Prime target*: **customers** duped by bogus banks that use the web as a *transitional target* to set up fraudulent websites. Bogus company that promises to turn iron-ore rocks into gold, and many more.[34]	Securities scams run by organised crime: 35 companies in the USA exposed by FBI in 2000. Frauds cost victims $50 million.[35]

Telemarketing fraud	*Prime target:* **customers** and groups of customers. The top ten telemarketing frauds of 2000 were (in order of incidence): prizes/sweepstakes, magazine sales, credit card sales, work-at-home, advance fee loans, telephone slamming, credit card loss protection, buyers clubs, telephone cramming, travel/vacations.[36] *Transitional targets:* fraudulent websites and e-mail used to promote scams.	Estimated cost in the USA of $40 billion a year through telemarketing fraud; 92 per cent of adults in the United States report receiving fraudulent telephone offers. The FBI estimates that there are 14,000 illegal telephone sales operations at any given time.[37]
Sale of stolen or illegal goods	*Transitional target:* **Internet auction sites, bulletin boards, news groups.** Man uses aliases to sell pirated Adobe software on Ebay auction site.[38] Four high school boys purchased DXM, an hallucinogen, on web auction site.[39]	16 million users of auction websites per month; 87 per cent of fraud cases online estimated to be related to auction websites.[40] Consumer complaints in the USA rose from 1,280 in 1987 to 10,660 in 1999.[41] There are over 1,000 auction sites on the Internet.[42]
Identity theft	*Convertible target:* a husband/wife team (the 'modern Bonnie and Clyde') stole the **identities** and emptied the **bank accounts** of their victims in over six US states.[43]	Identity fraud accounted for 96 per cent of Visa members' bank credit card fraud losses of $407 million in 1997 (United States General Accounting Office, 1998; see also Jones and Levi, 2000).

Table 3.3 'Frontier' crimes of the computing environment having direct and indirect effects on e-commerce.

Crime type or incident	Examples	Estimates of extent or cost
Gambling	*Attractive targets*: May or may not be illegal in various countries and regions, which is a major part of the problem (McMillen and Grabosky, 1998). The web is the *transitional target* for promoting these attractive activities.	Worldwide online gambling revenue has increased from $651 million in 1998 to $2,238 million in 2001.[44]
Tax evasion	*Convertible target*: Barnes&Noble.com sued by Amazon.com for **not charging sales tax** because it gave them an unfair competitive price advantage.[45]	Sales tax and trade embargoes make otherwise ordinary products 'hot'. Cuban cigars are sold widely on the web.[46]
Criminal conspiracy	International networks to trade in pornography, the 'Wonderland Club'. Organised crime in smuggling, drugs, gambling and prostitution all enhanced by *convertible target* of the **computing environment** (Grant and Grabosky, 1997).	100 arrests in 1998 and 100,000 images seized world wide (Grant and Grabosky, 1997: 41).
Aiding and abetting crime	*Convertible target*: **intelligence** provided by how-to news groups: bomb-making, lock-picking, counterfeiting, encryption fixes, smart card cloning (Mann and Sutton, 1998).	Alt.hacker newsgroup is one of many in which 'newbies' and seasoned hackers exchange information.

Criminogenic attributes of the computing environment

The picture of the computing environment emerging from Tables 3.1–3.3 is one that is ripe with crime. So much so, that we are led to speculate that there are attributes about the computing environment – the information system that makes e-commerce possible – that themselves make certain types of crime possible, and provide opportunities for crime which criminals cannot resist. That is to say, from a situational crime prevention perspective, situations present themselves in the computing environment that may either provoke or tempt individuals to commit particular kinds of crimes, or make it easier for offenders to carry out crimes. Clarke (1999) applied this perspective to an understanding of 'hot products' by identifying attributes of product designs that made their theft easier, more attractive and more possible. He summed up these attributes with the acronym CRAVED, designed to describe the vulnerability to theft that may be contained in the design of manufactured products. These attributes were: Concealable, Removable, Available, Valuable, Enjoyable and Disposable. When we examine in the following chapters elements of e-commerce transactions we will consider the idea of hot products in the e-commerce environment further. For the moment, we wish to apply this perspective to an understanding of the computing environment that makes e-commerce possible.

If we think in broader terms of the information system providing situations that are imbued with attributes that make certain crimes more possible, we can identify the elements of the information system itself that are conducive to crime with the acronym SCAREM: Stealth, Challenge, Anonymity, Reconnaissance, Escape and Multiplicity. The six features identify not only features of the information system that are 'hot' in and of themselves, but also tie these to the known motivations of potential offenders.

- *Stealth.* Stealth is certainly a 'convenience' provided to all who use the Internet. It makes carrying out furtive crimes obviously much easier. Consider the fantasy of the invisible thief who can just walk into a bank and remove as much money as he wants, all the time remaining undetected! Just such a possibility exists on the Internet as clearly outlined by Denning and Baugh (2000). Criminals use encryption, mimic the actions of a systems operator, obtain passwords, use steganography and use remote storage on an innocent third party's computers, to identify just a few techniques. These thieves are virtually invisible.[47] And on newsgroups, even non-criminals can use assumed identities.

- *Challenge.* The literature on computer criminals who are hackers is replete with one primary motivation: to 'beat' the computing system. Many seem unable to stop or even delay their mission to break into a computing system, once they have begun their task. They work very long hours, become obsessed with the challenge and completion of their task (Clough and Mungo, 1992). This obsession is not, however, to the detriment of getting caught. Indeed, part of the challenge seems to be to carry out the intrusion virtually under the noses of computer administrators. Depending on the particular situation, the risks of getting caught can be reduced possibly to zero in cases where one can intercept the transmission of information and deflect it to an anonymous account or place. Timing here is of prime importance. Messages, such as those containing funds transfer, move almost at the speed of light. It follows that the less time necessary to carry out the criminal act, the less chance of being caught. Considerable preparation is needed in order to gain access to these transmissions: one must gain entry into the bank's or other institution's computer system. Almost all major break-ins of computing systems have resulted from persistent activity by the hacker over long periods of time, from one month to several months.[48]

- *Anonymity*. Long periods of intrusion are made possible by the anonymity offered users of the Internet. Anonymity differs from stealth which is sneaky and secretive. Anonymity is a traditional value of regular commerce, though it is fast disappearing. When cash purchases are made at a department store, it is irrelevant who the buyers and sellers are. This is a trusted transaction between two strangers, both of whom protect their identities. Adam Smith marvelled at the market economy that actually thrived on the basis of transactions among strangers. Anonymity and its close sibling, deception, abound on the Internet. E-mail addresses can be obtained for free in many places on the Internet, with little or no personal data (or if required little or no verification of personal data). Sophisticated hackers can also mimic the IP addresses of others ('spoofing'), making their e-mail extremely difficult to track (Ahuja, 1997: 12). This therefore allows such hackers to spend long periods of time online attempting to gain illegal entry into an institution's information system with little chance of being detected, or if detected little chance of the offence being tracked specifically to the offender. Finally, in his review of 'situations that permit' Wortley has shown that there is strong research evidence in psychology linking anonymity to deindividuation, a psychological condition that allows individuals to act irresponsibly or criminally (Wortley, 1997). Anonymity is an especially important attribute of the information age to which we will return in the final chapter of this book when we discuss its relationship to authenticating identity.

- *Reconnaissance*. Perhaps the most important element in the rational choices that a criminal makes in carrying out his crime is the choice of a suitable target. The Internet makes it possible to scan thousands of web servers and even millions of personal computers that are connected to the web, looking for 'holes' or gaps in security through which the criminal can enter and carry out any aspect of his crime – whether to deposit stolen files on an unsuspecting computer, or to steal passwords or credit card information for use in a later crime, or to intercept funds transfers, and so on. This scanning for targets can be done automatically in the computing environment using software easily obtainable on the Internet. Cornish and Clarke (1986) have described criminals as demonstrating 'limited rational choice' in the process of carrying out their crime. The picture is that criminals may have a specific goal in mind, say stealing items from an automobile, but will tend to take the path of least resistance in order to accomplish this crime or something like it. Thus they may break into cars that are unlocked (proximate targets as we noted at the beginning of this chapter) or cars that are parked late at night in poorly lit streets. This is a picture of criminals taking advantage of surrounding circumstances of the moment. In contrast, the Internet provides a context in which the informed criminal can take a careful survey of all possible targets, then act accordingly. Much more planning is involved. Rational choice seems less limited than it is enhanced!

- *Escape.* There is little sense in planning and carrying out a crime if it is obvious that the chances of getting caught at the time of the act are very high, or that a trail of evidence is left that will lead inevitably to detection. It is true that some criminals do not think much about the consequences of getting caught when committing their crimes (Katz, 1988). However, it is surely obvious that the crime-inducing aspects of the information system environment of anonymity, deception and stealth all combine to make it extremely difficult for law enforcement to track down the crime to the individual perpetrator, especially when the crime itself may never be detected, even by its victims. In the major case of the US military network break-in mentioned in Table 3.1, the perpetrator first hacked into the Harvard University computing system, and worked from that address. Thus he was able to cover up his own location or 'true identity' (Ahuja, 1997: 14).[49]

- *Multiplicity.* A traditional theft, such as a bank robbery, is a relatively finite act. However, if an offender hacks into a bank's files, this one crime can be multiplied exponentially, since it makes available to the offender a huge number of new opportunities to commit crime by exploiting access to the bank's accounts. While it is true that some traditional crimes such as burglary do create the opportunity for additional burglaries of the same premises, these are limited to one or two additional times, and do bring with them substantially increased risk. But hacking into valuable databases makes many more crimes possible and attractive. These are not just confined to theft from bank accounts, but can also involve extorting money from the bank for return of the database.

The SCAREM of information systems provides a benign setting for the commission of crime on the Internet and other computer networks. We would argue further that, not only do the information systems of e-commerce provide special opportunities for crime, but information itself contains attributes that makes it an attractive target of crime. And since information is the stuff of e-commerce, its targeting threatens the entire fabric of e-commerce. In the following chapter, we analyse the criminogenic attributes of information.

Notes

1 It is likely that this figure considerably underestimates the costs of computer-related crime because it is limited to scams and cons and excludes certain types of hacking, vandalism and other types of computer crime that do not have direct monetary effects on specific victims, but whose costs are far broader and non-specific.

2 The distinction between computers as targets and instruments of crime has also been made by Grabosky (2001). Strictly speaking it is often hard to distinguish exactly what is the target: the computer that contains and transmits the data, or the information systems contained therein. Grabosky uses the latter term, and the Department of Trade and Industry (2001) paper uses the former. See also Grabosky, Smith and Dempsey (2001) for a more extensive treatment of targets and guardians in relation to electronic theft.

3 A contrary argument could be made that pornography and gambling are positive elements of the Internet simply because they increase traffic on the Internet, thus increasing the number of potential customers. The question of whether these enterprises create negative or positive externalities has yet to be researched.

4 Grabosky and Smith (2001) subsume almost the entire range of 'digital crime' within telecommunications fraud.

5 Staff (2000) 'Attorneys in video hacker court case predict mass piracy', *Reuters, CNN.com*, 18 July. A new DVX compression format now makes it possible to compress extremely large movie files into small enough files to make it practicable to download from the Internet. This technology is now widely available. See: Borland, John (2001) 'Hackers' video technology goes open source', *CNET News.com*, 17 January.

6 Staff (Reuters) (2000) 'Video game makers sue Yahoo! in piracy complaint', *Business News*, http://internet.com.

7 Staff (2000) 'Attorneys in video hacker court case predict mass piracy', *Reuters, CNN.com*, 18 July.

8 Wheeler, Marilyn (2000) 'Forget streaming video. Bootleg versions of nearly every movie you can name are already available online', *ZDNET News.com*, 15 May.

9 Staff (1999) 'U.S. and video game makers lost more than $3 billion worldwide in 1998 due to software piracy: Greater China, Paraguay, Thailand and Malaysia top list', *Business Wire*, 16 February http://www.businesswire.com.

10 Arlen, Gary (2001) 'Always on: Dutch video piracy prelude to a corporate threat', *Broadband Week*, 16 April. This figure contrasts with the US figure of 534,668. Clearly the Netherlands figure is disproportionate to the population.

11 Meyer, M. and Underwood A. (1994) 'Crimes of the Net', *Bulletin/Newsweek*, 15 November: 68–9.

12 Castelluccio, Michael (2001) 'Intellectual property online: a landmark case', *Strategic Finance*, February: 52–7.

13 United States Information Infrastructure Task Force (1995) *Intellectual Property and the National Information Infrastructure: Report of the Working Group on Intellectual Property Rights* (Bruce A. Lehman, Chair). Washington: US Patent and Trademark Office.

14 Eichin, M. W. and Rochlis, J. A. (1989) 'With microscope and tweezers: an analysis of the Internet virus of November 1988', *Proceedings of the IEEE Computer Society Symposium on Security and Privacy*, May: 326–42.

15 Christy, Jim (1998) Rome Laboratory Attacks: Prepared testimony of Jim Christy, Air Force Investigator, before the Senate Government Affairs Committee, Permanent Investigations Subcommittee, 22 May 1996.

16 Staff (1998) 'Cyber terrorism', *Terrorism Update*, Anti-defamation League, Winter: http://www.adl.org/terror/focus/16_focus_a2.html.

17 Barker, Garry (1999) 'Australia: Internet terrorism escalates the new info-war', *The Age* (Melbourne), 13 July: 9.

18 See Wasik (1991: 42–54). The accomplishments of hackers are shrouded in myth and full of apocryphal stories. It is particularly difficult to tell fact from fiction in many cases. See, for example, Levy (1984) and Taylor (2000).

19 Miller, Greg (2001) 'Firms say hacker cost them $291 million', *L.A. Times on Channel 2000*, http://www.channel2000.com. Pro-hacker websites and publications dispute this estimate. See http://www.2600.org.

20 Ricciutti, Mike (1996) 'Hacking cost business $800 million', *CNET News.com*, 6 June, 12:15 p.m. PT, http://news.cnet.com/news/0-1005-200-311476.html?tag=prntfr.

21 Knight, Will (2000) 'Hacking will cost world $1.6 trillion this year', *ZDNET news*, 11 July, http://news.zdnet.co.uk/story/0,,s2080075,00.html. However, other experts doubt the claims of some hackers' achievements. See Nuttall-Smith, Chris and Flavelle, Dana (2000) 'Experts doubt claims by Canadian hacker', *Toronto Star*, 16 February.

22 Gibson Research Corporation (2001) 'Denial of service investigation and Exploration', http://grc.com/dos/. Also contains 'how it was done' information. A most publicised case of distributed denial of service was that of Mafiaboy and others in which several major e-commerce businesses such as Amazon.com, Etrade and others were brought down by Mafiaboy's claimed attack (Verton, 2002).

23 Staff (2000) 'E*Trade, ZD Net latest targets in wave of cyber-attacks. Earlier strikes hit Ebay, Amazon, CNN.com, Yahoo!' *Insurgency on the Internet*, http://www.cnn.com/2000/TECH/computing/02/09/cyber.attacks.02/index.html, 9 February, web posted at 1:33 p.m. EST (18:33 GMT).

24 Parker, Nicholas (2000) 'Mom, Moldova, and how a boy lost his innocence (plus $375)', *Fortune*, col. 141, issue 11: 274–5.

25 *United States of America* v. *Adam Quinn Pletcher*, United States District Court, Western District of Washington Seattle, Magistrate's docket, Case No. 97-179M, 9 May 1997.

26 Staff (1996) 'Banks appease online terrorists', *CNET News.com*, 3 June.

27 Staff (1996) 'Companies give cell phone bandits a new hang-up', *CNN News*, 10 December, http://www.cnn.com/TECH/9612/10/cellular.cloning/.

28 Richtel, Matt (2002) 'Credit card theft is thriving online as global market', *New York Times*, 13 May, p. A1.

29 Sullivan, Bob (1999) 'Just how bad is online fraud? No one really knows how safe your credit card data is', *MSNBC*, http://stacks.msnbc.com/news/590609.asp, June 25.

30 Richtel, Matt (2002) 'Credit card theft is thriving online as global market', *New York Times*, 13 May, p. A1.

31 Staff (2002) 'Accounting for change', *The Economist*, 29 June, pp. 13–14.

32 Cyberangels (2000) *About Cyberstalking*, Cyberangels, http://www.cyberangels.org/stalking/intex.html.

33 Fint, J. (2000) 'Stalker terror, girl tracked and taunted', *Sunday Herald Sun*, 4 June, Melbourne, p. 1 and p. 3.

34 Wyatt, Edward (1999) 'SEC sweep focuses on bogus securities offerings on the web', *New York Times*, 13 May, Section C, p. 9. Bulkeley, William M. (1999) 'Arrest made in PairGain Internet hoax', *Wall Street Journal*, 16 April Section C, p. 1. Lowry, Tom (1998) 'Bogus cyberbanks pose increasing threat', *USA Today*, 6 April, Section B, p. 1. *On credit card scams*: BT (1998). 'Three real cons in the virtual world', *Good Housekeeping*, vol. 227, no. 3, p. 163. *On bogus HIV test kits*: Kurtzweil, Paula (1999) 'Internet sales of bogus HIV test kits result in first-of-kind wire fraud conviction', *FDA Consumer*, vol. 33, no. 4, July–August. *On 'cramming' by sending fraudulent invoices to businesses who subscribe to 'free' web hosting*: Gross, Liza (1999) 'FTC says to beware of web site scams', *Graphic Arts Monthly*, vol. 71, no. 9, September, http://www.gammag.com. *On fake e-mail messages to elicit personal information such as credit card numbers*: Davis, Kristin (2000) 'You've got bogus mail', *Managing Kiplinger's*, vol. 54, no. 11, November. *On bogus drugs*: Leff, Michael (1999) 'Too good to be true', *Consumer Reports on Health*, vol. 11, no. 6. p. 2.

35 McEvoy, Aoife, Albro, Edward N., McCracken, Harry, Brandt, Andrew and Spring, Tom (2001) 'Dot cons', *PC World*, May, vol. 19, no. 5, pp. 107–10.

36 National Consumers League at 1701 K Street, NW, Suite 1200, Washington, DC 20006, (202) 835–3323, info@nclnet.org, http://www.fraud.org/telemarketing/00statsfinal.htm.

37 *Ibid*.

38 US Department of Justice (2001) press release: *Man indicted for auctioning pirated software*, US Attorney Northern District of California, November, http://www.cybercrime.gov/niemi_indict.htm.

39 Hancock, Bill (2000) 'Isn't it interesting what you can buy at an auction site? TVs, computers, drugs', *Computers and Security*, vol. 19, no. 5, pp. 404–5.

40 Haney, Clare (2001) 'Auction sites hit hard by electronic crime', *InfoWorld*, vol. 23, no. 3, 15 January, p. 25.

41 Messmer, Ellen (2000) 'Ebay acts to curtail Internet fraud', *Networld*, 24 July http://www.nwfusion.com.

42 Blake, Kevin (2000) 'Cyber fraud crackdown', *Consumers' Research Magazine*, March, vol. 83, no. 3, p. 6.

43 Kristin, Davis (1998) 'The Bonnie and Clyde credit card fraud', *Kiplinger's Personal Finance Magazine*, July, vol. 52, no. 7, p. 65.

44 NUA surveys, http://www.nua.org.

45 McWilliams, Brian (1997) *PC World News Radio*, Friday, 22 August.

46 Karp, Jack (2001) 'A growing number of foreign websites sell Cuban cigars to US residents, and there's nothing law enforcement can do about it', *TechTV.com*, 6 November. http://www.techtv.com/cybercrime/print/0,23102,3336772,00.html.

47 The invisibility fantasy is at least as old as the Greek myth of Gyge's ring, the wearer of which became invisible. In Plato's *Republic* Glaucon argues that any man wearing the ring would commit immoral or criminal acts. Socrates argues that a moral man would not. Fortunately, situational crime prevention does not have to answer this question, which is essentially one of human nature. Rather, it only has to define the situations in which opportunities occur to commit crime, and then modify the situations, without direct concern for the human nature (probably unchangeable anyway) of the individual actor. See Kleinig (2000).

48 A shortlist includes: the Internet worm released in 1988; 'Hacker in the cuckoo's egg' in which an East German spy penetrated the US Department of Defense network in 1989; intruder stole IDs and passwords from a NYC Internet Service provider in 1993; in 1995 source address spoofing resulted in widespread denial of service; in 1995 $10 million stolen from Citibank computers by Russian who deflected fund transfers to his own accounts; in 1996, after a break-in to Harvard's computers, hacker penetrated US government network (Ahuja, 1997).

49 Ahuja, 1997: 14.

Chapter 4

Information as a hot product

We have already referred to Clarke's (1999) work in identifying consumer items that, because of their design, were more vulnerable to theft than other products. These he called 'hot products' and he described their criminogenic attributes with the acronym CRAVED (Clarke, 1999): Concealable, Removable, Available, Valuable, Enjoyable and Disposable. In later work, Clarke and Newman (2002) showed how a variety of consumer items might vary according to these criteria. For example, a refrigerator is not as removable or enjoyable as a piece of jewellery, but both are valuable and their disposability may depend on local circumstances such as the presence of a fence or willing buyer. In the previous chapter we argued that a prime ingredient of all products found in e-commerce was information, and that this ingredient was often the target of crime. Here we will extend this idea further to suggest that information itself may be thought of as a hot product by showing how it fits Clarke's CRAVED descriptors.

We identified in Chapter 3 the kinds of information that are targeted by crime in the e-commerce environment as intellectual property, intelligence, systems and services. Table 4.1, which uses the listing of crimes from Tables 3.1 to 3.3, matches crimes to types of information and to targeted products. The classification is very general and only suggestive, but it serves the purpose of demonstrating that there are links between types of crimes and types of information. We would go further, however, and suggest that there probably is a link between types of crimes and the portion of a product that is information based.

To explain what we mean by this, let us consider the example of the credit card, which is the transitional product that links the old model of commerce to the new e-commerce. It is a piece of plastic, a physical product which has almost no intrinsic value. Ordinary customers do not buy credit cards nor do they own them. The banks or other card-issuing organisations own them. However, the card issuers provide the cards to customers in order to market a service – a product actually – which is credit. Thus the portion of a credit card that is composed of information is 100 per cent. Similarly, the portion of a cell phone that is information is probably close to 80 per cent or more. The phone is a marketing device for the service provided.

Typical consumer products are becoming increasingly like credit cards, because their marketing and pricing is increasingly bound to services provided as part of the product. Customers are solicited to buy service contracts for a product, especially an electronic product. Software is now largely licensed to users and updates or services to that product are part, often a major part, of the revenue collected for that product. New and used cars are sold along with extended service contracts, as are computers which become cheaper by the day, but whose information portion – the service contracts – increasingly become a significant part of the product. The blurring of the line between products and services means that traditional consumer products are increasingly redefined not so much in physical terms, but as items whose main ingredient is service, which is to say *information*. Thus if we are able to

Table 4.1 Information, crimes and targeted products of e-commerce.

Information type	Crimes	Product or target
Intellectual property	Video piracy, software piracy, copyright violation, counterfeiting.	CDs, videos, music, software.
Intelligence	Industrial espionage, extortion and blackmail, credit card fraud, accounting fraud, identity theft, aiding and abetting crime.	Proprietary information, business plans and formulas, databases of credit and personal information, accounting records, credit card users, newsgroup users.
Systems	Vandalism, terrorism, electronic funds transfer fraud, hacking, denial of service, accounting fraud.	Bank accounts, websites, databases, accounting records.
Services	Theft of telephone services, electronic funds transfer fraud, cross-border crime, denial of service, cloning of cellular phones and phone cards, credit card fraud, stalking, harassment, money laundering, investment fraud, telemarketing fraud, gambling, tax evasion, criminal conspiracy.	Cell phones, phone cards, bank accounts, credit cards, Internet users, personal identity, banks and credit institutions, fake lotteries and prizes, illegal drugs and services, newsgroup users, pornography. Sale of stolen or illegal goods easy at online auction sites, though maintaining anonymity is increasingly difficult.

show that information contains criminogenic attributes similar to the hot products described by Clarke then we have a strong case for assessing the criminogenic features of many consumer items of e-commerce, depending on the amount of information bound into them. This would also explain, in part, the distribution of products, crimes and information types shown in Table 4.1.

CRAVED information

If we say that information is the prime target of computer criminals, we must also add that it is a constantly moving target. The information that the criminal seeks either to steal or disrupt may be 'on the move', and it may be stolen by intercepting it between one computer and another. And as wireless computing becomes more pervasive, information that is on the move truly does exist in space. It is the fleeting existence of information in cyberspace that makes it so efficient to transmit, but it is also its cyber characteristics that cause it to resemble 'hot products' that are especially or even inherently prone to criminal attack or misuse. Indeed, the CRAVED analysis that follows clearly shows that it fits information in e-commerce almost perfectly.

- *Concealable*. What better way to conceal an item one has stolen than in cyberspace, a vast territory with so many nooks and crannies that one can hide stolen information, and do it so quickly, that one may never be seen carrying it? Thieves may have thought it easy to remove a magazine from a stand in a store and conceal it under their coat. On the Internet it is even easier to steal. In fact, using the Internet, one can steal information without ever having personally to possess it, and can do so from half way around the world. Not only that, using the standard services and procedures provided by the Internet, users can easily fake or otherwise obfuscate their identities. In fact, in cases where the criminal simply wants the information and does not want to deny it to someone else, the information can be copied and the original left alone. In such cases, there is no trace of the theft. And if so many copies are made of the information, such as, for example, in the case of copyright infringement of software and audio files, which one is the original? This is the ultimate in concealment.

- *Removable*. We hardly need to make comment here. The whole *raison d'être* of the Internet is that information is removable. In fact, it is constantly on the move. It is therefore intrinsically vulnerable to interception and deflection to places that it was not originally intended for. As noted in Table 3.1, electronic funds transfers between banks can be intercepted and deflected to a criminal's own bank account. E-mail can be easily intercepted and personal information stolen. Software files can be downloaded which makes the object of the crime – software – removable, yet still leaves the original file in place. In this sense information is removable and replicable countless

times. While various locks and access controls ar
environment, criminals find ways to break those (

- *Available*. The Internet calls out loud and clear t!
able. Some argue that the true revolution of
made *all* information potentially available to (
been likened to the invention of the printing
displayed on the Internet on all manner of subjects
information on how to break access codes and obtain inform
available, but ostensibly not removable. One may argue that consume
products are not available as they are on a shelf in a regular store, so that
this makes them less 'hot' to steal. Clearly, this is true. A book cannot be
stolen in such a direct way on the Internet as it can in a bookstore (unless
of course it is an electronic book). However, while slightly more complex,
one can nevertheless steal a book on the Internet by making a fraudulent
credit card purchase, using any number of fraudulent techniques such as
pretending non-delivery or using another's credit card. In this case, one
does not even have to risk going into the store to steal the item, rather one
can have it delivered right to one's chosen address.

- *Valuable*. In the information society, information is like money (actually, in
the case of banks it *is* money). Companies and individuals are now taking
great steps to protect their proprietary information. The paradox is that the
ethos of the original Internet was that all information on the Internet
should be openly shared and be free (the 'hacker's ethic'[1] – see Table 4.2).
Thus, criminals are provided with a ready-made excuse for attacking protected bodies of information. Since they are placed on the Internet 'they
ought to be free'. There is also much information on the Internet that has
immediate value to potential criminals. Because of the masses of personal
information now being accumulated on the web as a result of e-commerce,
access to such information by criminals gives them valuable credit card
numbers and bank accounts which they can use to commit a wide variety
of fraudulent crimes. Online store fronts are cheap and easy to establish,
providing fraudsters with access to millions of potential targets.

Table 4.2 The hacker's ethic

- Access to computers should be unlimited and total.
- All information should be free.
- Mistrust authority – promote decentralisation.
- Hackers should be judged by their hacking not bogus criteria such as degrees,
  age, race or position.
- You create art and beauty on a computer.
- Computers can change your life for the better.

Source: Levy (1984).

able. Joyriding was a favourite delinquency when automobiles became pervasive in the twentieth century. The literature on hackers, who are often clever schoolboys (and sometimes mischievous adults), clearly demonstrates the joy that they experience in overcoming the challenge of breaking into protected computer environments (Levy, 1984). Many appear to do this for the pleasure of the challenge, not for the money – although there are many who also do not mind making money out of their enjoyable enterprise as well. The world of computing also changes dramatically almost daily, creating a yearning by hackers and others to acquire the latest technology and modish gadgetry. For some computer criminals, especially hackers, much of the enjoyment is obtained by making public the results of their hacking. Acclaim is especially sought from other hackers, as is clear from even a cursory perusal of hacker websites and newsgroups (e.g. alt.hackers). Making their achievements public is somewhat paradoxical, for it often leads to their arrest and prosecution. In this respect, the activities and rationales of hackers resemble closely those of graffiti artists.

- *Disposable*. The Internet provides a ready means to dispose of stolen property. Newsgroups and IRC (Internet Relay Chat – online real-time communication that is typed into the computer and is less public) can be used to find individuals who are willing to purchase stolen property. However, by far the greatest venue for disposing of stolen property is the online auction, such as Ebay and its competitors. This convenient and cheap way of selling goods (one should add that most items are legitimately sold) provides an easy way to advertise and sell any used item, whether 'hot' or not. The literature on disposal of stolen goods has suggested that the availability of a fencing operation enhances the chances of particular items being stolen (Sutton, 1995). Thus, the mere existence of online auctions provides a ready market for stolen and counterfeit items. Information, this time in the form of matching a buyer to a seller, once again displays its inherently crime-prone quality. Depending on the type of information and type of computer crime committed, disposability may or may not be an important attribute of the information. In fact, for many hackers, an important element to the enjoyment of their activity is disposing of their criminal theft – making publicly available the results of their labours. Thus, for example, the individual who cracked the code of DVD protection posted this information on the web (see Table 3.1). In this case, the criminal receives public acclaim and recognition for his deeds, rather than financial rewards, as he would do if fencing stolen goods. One can also note that it is the disposable nature of stolen information that is the most vulnerable aspect of the criminal's activity. The disposal of counterfeit movies in large quantities, for example, necessarily makes public the results of the crime. However, in the case of peer-to-peer exchange of copyright materials, such as the exchange or downloading of music files for personal use, such disposability is not public and remains largely invisible.

Perhaps the analogy between consumer hot products and information as a hot product is stretched a little too far? Information, after all, is not a physical product of the same kind as, say, a handgun. Although information may be contained at particular times in a physical product, such as a computer in a particular place on a particular desk (or in a laptop whose small size may make it a hot product), it can also exist in many places, especially cyberspace. Information also takes on many different forms and characteristics as we have shown in the classification of Table 4.1. But this table gives a misleading static picture of information. In fact, it may at one time be intellectual property, at others a list of names and addresses and credit card information, at others encrypted messages, at others a series of instructions to search the Internet, at others a series of instructions to make computers, telephones and networks accomplish particular tasks. Thus, the idea of information as a product is something that is far more complex than one particular criminogenic consumer item, such as a handgun. Yet the CRAVED exercise shows very clearly that information is inherently vulnerable to criminal misuse, rather similar to a handgun. Unfortunately, the complexity and variety of information, unlike a simple consumer item, makes it especially difficult to suggest specific design changes, such as safety locks on handguns, that could eliminate or reduce its inherent vulnerability to criminal misuse.

Some changes to the design of information in order to protect it from theft have been developed of course. Encryption is one excellent example, but it is used only in very specific situations or circumstances. It is significant that the majority of successful criminal intrusions into computing systems are made possible by bugs or errors in programming languages, which the sophisticated hacker can turn to his advantage. Programming languages such as C, C++, Microsoft's Visual Basic and Java all have errors contained in their design. Many of these errors are widely disseminated on the Internet, and in fact there are programs that will scan systems to find such errors or 'holes'. Security managers depend on such programs, but unfortunately hackers can also make use of them. No programming languages have been written with security or defence against intrusion or attack built into their design (Garfinkel, 1997: 41f.). Thus attempts to prevent intrusion have to concentrate on other aspects of the e-commerce delivery system. This requires an analysis of the situations in which information is used, stored or transmitted. The application of the basic principles of situational crime prevention should be applicable to uncover the opportunities that various information systems make available to potential criminals, and the vulnerabilities that are not only inherent in information itself, but in the system within which the information resides. The criminogenic features of the information system (SCAREM) we have already described in Chapter 3.

That defensive actions to make access and misuse of information have been developed raises an additional caveat concerning our CRAVED analysis of information as a hot product. It follows that, not only will a particular consumer product of e-commerce contain the criminogenic elements of information depending on the amount of that product that is composed of information, but that also its vulnerability will depend on the amount of effort or skill needed in order for the criminal to steal or damage that product. Much of situational crime prevention is concerned with making it more difficult for an offender to carry out his crime, as we will see in Chapter 6. There is a now familiar analogy here to the misuse of automobiles to carry out crimes early in the twentieth century. In order to use a car to carry out a bank robbery, the offender first had to reach the entry level of skill, which was being able to drive a car (preferably well and at high speed). Similarly, in the information age, one has to be able to use a computer (or minimally a telephone) and use the Internet in order to be able to carry out any cybercrimes. Once one reaches the entry level of skill, however, the level of skill and effort needed to steal or interfere with information online varies from very little to extremely high. The amount of skill needed has much to do with the target of criminal activity. In the case of a burglary, for example, if the ultimate target is jewellery, the amount of effort or skill needed in order to access that jewellery has nothing to do with the product itself (though it may have a lot to do with its disposability). In contrast, many of the crimes committed on the Internet require considerably developed skill and effort on the part of the criminal. We touched upon some of these attributes when we introduced the SCAREM attribute of the challenge that committed hackers find in their 'work'.

Table 4.3 is a first attempt to classify types of e-commerce crime according to the amount of effort or skill needed to accomplish them. We should note at the outset, however, that the introduction of software that made it easy to (a) access the Internet and (b) construct web pages having to write no or little code, reduced the level of skill needed for entry into the Internet considerably. To continue our comparison with the automobile, this was like the introduction of automatic gear change that made driving a car much easier for beginners. In addition, as we move up the scale of skill, there is also the need of specialised equipment, such as souped-up cars or souped-up computers and software. Finally, the wide availability of 'how to' information on Internet websites, newsgroups and chat rooms concerning hacking or doing any other crime has also made the acquisition of skills needed to carry out criminal activity much easier.

As noted in Chapter 3, many of the crimes listed in Table 4.3 do not have direct impact on e-commerce buying and selling, but all of them do affect the 'neighbourhood' in which e-commerce conducts its business: that is, increasingly, the Internet. We have also shown in previous chapters that the core ingredient of e-commerce (in fact all commerce) is trust, so that if it is violated or suspect in any way, customers and users of e-commerce will look elsewhere to do their buying and selling. The type of product sold online can very much affect the ways in which trust in buying online is undermined or affirmed. In the following chapter where we analyse the risks of online shopping we examine two examples of particular products that are widely sold on the Internet and that are highly vulnerable to fraud of various kinds: financial services fraud and medical services fraud. We would place these products in the category of fraudulent services, and classify them, depending on the level of sophistication of the operation, as requiring moderate to high skill or effort to carry them out. However, compared to fraudulent marketing of these products offline, the effort and skill level required is much less.

Table 4.3 Skill, effort levels, crimes and information types.

Information types	Crime types	
	High skill	*Low skill*
Intellectual property	Professional counterfeiting requires sophisticated equipment and criminal organisation for marketing and distribution. Construction of websites that promote downloading of copyright material requires considerable design and computing skill.	Casual video piracy, software piracy, copyright violation, counterfeiting made easy by wide availability of cheap CD burners, and websites offering pirated products.
Intelligence	Industrial espionage, extortion and blackmail, credit card fraud, accounting fraud, identity theft require skilled and persistent application of computing and software skills. Card counterfeiting (magnetic strip readers) equipment also needed.	Aiding and abetting crime requires minimal skills to post information on widely accessible newsgroups.
Systems	Electronic funds transfer fraud, hacking, denial of service, accounting fraud require advanced knowledge of computer programming. While software is freely available to assist in hacking, high knowledge level and persistence is still needed to apply these programs.	Vandalism, terrorism. Some knowledge, though not highly advanced, is needed in order to release a virus or worm, all of which can be downloaded from Internet websites, with instructions on how to use them.

Services	Theft of telephone services, electronic funds transfer fraud, cross border crime, denial of service, cloning of cellular phones and phone cards, credit card fraud, money laundering, investment fraud mostly require sophisticated equipment and high skill level as for Systems above, to conduct on professional basis.	Theft of telephone services can be achieved by low-tech methods such as watching someone dial a PIN number. Stalking and harassment require minimal skills of accessing newsgroups. Telemarketing fraud, sale of stolen or illegal goods, gambling, and tax evasion websites require moderate amount of skill to construct convincing fraudulent websites. Criminal conspiracy, such as pornography exchange via e-mail and newsgroups, is not difficult.

Obviously, one way of counteracting the opportunities for crime in the e-commerce environment is to increase the skill level needed to carry out the cybercrime. The history of credit card fraud (see Chapter 8) reveals how efforts to use both technology and changes in the information systems of processing credit cards have been successful in reducing credit card fraud but have also had the effect of contributing to an 'arms race' (Ekblom, 2000) between the offenders and suppliers of credit card services. For example, the requirement of a signature was the original method of establishing the link between the credit card and its legitimate user. However, it became widely recognised that, due to the pressures at the POS, verification of signatures was cursory and, as well, signatures were not a reliable way of establishing identity anyway. These were followed up by the addition of magnetic stripes on the cards that supposedly provided unique information identifying the user. However, criminals soon obtained magnetic stripe technology and added their own stripes to their cards. Next steps in the arms race have included various efforts to establish identity through biometrics, PINs and various smart cards, all of which criminals have sought to overcome by acquiring new skills and technology. And when the level of skill has become too high, they have turned to other aspects of the credit card system that were vulnerable, such as acquiring the identity of the person who carried the credit card. In Chapter 7 we will examine in more detail the history and methodology of credit card fraud, which is a classic example of both the broad and narrow approaches of situational crime prevention in the reduction of a specific crime.

In this chapter, our analysis of the opportunities for crime in the e-commerce environment has remained fairly general. As noted in Chapter 1, situational crime prevention includes both broad and narrow approaches. Using a broad approach, we have sketched in the criminal opportunity structure that prevails in the e-commerce environment, and have tried to provide some conceptual and systematic ways of understanding that environment. In the following chapter we adopt a narrower focus by offering a detailed analysis of the risks and opportunities that are afforded criminals in one specific aspect of e-commerce: online shopping.

Note

1 There is an emerging controversy concerning the authenticity or claims by hackers with regard to their accomplishments and even the actual existence of the hacker's ethic, especially in terms of a 'culture' that engenders and promotes this ethic (Taylor, 2001). A recent book (Verton, 2002) portrays hackers as gifted, though irresponsible, adolescents living an isolated suburban life. They are, according to Verton, outlaw-heroes, 'Mafiaboy' being the typical example.

Chapter 5

Risk analysis of online shopping

The situational crime prevention approach directs us to examine the detailed situations in which the opportunities for crime arise. In Chapter 2, we identified in Figure 2.2 the route that a product takes from manufacturer to customer and the main points of interaction that occurred between businesses and between customers and businesses along the way. Opportunities for crime occur at each point. For example, theft of a product may occur at the beginning of the chain within the manufacturer's premises, theft from vehicles may occur when the product is en route to the retailer, or in the e-commerce value chain, en route directly to the customer. Theft of product may occur from the retail floor in several different ways, such as by employee theft, shoplifting or employee–customer collusion. Finally, theft of a product may occur at the point of the customer receiving the product through home delivery by dishonest customers who claim non-receipt of the product. The solutions to all of these kinds of theft are usually found by examining in minute detail what actually happens during a particular transaction at a particular point in the value chain.

We propose in this chapter to examine in detail two such transactions of the e-commerce environment, the purchase of an item using a credit card and the delivery of the product to the customer who has purchased an item online, whether by telephone or on the web. This exercise may seem mundane, even an exercise in the obvious. Yet, as Paco Underhill (2000) noted in *Why We Buy*, 'the obvious is not always apparent'. Without knowledge of all the factors that contribute to a situation, it is not possible to devise a way of modifying it. Along the way we will also point out, where applicable, the advantages that each transaction brings to e-commerce because modifying situations that provide opportunities for crime may sometimes – perhaps often – need to be weighed against the commercial benefits that are derived from that transaction and its setting. For example, making a customer wait (one of the most common reasons for shoppers turning away from a purchase) while a credit card check is run may militate against careful security checking of a customer's credit card account. Often, technology offers a solution to such problems as we will indicate in Chapter 7. But it is important to recognise that there is a basic underlying tension between maintaining security and maximising selling, though the two do not need to be antagonistic and can often work together.[1]

In what follows, we will analyse the basic elements of an online e-commerce purchase and identify the risks of crime embedded in that transaction. Even here, though, we must necessarily simplify the analysis. As we have seen, an entire value chain lies behind a seemingly simple purchase of a single consumer product or service – whether a traditional purchase at POS in a retail store or whether a simple purchase with 'one-click' shopping online. Thus, when we identify the basic elements of a purchase transaction, we must extend these elements beyond the specific situation in which money changes hands.

An online e-commerce purchase is composed of three elements: (a) the method of payment; (b) the parties involved in the sale or transaction; and (c) the delivery of the product. Of course, a fourth element, already described in the previous chapter, the type of product or service, will affect each of these elements of an e-commerce transaction. The opportunities for crime (and the opportunities for commerce) may be variously conditioned by each of these elements. The division of the transaction into these elements is largely didactic since there is considerable interaction among them. The type of product is often related to the type of delivery (e.g. software and music downloads), and the parties involved may also be related to the method of payment (e.g. online auctions).

Methods of payment

Methods of payment online fall into two categories: (a) methods that allow for online payment at the time of the purchase, such as credit cards or various forms of electronic or digital cash; and (b) payment offline after the purchase, such as follow-up with phone call and credit card information, a cheque, a money order or COD. Offline payments are more common with other kinds of transactions such as auctions, so discussion of these payment methods will be reserved until discussion of those transaction types where the parties involved also vary. Since credit cards are the most common method of payment for online purchases (Chen and Mayer, 2001) in a typical transaction between a customer and an online retailer, an analysis of this transaction and its benefits and vulnerabilities follows.

Online credit card payment

The diagrams of the e-commerce value chain in Chapter 2, though detailed, nevertheless are a simplified schematic representation of a series of typical e-commerce transactions. We should pause to note that we are not here conducting an analysis or explanation of 'credit card fraud'. The crime of credit card fraud contains several different kinds and techniques of fraud that relate to the complexities of manufacture, delivery and processing of credit cards themselves, upon which we will elaborate further in Chapter 7 when we review the mechanisms and organisation of e-commerce policing. For the moment, we simply note that, because of the many known opportunities for fraud exploited by criminals in the use of credit cards, procedures have been introduced to ensure validity of the credit card account, verify the cardholder's identity, check the card against a list of known stolen cards, and check that the card is not counterfeit (Levi, 2000; Levi and Handley, 1998a, 1998b; Levi, Bissel and Richardson, 1991).

An understanding of the complexity of the online credit card purchase should reveal opportunities for interception by a sufficiently skilled and motivated offender at any point in the transaction.[2] A typical card transaction involves up to five different parties: the consumer, the merchant, the consumer's bank or institution that issued the credit card, the merchant's bank (acquiring bank) and the network that links the banks together in order to settle the transaction. Table 5.1 displays the series of steps involved in a credit card transaction on the Internet.[3]

Table 5.1 The online credit card transaction.

---

1. If new to the e-commerce website, the customer enters card number onto secure form, usually provided at the 'virtual checkout' when the 'shopping cart' is reviewed.

---

2. If a registered customer (i.e. one whose credit information is stored on the online retailer's database), customer checks box to give e-commerce retailer permission to use the credit card information from his or her personal profile.

---

3. Depending on local arrangements, the card account may be checked with a third-party database to verify authenticity and check against database of stolen credit cards.

---

4. Seller sends request to acquiring bank for authorisation.

---

5. The acquiring bank sends a message via the interbank network to the consumer's bank or card issuing institution asking for authorisation.

---

6. Consumer's bank sends message to acquiring bank verifying account status and debiting amount from consumer's credit line.

---

7. Acquiring bank notifies seller that the charge has been approved.

---

8. The web retailer fills the consumer's order (i.e. a message goes to the e-commerce retailer's supplier who ships the product to the consumer, or the consumer receives a key to unlock a file to download, such as software or audio files).

---

9. The web retailer's bank sends a settlement request to the customer's bank.

10. The amount of sale is deducted from the consumer's credit card account and the money placed in an interbank settlement account.

11. The acquiring bank credits the web retailer's account for the amount of sale (minus fees paid to the acquiring bank), and withdraws the same amount of money from the interbank settlement account.

Benefits of the transaction

- *Swift authorisation*. In the 1970s in the US, the time taken for a typical charge card authorisation was around a minute, and in that period, only charges above a threshold of typically $50 were checked. Today, the time for authorisation is less than five seconds. One can see that a wait of over a minute during an online transaction would eliminate many customers. Swift authorisation procedures that make it possible for 100 per cent verification of all charge amounts have helped reduced credit card fraud considerably over the past decade.[4]

- *Swift and reliable payment*. Compared to other means of payment, most merchants appear to prefer credit card payments because they represent, generally, virtually immediate payment for the item directly into their bank accounts. In contrast, cash may be counterfeit and cheques often bounce. In addition, a credit card transaction establishes an accounting trail that can be followed to identify a bogus transaction. Typically, also, the acquiring banks are those that foot the bill in the case of a fraudulent transaction. It is well known, of course, that the consumer is only liable for a maximum of $50 on any fraudulent transaction. In fact, many card issuing banks do not even charge their customers that amount.

- *Persons eliminated from transaction*. Online transactions eliminate a person-to-person contact between the sales clerk and the customer. The opportunity for clerk–customer collusion to defraud the merchant is therefore almost eliminated. In order for collusion to occur, more elaborate arrangements would have to be made between an employee of the online retailer's website and accounting department and a customer/hacker.

- *No physical contact with products in online purchase*. There is no physical contact between the customer and the product to be purchased. Thus it cannot be, in principle, concealed on the person and stolen from the store, as a shoplifter can do typically in a department store. The disadvantage to this, which applies to all web-based retailing, is that a significant factor influencing shoppers to buy is the habit of touching, feeling and examining the physical product (Underhill, 2000).

- *Computer as sentinel.* The Foresight Panel of the UK Department of Trade and Industry (2001) noted that an important function of computers in e-commerce is to serve as a sentinel (to monitor activities and flag events or patterns of behaviour that deviate from established profiles). This approach has been used effectively to flag deviant spending patterns on credit card accounts, thus warning of potential fraudulent use.[5] The collection of detailed information from customers in the value chain of e-commerce should make the use of such databases even more effective.

Vulnerabilities of the transaction

- *Many points of interception.* Table 4.2 demonstrates clearly that there are many points of interception for a hacker to find in order to deflect payment. Although information moves with great speed from point to point, nevertheless in a network environment, the more points of passage, the more the opportunity for interception.

- *Proximity to the Internet.* While there is, in theory, no need to link the online retailer's website to the banking network, there remains the possibility that this may happen when the web retailer transmits information concerning a transaction to the online retailer's bank. The interbank network is not part of the Internet, but it is an 'intranet' – a network of computers closed to outsiders and dedicated only to the service of its members. In these days of interconnectivity, however, it cannot be guaranteed that such a connection will not be made by any online retailer for reasons of convenience and to speed up the process even more. It requires only one link to be made between the retailer on the Internet and a banking network, and this is enough to provide a door into the entire system.

- *Dial-up vulnerability.* Even if the interbank network is physically separated from the Internet, there still remains the vulnerability of transmissions between the different bank computers that are certainly open to attack. In fact many of the serious intrusions into bank computing systems have been made using means that did not require the open architecture of the Internet. Rather, all the sophisticated hacker need do is find a way into the closed network: either through a telephone dial-up which almost all closed networks or intranets have or through a complicit employee.

- *Employee vulnerability.* If the intranet does not have a dial-up entry into its system, there is one other way to obtain entry: through insider information from an employee or by a rogue employee. Thus it is essential that security procedures be adopted within the network itself to prevent attacks from within, just as much as to prevent attacks from outside. In fact we have already reported some evidence from the FBI that major portions of losses occur as much from internal threats as from those of outside hackers (Bernstein *et al.*, 1996: 23, 26f.)

- *Valuable databases become convertible targets.* A more serious vulnerability is that these e-commerce websites, as a part of their efficient value chain, collect extensive information concerning their customers – their website behaviour, their personal information including credit card information and even sometimes their bank accounts. By placing such high value on this aspect of e-commerce, they have created a most attractive target and a potentially lucrative one. Given that the online environment of retailing has closed off some avenues for theft, such as shoplifting, one may speculate that a special form of displacement may emerge in which the target becomes the databases of online retailers instead of the actual products that they sell. These databases can be used for a number of criminal activities: credit card information can be used to make fraudulent purchases, the credit card databases can be sold to other criminals for their use, or perhaps worse, the database can be used to extort money from the seller. At least one major incident of this type has already occurred.[6]

The above vulnerabilities clearly reflect the problems of the SCAREM information systems environment. There are other vulnerabilities in the online transaction, but these also apply equally to other kinds of online transactions that will now be considered. It should be added that these vulnerabilities are only those relevant to online payments. There are many other difficulties incurred in using credit cards for payment in the traditional POS (point-of-sale) situation. Various Home Office reports have carefully examined these issues and recommended many successful solutions for the prevention of credit card fraud (Levi, 2000; Levi and Handley, 1998a, 1998b; Levi, Bissell and Richardson, 1991). These solutions resulted from partnerships among the several parties involved in credit card transactions that we will describe further in Chapter 7.

Digital cash

For those who do not wish to use credit cards, there are various forms of Internet online payment services available which are known as 'digital cash' (or sometimes 'electronic cash'). The procedure for establishing digital cash usually requires three steps:

1. *Enrolment*, in which the consumer establishes an account with a payment system. This may require giving a bank account number for the automatic debit or credit of the bank account by the digital cash agent, or simply that the consumer place into the particular account a certain amount of money to keep it operative.

2. *The purchase*, in which the vendor (who is usually registered with the payment system) must agree to accept the digital cash payment.

3. *Settlement*, in which the amount is deposited in the vendor's bank account. Again, the bank must agree to accept these payments, and is usually registered with the payment system to receive the amount.

The advantages claimed for these forms of payment are:

- reduced transaction costs (credit card payments cost anything from 25 to 75 cents per transaction in the US);

- because of low cost, suitability for multiple small transactions, such as small fees charged by online databases for downloading of information or articles;

- anonymity – as we have seen, credit card payments require the consumer to give up considerable personal information online, which makes their personal information vulnerable to attack. Some merchants also think that they could increase sales if consumers were not required to give out this information;

- extension of the market to those not eligible for credit cards (although given the competition among issuing institutions, one doubts that there would be many people these days who could not obtain one).

Typical systems include: PayPal,[7] Cybercash,[8] Digicash (now defunct[9]) and various systems requiring passwords, such as Virtual PIN.[10] Depending on the payment system, the features offered may include:

- guaranteed anonymity, in which it is 'mathematically impossible' for the bank or merchant to learn the consumer's identity. One can recognise that this feature is almost identical to a simple cash sale in any store. This transaction occurs usually between two strangers (the sales clerk and the customer). Online, the transaction occurs in even greater anonymity where there is no face-to-face recognition of either party involved;

- guaranteed privacy, in which the merchant does not know the identity of the consumer but the information is available within the organisation that operates the payment system;

- individuals, as well as businesses, once enrolled in these services can accept online payment.

None of these methods of online payment, however, solves the problem of the SCAREM information systems environment. All of these methods of online payment create multiple targets for crime. Committed intruders can break into any of these systems. Fortunately, computer experts have been especially sensitive to this problem and have devoted much time and money to its solution. Businesses and governments have also worked together through Commercenet[11] to collect information and work towards an industry standard for electronic payment procedures. At bottom is the issue not only of stopping criminal abuse of the online environment, but also the challenge to develop an online payment system that consumers feel they can trust. Industry efforts appear to assume that advanced technology can solve both problems: achieve actual secure electronic payment systems and engender trust among its users. Electronic payment technology is discussed in more detail in Chapter 6.

Digital payment systems have also turned out to be extremely useful and popular in another type of sales transaction that occurs on the Internet, that of online auctions. The online auction and other kinds of online sales opportunities involve arrangements of the parties of the transaction that are somewhat different from the common sales transaction of retailing. Because of their guaranteed anonymity they have also played a large part in fuelling the growth of online gambling and purchasing of pornography. In fact, it has been estimated that close to 10 per cent of PayPal's revenue is attributable to online purchases in gambling and pornography.[12]

The parties involved

In the previous section we used online credit card and digital cash payments to focus on the actual physical and cyber elements of the payment in e-commerce. The parties involved, apart from the buyer, included a range of individuals and organisations from the retailer's sales representative, the banks, web designers and so on. In this section, we will address two kinds of parties that introduce the opportunities for theft or fraud: (a) fraudulent retailers; and (b) online auctions where the exchange between buyers and sellers is, perhaps, a modern representation of the primitive form of market economies, yet where the element of trust is essential for their success. In the former, of course, fraudulent retailers exploit trust in order to con their victims.

Fraudulent retailing

Fraudulent retailing represents an important example of the relationship between the type of product (one that is too good to be true – a truly 'hot' product) and the other elements of the online transaction. In what follows, a brief account of two of the more common product-specific Internet frauds is provided: (a) financial services fraud; and (b) fraudulent medical services/products. Both these types of fraud are not new by any means. There are centuries-old scams attached to both of these products. However, as noted often throughout this book, the Internet makes it much easier and more effective to carry out frauds related to these products. All the advantages of SCAREM offer an enticing environment for fraud, and the CRAVED attributes of these products makes them an ideal 'hot product'. Specifically, the Internet offers several advantages for fraudulent selling:

1. Start-up costs are minimal. One can set up a bogus 'storefront' on the web using excellent quality software that will make a website look as good as any professional and legitimate site. The costs of web design software and obtaining an Internet service provider (ISP) are minimal. Thus individuals with little capital can undertake major investment scams that were previously the province of organised crime.

2. The Internet gives the fraudster instant access to millions of potential victims. In a second, one e-mail solicitation can be sent to millions.

3. Costs of maintaining the bogus operation are also low. Expensive printing of fancy brochures and expensive mailing of them is not required (though some do follow up with these, especially in the case of travel scams). All this can be implemented on the Internet.

4. All the services and power of the web are at the fraudster's disposal: e-mail for distribution, websites for deceptive advertising, electronic newsletters to obtain subscribers and bulletin boards for manipulation of opinion.

5. With a little more knowledge, a fraudster can mimic legitimate techniques of web page operations and use consumers as transitional targets to obtain their personal information. For example, a fraudster can monitor activity on your computer when you are visiting a website. Should you enter a credit card number or other personal information, even if encrypted, the fraudster can program a legitimate looking window to pop up and say something like 'the card number you entered did not match the record we have in our database. Please re-enter the information.' The unsuspecting user dutifully enters in the credit card information, which is then retrieved by the fraudster. This is a case in which all the encryption of keyboard entry does nothing to prevent theft of valuable information.

Financial services fraud

There are two main types of fraud operated in the financial services arena. The first is the kind that applies across the board to many different types of products: the operation of a bogus company (website) offering services or products that are either non-existent or not what they appear to be. They always involve offers that are too good to be true, and of course they are not true! The US Securities and Exchange Commission on its website gives an extensive description of the many different kinds of bogus investment scams currently being promoted on the web.[13] These include:

1. online investment newsletters identifying false 'hot stocks' that they have paid stockbrokers to tout. When readers of the newsletter bid up the stock, the fraudsters unload theirs at a higher price. One convicted fraudster sold 42 million shares in a bogus stock and issued false press releases touting the company;

2. bulletin boards on which fraudsters collaborate and invent multiple aliases to join the bulletin boards (extremely easy to do), pump up the stock and again unload them at a higher price ('pump and dump');

3. e-mail 'spams' sent to millions pushing worthless stock. For example, one convicted fraudster built bogus websites and sent 6 million e-mails to promote two thinly traded stocks;

4. the classic pyramid schemes in the US that often read: 'Make money from your home computer, turn $5 into $60,000 in just three weeks!' In reality this is a version of the old 'chain letter' scheme in which partici-pants try to make money by recruiting new participants;

5. 'risk-free' fraud – enticements to invest in exotic projects such as wire-less cable projects, eel farms and $3.5 million worth of prime bank securities (no such thing);

6. offshore frauds, especially offshore banks as tax-free safe havens.

The second type of financial services fraud involves the manipulation by fraudsters of the transmission of funds from one bank account to another. This can take two forms: the hi-tech form and the low-tech. The high-tech form involves sophisticated hacking into funds transmissions, as was the case described in Table 3.1, in which a Russian diverted inter-national transfer funds from Citibank in New York to his own accounts in Russia. However, something similar can be achieved by decidedly low-tech procedures. For example, at the inception of the new online bank X.com, customers opening new accounts could open them in any name and then nominate a bank account from which they wanted to transfer funds to begin the new account. The bank allowed this transac-tion to take place completely on their website, but unfortunately did not bother to verify that the customer owned the rights to the transfer funds bank account. Thus it was possible for individuals to transfer money into their own accounts, needing to know simply the name and number of someone else's bank account – not an especially difficult piece of information to obtain. The serious implication of this fraud was that the bank Automated Clearinghouse (ACH) system depends on the integrity of its member banks to make accurate requests. Thus this breach in security threatened the entire basis of trust of the online banking industry.[14]

A case using both hi-tech and traditional security lapses, fortunately uncovered before it was completed, was that of a Mafia attempt to 'clone' an online branch of the Banco di Sicilia. Using computer technology and the assistance of bank employees (low-tech), they stole files, codes and passwords from the bank and set up their own operating clone of the bank's online system. The plan was to steal 264 billion lire by, at an agreed time, switching off the bank's computing system and substituting the Mafia's clone. The money, once stolen, would be transmitted electronically to overseas bank accounts. The operation was discovered only because of informants. Subsequently an undercover police officer posing as a crooked bank director was able to expose the whole operation.[15]

Finally, brief mention should be made of money laundering as it operates in the financial services sector. As noted in Table 3.1, approximately $1 trillion are laundered every year. These criminal funds are typically proceeds of drug trafficking and the smuggling of human beings and guns. The typical problem for the launderer is the preponderance of cash that has to be turned into respectable money without attracting the notice of bank officials. In fact many countries have regulatory agencies whose job it is to monitor suspicious use of accounts and the movement of money. The OECD Financial Action Task Force, for example, maintains a register of 'suspicious activity' which is continuously updated.[16] The difficulty that the launderer faces is that banks and other agencies are attuned to watch for unusual patterns in trading, deposits and withdrawals. Thus launderers devise schemes to make their banking transactions seem legitimate. One of the most typical features of crimes producing lots of cash is that they tend to be crimes that involve crossing borders. Since the Internet operates without restriction of national borders, it is the ideal place for disposing of money in ways that ignore national borders. Although there appears to be no case on record as yet in which the Internet itself was used to launder money (though there are many using banks and electronic bank transfers[17]) the OECD Financial Action Task Force has outlined ways in which it anticipates criminals may do so. One scenario would be for the criminal to set up a bogus Internet company (such as, for example, an Internet café), use the services of this company pretending to be an actual customer, charge the costs of these services to 'legitimate credit cards' (obtained using fake IDs) then receive the proceeds from the credit card acquiring bank.

This case is significant because it points once again to the complex transactions that take place between buyers and sellers of services and products on the Internet and the ways in which the Internet's qualities, such as the ease of setting up a presence and the ease of using false identities, match nicely the qualities valued by a money launderer. In this case, none of the legitimate companies involved – the Internet service provider, the credit card issuing bank or the credit card acquiring bank – would have any reason for suspicion. While money laundering does not impact directly on the regular business of e-commerce, it most certainly could affect or even poison the regular transactions that are involved in everyday e-commerce.

Medical services/products fraud
Traditional medical fraud is perfectly suited to the Internet where quacks can ply their false medicines and cures using all the advantages the web has to offer: cheap set-up, anonymity, easy construction of deceptive advertising and websites, instant access to millions of potential dupes. However, modern health care offers many more opportunities for fraud. In 1998, 22.3 million adults in the USA sought medical information on the Internet and this was predicted to rise to 30 million by 2001. Seventy per cent of those seeking information on the Internet did so just before visiting their doctor.[18] Types of medical services and health care fraud online include: making false statements, kickbacks and self-referrals, unauthorised distribution of drugs and medical devices, violation of privacy laws relating to personal health information, deceptive trade practices in submitting claims to healthcare plans, and violating rules set down for healthcare providers that receive reimbursement from federal or national health programmes.[19] Of these, online pharmacies are the retailers most relevant to this issue.

Online pharmacies have blossomed in recent years. It is estimated that legitimate sales in online pharmacies will reach $15 billion by 2004[20]. There are over 300 websites selling healthcare products, and one study revealed that there were at least 86 websites selling Viagra, the anti-impotence drug, without a doctor's prescription.[21] These pharmacies have developed a large following of customers even though they operate in what seems to be a confused edge or grey area of the law. The first reason why any e-commerce retailer is popular is that the merchant is providing a product or service that customers want. And the benefits that online pharmacies offer customers are as follows:

- *Generally cheaper drugs.* Bulk purchases by pharmacies can produce savings, but also different regulatory laws governing the pricing of drugs in different countries can create a large difference in price for the same or similar prescription drugs between one country and another. For example, many Canadian pharmacies (online and offline) sell to US customers because their prices are close to half those in the USA.[22] The FDA estimates that some two million parcels containing prescription drugs enter the USA from other countries each year.[23]

- *Privacy.* Customers may purchase drugs from the privacy of their own homes.[24]

- *Convenience.* Those who are house bound because of infirmity are easily able to purchase prescription drugs they need. Online pharmacies are also available 24 hours a day, seven days a week.

- *Easier access to written product and other medical information.*

- *Easier comparative shopping for preferred prices and products.*

The points of vulnerability and opportunities for crime in the online pharmacy transaction (see Table 5.2) can be identified as follows:

- Customers' personal information, especially if they fill in forms concerning health insurance and health history, not to mention credit card information, is collected and stored on the online pharmacy's website. This information, as noted several times throughout this book, creates an attractive database to hackers who can make use of the information by either selling it or by extortion.

- The obvious 'legal frontier' of these pharmacies, especially those that sell across national borders, makes for even greater opportunity for fraudsters to operate and avoid legal responsibility for their acts.[25] It provides them with an easy avenue of escape should they be caught. And of course, in a grey area of the law, it is difficult to be sure just what it is that the online pharmacy is being 'caught' doing.

- There is ample room for deception on the part of fraudsters to pose as legitimate customers, but who in fact seek to purchase prescription drugs in order to resell them on the illegal drug market or for their own drug abuse. Because of the anonymity afforded by the Internet, it is relatively easy for customers to invent identities, and for them also to invent doctors who call in or e-mail prescriptions.

- If pharmacies are not registered with the state or licensed in some way, there is no way to guarantee the quality of the product purchased. For example, in the mid-1980s, two million bogus birth control pills flooded the US market. Because of the SCAREM attributes of the information system, unregulated websites dispensing drugs easily become the outlets for counterfeit and otherwise illegally obtained drugs.

- There is ample room and temptation for professionals (pharmacists and medical profession) to collude with each other in order to exploit the obvious very strong demand of the public to purchase many of these prescription drugs online. The fact that the US Congress has not yet managed to pass the various bills to control online pharmacies is strong evidence of this public demand.[26]

- When collusion occurs among different personnel and organisations of the healthcare system, the privacy policy on the part of the online pharmacy is put at risk, and arguably it is health information that is considered by the public as a most important aspect of healthcare that must be protected.

Table 5.2 Online pharmacy transaction.

1.	In the USA the online pharmacy obtains licences to sell prescription drugs from the state in which it operates and from states to which it sells. Different rules may apply in different countries. Pharmacies outside the USA appear not to be covered by these rules.
2.	Customers open an account with the pharmacy, submitting credit card and insurance information.
3.	Customer submits a valid prescription. This can occur in a number of ways. Customer's doctor may call in, fax or e-mail the prescription. Or the online pharmacy provides a doctor online to write the prescription, usually based on the customer filling out a patient history form online. Again, different rules apply in different countries, so it is not clear whether in fact this stage is legally required in all counties or, if it is, how enforceable it is by countries outside the customer's domicile.
4.	Some sites provide the possibility for the customer to ask questions of the pharmacist concerning the product. In the USA the customer should be directed or otherwise asked to read the online pharmacy's privacy policy. This rule may not apply in other countries, or even in different states in the USA.
5.	Customer completes purchase, customer's charge card is submitted for approval and sale is completed appropriately.
6.	Order is shipped to customer.

Based on Henkel, John (2000) 'Buying drugs online: it's convenient and private, but beware of rogue sites', *FDA Consumer*, January–February, online revision June 2000, http://www.fda.gov.

It should be added that there is no strong evidence of actual serious health damage done to customers who purchase prescription drugs online. While there are an estimated 100,000 deaths in the USA attributed to adverse drug reactions, there is no research to identify what portion of these resulted from online prescriptions. Furthermore, it is well known that individuals who are committed to obtaining particular prescription drugs are able to 'doctor shop' to find a doctor who will write a prescription. Thus it is not at all clear that online prescription writing may be any worse than that obtained from a regular doctor's visit. Only an occasional case has been reported, such as a male adult with a history of heart problems who purchased Viagra after filling out an online medical questionnaire and who subsequently died of a heart attack.[27] And of course, there is the standard problem of Internet retail sales to minors of products that may be controlled by various regulations. One case was reported of a 16-year-old who purchased the diet drug Meridia and Viagra online using his mother's credit card.[28]

Opposition to legislation to control online pharmacies in the USA has also been voiced by those who claim that there are plenty of laws and regulations already existing to control their practices. In the US, primary control of healthcare systems is left to the states which license healthcare professionals and pharmacies. However, certain federal agencies such as the FDA and FTC and the Federal Food, Drug and Cosmetic Act provide considerable opportunity for law enforcement. Thus, because of the myriad of jurisdictions, prosecution has been difficult. However, there have been some major cases in which online pharmacies have been shut down, even those operating outside the state that brought the charge.[29] And in February 2000, the US Department of Justice announced that it had conducted 134 investigations into healthcare fraud, 54 of which involved online pharmacies. In addition, 17 convictions had been achieved as a result of FDA actions against the illegal sale of drugs (not necessarily by pharmacies) or medical products over the Internet. The best the US law enforcement has been able to do in regard to foreign-based online pharmacies is to send them a warning letter.[30]

Auctions

The mission of online auctions is to bring buyers and sellers together rather than to market an inventory of products to customers. These transactions are commonly known as 'peer-to-peer' transactions, which exploit the natural infrastructure of computer networking. Online auctions act as the 'middleman' who provides the service of bringing together buyers and sellers. This is, perhaps, the oldest form of an open market. These venues look like massive online garage sales or swap meets.

This kind of online e-commerce transaction differs from retailing, since private individuals use the online auction to get rid of their excess baggage, as it were, so the value chain as we have described it for online retailing does not quite apply (though the delivery part of it would). However, there are many small home businesses, perhaps accounting for the majority of auction use, which use online auctions as their means of marketing or as their retail sales outlet. The value chain for such businesses would also differ from that of Figure 2.2, since the relationship between the 'retailers' and their suppliers is largely unknown. However, in an auction, the merchant acts as a trusted third party who provides a service that matches buyers to sellers. This type of e-commerce is included here because it has over the last five years assumed a place in online transactions that has been extremely popular, and has also brought with it extensive amounts of fraud, by some measures accounting for the greatest amount of fraud that occurs on the Internet. It has also been an extremely successful business model. Ebay, the largest auction site, has been the most successful company on the Internet, having turned a profit every year since its inception in 1995, which is quite an accomplishment compared to the majority of dot.coms that have operated in the red, most of which, even the more successful, have yet to turn a profit. Ebay promotes itself as 'the leading online marketplace for the sale of goods and services'. It has upwards of 37.6 million registered users worldwide and transacted more than $5 billion worth of sales in 2000. Its mission, Ebay says without modesty, is 'to help practically anyone trade practically anything on earth'.[31]

Ebay is not strictly speaking an auction, although it provides online access to live auctions. Rather, it provides a marketplace in which buyers and sellers can meet. Ebay provides the organisation, listing, the venue for sellers to show their products and services and also a secure way for money to change hands between buyers and sellers. The online transaction for a typical auction works as shown in Table 5.3.

Table 5.3 Online auction transaction.

---

1. Seller registers certain personal details with Ebay such as a credit card account and address attached to that credit card account.

---

2. Once registered, seller places item on Ebay's list of items according to selected categories, and also includes information about the product, the minimum amount and bid accepted, how long the auction will last (usually five to seven days) and payment options.

---

3. Buyer searches database for item to buy.

---

4. Once the item has been located, buyer checks out the comments on seller's previous transactions, especially to check on shipment, honesty and previous customer satisfaction with the seller.

5. Buyer places bid, or in some instances, if seller has included a specific price acceptable for an immediate sale, buyer may offer to buy.

6. Buyer wins auction.

7. Seller checks out buyer's payment history in the feedback file.

8. Ebay also notifies by e-mail each party of the successful completion of the sale.

9. Seller contacts buyer within prescribed time (usually three days), either by e-mail or by phone, to arrange payment.

10. Payment options initially are money order or cheque (product shipped when cheque is cleared or when money order is received). Obviously, this is a high-risk situation since there is no guarantee that the seller will ship the product (it is rare that the shipper ships a product without having received a payment). This is why buyers and sellers leave feedback concerning their satisfaction with the transaction in the Ebay feedback file. Buyers and sellers are urged by Ebay to check out this information, which presumably is assumed to provide a kind of informal self-policing of the 'Ebay community'.

11. Seller may register with Ebay's credit card processing service (*Billpoint*) so that the seller can accept credit cards as payment. This involves the seller providing additional information to Ebay's Billpoint service, in particular a bank account number as well as the credit card number. Other third-party services such as PayPal (taken over by Ebay) offer similar services. In either case, the processing of the credit card payment of the buyer is carried out in the same way as any other online credit card payment. The difference is that Ebay acts as both the buyer's and seller's agent, and charges a small fee for the service.

12. When payment is settled, item is shipped by seller according to shipping instructions included in the original notice of sale.

13. Upon receipt of the product, buyer posts comments concerning satisfaction with the transaction on Ebay's feedback file. Seller does likewise for the buyer.

Benefits of online auctions

The obvious benefit of this variation on e-commerce is the business model of bringing buyers and sellers together in a trusted environment. There are different kinds of models within this basic idea. The Ebay model allows almost a 'free-for-all' in which buyers and sellers deal with each other with minimal interference of the third party. The third party makes money by charging a small fee to the seller for listing the product. In other models, the third party plays a heavier role. Half.com, for example, requests the seller to set a specific price (usually following guidelines suggested by Half.com) and lists the item description that it has itself assembled. (Half.com has also recently been taken over by Ebay and the fixed price model continued.) The only input of the seller is to check off the condition of the product. Half.com therefore sells the item as if it were a regular catalogue retailing transaction, charging shipping, then paying the seller after the transaction is settled. Registration is required of both seller and buyer, and Half.com therefore takes the responsibility of seeing through the transaction to the end, although actual delivery of the product is left to the seller. Another variation is that adopted by Crossmarket.com, which requires sellers to sign legally binding agreements that they will ship their products to the highest bidders. In this case, Crossmarket takes full fiduciary responsibility for all transactions.[32] Utrade.com also takes stronger charge of the transaction, requiring buyers to send their money to utrade.com, which then transmits the payment to the seller once it has verified that all requirements of the transaction have been met.

An obvious advantage to this business model is the sheer mass of buyers and sellers that are brought together. As noted above, there are over 37 million registered users on Ebay throughout the world, which makes it possible for sellers to sell just about anything. There is always someone somewhere who wants or needs something that the seller has to sell. And because of the sheer mass of transactions, the small amounts that the auction sites charge for listing a product makes them even more popular. It must be the cheapest venue for advertising a product ever invented. For a few pence, one can reach millions of potential customers.

Vulnerabilities of online auctions

Unfortunately, with the great benefits of this business model of e-commerce come extensive opportunities for fraud and vulnerability to attack. These include enhancement of opportunities that already existed before online auctions, as well as new ways to commit fraud because of the online environment. We should first note that the online auctions account for by far the greatest portion of online fraud. In 2001 in the US, 63 per cent of online frauds were at auctions, followed by the next highest of 11 per cent for general merchandise sales, although the average loss per person was higher for general merchandise sales ($845) compared to auctions ($478).[33] In terms of overall amounts lost in the USA $4,371,724 were lost by consumers to online fraud in 2001, an increase of some 30 per cent over the previous year. The opportunities for fraud in the online auction may be summarised as follows:

- *Bid shilling.* A seller or seller's associate may assume a false identity and bid up the price of the item. Variations of this could, of course, occur in a regular offline auction. However, the ability to create multiple identities to bid in an online auction is extremely easy, and difficult if not impossible to detect.

- *Bid shielding.* A buyer and partner make a ridiculously high bid, thereby scaring other bidders away. At the last moment, the high bid is withdrawn, and the associate wins the auction with a low bid.

- *Non-delivery.* Seller receives payment and does not deliver the merchandise, or delivers a cheaper product than that advertised. This accounts for some 90 per cent of all frauds on online auctions.[34] As can be seen in Figure 5.1, the problem here is reflected in the method of payment. When buyers send the seller a money order, cashier's cheque or personal cheque, there is virtually no recourse.

- *Non-payment.* Bidder does not honour the bid and does not send payment. While the cost is minimal (the seller will have to list the item again) nevertheless the cost in terms of loss of trust in the process is considerable. In fact, every time someone is victimised in online trading, whether it is the seller or the buyer, it is trust that is the victim.

Figure 5.1 Online auction frauds by method of payment (Jan–Oct. 2001).

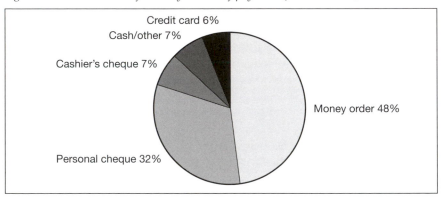

Source: Internet Fraud Watch.

All of the above are transaction-related frauds. Of course, one obvious opportunity created by this wonderful business model is that it can be used most easily as a venue for disposing of stolen goods. Indeed, the online auction with its millions of registered subscribers (many registered with identities that are not immediately traceable) is a perfect place to sell counterfeit copies of software, videos, music and many other 'name brand' consumer products. While counterfeit versions of name brand products are commonly found on auction, by far the most extensive counterfeit and black-market trade is conducted in software.[35] While much of this trade is conducted by organised gangs, the fact is that there are many willing buyers. Also, much of this software is indistinguishable from its original, and much may be 'grey market' – legitimate software marketed by special agreement to specific markets, such as educational markets. This makes for considerable difficulty in identifying what software is counterfeit or illegal and what is not. The wide availability of low-price CD burners also makes it very easy to produce copies of software and music (and soon videos) that can be sold at auction sites.

Peer-to-peer transactions

Selling copies of music that have been made on a personal computer with a CD burner is in fact not likely at auction. This is because one can get music at no cost illegally from websites that operate under a different e-commerce model. Actually, it is not altogether clear whether such a model should be included as 'e-commerce' or not, although since businesses do make money out of these trading sites, it is reasonable to include a brief note concerning these business models. They also represent what is likely to be one of the more significant changes in online Internet models of computing, one that exploits the major strength of the Internet – its decentralised architecture. That is, peer-to-peer computing.

Peer-to-peer transactions occur as a result of software solutions that make it possible for millions of users to be directly connected with each other via software that they download from a particular website that hosts the peer-to-peer transactions. The most well-known example of this arrangement was Napster which made it possible for millions of its software users to directly exchange songs and music (in various file formats, usually MPG3) that reside on their own personal computers with those of other personal computer users. The business model here is that the third party (that is the website) provides the software that enables individual users to both list the files they have available for swap and to search the computers of other users for files they would like to download. The listing of files changes constantly, depending on which and how many users are logged on at that particular moment. This can number in the millions. Once users find the songs they want, they simply download them directly from the other computer user's computer. Millions of college and high school students do this on various websites throughout the world. The host of the website makes money through advertising and providing access to information concerning its users. Users pay nothing, though they do give up considerable amounts of their computing privacy, probably without knowing it.

There are some interesting implications of this model of 'e-commerce' in which 'customers' pay nothing to the host or to each other. Essentially, it is like a swap meet. Of course, the problem lies in the fact that the music exchanged is copyright (most of it) and therefore violations of copyright occur every time an individual downloads a song. Legitimate owners of the copyright are therefore denied payment. Does it amount to theft? That is the argument made by those who brought the suit against Napster, which eventually succeeded in putting Napster out of business.[36] The large media companies have since attempted to start up websites that allow for exchange of music for a small fee so that the artists can receive their remuneration, but it remains to be seen whether this business model will succeed. In the meantime, as quickly as Napster was put out of business, others have taken its place providing much the same service.[37]

Napster and its successors demonstrate the highly fluid nature of cyberspace trading, and point to a possible direction for the future. The deeply entrenched 'ethic' on the Internet that 'everything should be free' lends strong cultural support for this kind of peer-to-peer model. Napster was certainly held up as the 'hero' in defending little people from the large corporations in the lawsuit that eventually put it out of business. At its height, it had 38 million file-sharing adherents[38] and it was at that time when the chairman of the huge conglomerate publisher Bertelsmann made an offer of partnership. When one considers that this massive customer following was accomplished in the space of less than three years, it is a sobering fact indeed to contemplate whether there is any way to counteract such a powerful force. The chairman of Bertelsmann obviously saw that it would be better to co-opt it if he could. As discussed below, there is some hope that technology may provide a solution.[39]

One might also expect that a computing environment (architecture) that allows strangers to access directly the personal computers of other strangers is fraught with opportunities for fraud. To date, no examples have emerged of any hacking or fraud that has been perpetrated in this environment. This may be because (a) there is no money changing hands and (b) the model fits closely with the hacker's ethic itself – that everything on the Internet should be free. On the other hand, businesses have begun to experiment with peer-to-peer architecture among businesses or within a large corporation[40] because it offers the advantages of security: a network of computers can be arranged so that all valuable data and programs are not stored in one or two central locations or computers ('servers') but may be distributed over a wide range of computers.[41] This is looked on especially as a useful safeguard against a catastrophic attack such as that of September 11 on the World Trade Center that destroyed many valuable databases that were stored in one or two places. While it is true that copies of such databases and sites were kept in back-up locations, the restoration of those databases took several days. In the online marketing and telecommunications world, being down for several days can be enormously costly. With peer-to-peer architectures, the databases are spread over many computers and if one computer or more goes down, others automatically take their place. One can also see that, given the numbers and increasing power of desktop computers, the potential in terms of rapidity of access to data and the amount of data that could be stored is close to limitless.[42] Applications that once required supercomputers could be run easily using peer-to-peer computing.[43] The downside, though, is that if many computers are involved in peer-to-peer computing, they offer many more points of entry for hackers.[44]

Napster and other online 'swap' websites are examples of variations in e-commerce that occur directly as a result of the type of product traded.[45] Exchanging and swapping songs among friends has been a popular pastime ever since the recording of songs was made possible in the mid-twentieth century. Napster and its successors, through the medium of connected personal computers, simply made this popular pastime possible not only among friends but among strangers via the Internet.

This overview of the different arrangements in exchanging money for goods, or sometimes goods for goods, among different parties obviously brings with it different arrangements concerning how such goods are delivered to the purchasers. In the peer-to-peer arrangement just described, one receives the product directly from the peer. However, in the typical online retailing sale, or the typical online auction sale, the product must be shipped from one location to the home or destination indicated by the buyer. The rise of companies specialising in the tracking and delivery of products over the past decade has been phenomenal, much of it owing to the increase in home shopping via the Internet. The following section examines the transactional points and other related issues concerning how online e-commerce retailers deliver products to the home purchaser and the risks that arise in doing so.

Product delivery [46]

The final point in the e-commerce online purchase is the delivery of the product to the customer, usually the customer's home or other designated location.[47] Opportunities for crime arise because of the transactions that must occur between the drivers of the delivery vehicles, their products and their customers. As shown in Chapter 2, Figure 2.2, a typical online order begins a complex process whereby an order is conveyed to the supplier who then ships the product through various channels of the supply chain. With the exception of direct delivery online by downloading a product (discussed at the end of this section), all deliveries to the customer involve some form of transportation in vehicles. McKinnon and Tallam (2002) summarise this process as follows:

> Losses of product along this complex chain of delivery result from a variety of factors that may or may not include crime, such as short orders received from suppliers, goods mislaid or misdirected, errors in inven-

99

tory/tracking records, and fraudulent denial of receipt by customers. In the case of home delivery of a product, there are seven transactional points in the home delivery system where loss may occur:

1. Inbound deliveries from supplier to the central warehouse/parcel sorting centre or hub where losses may result from short orders from suppliers or theft from the loading dock.

2. Activities within the central warehouse/hub where loss may result from pilferage of product in the warehouse by employees.

3. Truck movement from warehouse/hub to local depot, where trucks are sealed up, thus drastically reducing the opportunity for theft. This is the most secure stage in the supply chain.[48]

4. Local depot operations. Risks similar to stage 1.[49]

5. Local delivery to the home: either directly or via a courier network.

6. Receipt of goods at the home.

7. Return flow: following either a failed delivery or rejection by the customer.

The first four of these sources relate more to business-to-business transactions, which is not the focus of this chapter, though they do have significance for the customer since any loss contributes to business costs and consequently will be passed on to the consumer in the form of higher prices. We will therefore not address these points of risk. In addition they involve aspects of retailing such as employee theft that are widely reported and analysed in the retail security literature. It is, however, important to recognise that the last three stages in delivery are part of a complex supply chain, because as we will see in the following chapter, one of the solutions to reducing and preventing theft of products during delivery lies in being able to track precisely the movement of a product from source to consumer.

Receipt of goods at the home:

The study by MinKinnon and Tallam (2002) identified ten levels of security in the home reception operation (see Table 5.4). Most deliveries currently fall into categories 3 and 4, though categories 5 and 6 deliveries are also relatively common. They note in addition:

> No instances were found of companies delivering only to named individuals in a household, let alone individuals who could be formally identified by their signature. Parcel carriers usually require a proof of delivery (POD) from a household member or, if specially instructed, from

Table 5.4 Levels of security in home reception operations.

	Recipient	Nature of the proof of delivery
1	Named individual	Electronic POD
2	Named individual	Paper POD
3	Any member of household	Electronic POD
4	Any member of household	Paper POD
5	Specified neighbour	POD
6	Specified neighbour	No POD
7	Unspecified neighbour	POD
8	Unspecified neighbour	No POD
9	Package left outside	No POD, pre-arranged location
10	Package left outside	No POD, location at driver's discretion

Source: McKinnon and Tallam (2002).

a neighbour, but rarely leave consignments outside a home unattended. It is often the clients of the parcel carriers who stipulate the nature of the POD required from home customers. Some mail order companies and retailers allow their drivers to leave orders unsecured. This is normally done in accordance with the customers' instructions or on a regular basis for frequent customers.

Companies' home reception procedures have been adapted to the needs of their customer base and to strike what they regard as an acceptable balance between customer service, security and cost. They are prepared to sacrifice security for higher customer service levels and more economical delivery. Refusal to leave goods with a neighbour, for example, can result in a delay of several days until the vehicle is back in the area. Tightening security would inevitably increase the proportion of failed deliveries, necessitating one or more repeat deliveries at the carrier's expense. In the case of some courier networks, no payment is made for the return of goods to the depot. The courier is, therefore, given a strong incentive to make a successful delivery, even if this means leaving the order unsecured outside the home of a regular customer.

Unattended delivery: This practice, sometimes called 'door-stepping', involves leaving the consignment outside the house on the doorstep or at some concealed location around the property. This is normally done with the approval of the recipients and in accordance with their instructions. For at least one major catalogue mail order company and one high street retailer, this is quite a common practice. The retailer estimates that in some parts of the country around 15% of orders are left unsecured at the home. It relies on drivers' experience and judgement to assess whether an item can be safely left outside. This is clearly a very risky strategy, exposing the supplier and customer to various forms of crime:

Denial of receipt: As noted above, the customer can also exploit the lack of a POD and insecurity of this form of delivery by fraudulently claiming not to have received the goods. Although the customer can request an unsecured delivery, liability for the goods remains with the supplier. While a customer may abuse this form of delivery once, repeated attempts to do so would be detected and the supplier would subsequently refuse to provide unsecured delivery.

Burglary: The presence of a package outside a house usually indicates that the property is unoccupied and may increase the risk of burglary.

Entrusting deliveries to neighbours: Companies that are prepared to entrust goods to neighbours often require the customer to specify in advance to which address the delivery should be diverted in the event of them not being at home. For goods purchased online this must be done at the time of ordering. One supermarket chain [in the UK] with a home shopping service, for example, refuses to accept a telephone request to divert the delivery to an alternative address once the order has been placed.

Return flow of merchandise

McKinnon and Tallam (2002) report:

Direct marketing channels have typically been characterised by strong reverse flow of product. This occurs for two reasons:

a. *Failed delivery*: Merchandise that cannot be delivered is generally returned to the depot for redelivery at a later date. On arrival at the depot the order has to be re-registered or rescanned, and stored until the next available delivery slot. The companies consulted claimed that this reverse process was as secure as the outbound delivery and resulted in minimal loss of product. One company reported that some employees had ordered products for despatch through their network, giving a bogus address. After the delivery failed, the goods were returned and held in a special compound in the depot while the address problem was investigated. This compound was often a target for theft.

b. *Return of rejected product*: This presents a much greater security problem. On average around a third of catalogue mail order sales (by value) is returned. In some product categories, such as fashion clothing, the proportion is much larger.

It is claimed that these reverse channels are just as secure as the forward channels. In the reverse channel, however, the problem is not simply one of theft but also of the substitution of lower value products for the original content. For example, bricks are sometimes substituted for camcorders or cameras. Given their tight schedules, delivery staff do not have the time to check repackaged orders collected from the home. Although checking would largely eliminate the practice, the amount that this would add to delivery costs would substantially increase the value of lost merchandise. One mail order manager put the problem into perspective by estimating that there are a 'few thousand' instances of dummy substitutions per annum out of a total of 45 million parcels delivered.

Online delivery

There are many software e-commerce websites that now offer the option to consumers to download software into their personal computers at the time of purchasing online. This method of delivery avoids many of the risks and criminal opportunities offered by physical delivery systems (though the problem of denial of receipt persists), and furthermore offers the customer immediate acquisition of the product, just like in a regular store. In fact, it is better than buying software in a retail store because the product delivery and installation can be directly controlled by the software e-commerce site, thus avoiding user installation errors and also minimising the opportunity of the customer to claim non-receipt. The only opportunity for crime here is for the customer to either break the encryption methods used by the retailer (unlikely) or to have obtained illegally the ID of an individual and purchased the software using that person's information. There have been early difficulties in perfecting software download delivery procedures, but generally these have been solved. In fact the delivery system is so smooth, and the amount of bandwidth has expanded so much (that is the speed at which an individual can download a file using connections to the Internet that do not require dialling up), that many software companies now offer their software on a subscription basis that automatically updates itself on the user's own computer each time the computer is switched on and is connected to the

Internet. This approach has been adopted for virus detection software where constant updating is necessary to keep up with new viruses. Download delivery is also used by online software retailers who offer 'shareware' or variations of this, in which customers may download and run a program to 'try before they buy'. Should they like the program, they may pay for a 'key' (password) to unlock the program to run continuously or download the full version.

Conclusions

The analysis of the risks of buying and selling online provided in this chapter, while detailed and focused on one small aspect of the value chain of e-commerce, nevertheless remains general in content. By this we mean to acknowledge that a situational approach *in practice* would still need to identify the very specific local and systemic factors that contribute to whether particular individuals in particular situations will capitalise on the opportunities for crime afforded them. Some of the questions a situational approach would follow in regard to each of the elements of online sales transactions might include the following.

- *The online payment transaction.* Whether opportunities for theft will be taken up will depend on specific factors such as the skill or knowledge of the offender in capitalising on the SCAREM attributes of the e-commerce environment, the offender's motivations in doing so, the availability or accessibility to online transaction information, the kinds of products sold online, and the security procedures in place either at the website or in regard to protection of actual transmission of information essential to effect an online transaction.

- *The identities of the parties in the transaction.* Online retail shopping carries its own risks that are, perhaps, more loaded towards the seller rather than to the buyer, with the major exception of fraudulent retailers. However, when we examine online auctions, the risks appear to be more equally distributed between sellers and buyers. In all cases, however, much of the situational assessment of the risks of crime come down to identifying the particular factors that may be involved in the transactions: the identities and motivations of the buyers and sellers, which in turn in online trading relate to the ways in which the elements of trust and secure exchange are handled in the transaction (secure or encrypted messages, agreements and protocols for payment and acknowledging receipt of goods).

- *Home delivery*. While those online stores that also have large networks of local retail stores may use those facilities for online shoppers to pick up their items, many online retailers do not have such stores, so direct home delivery is the only option. In both cases, however, the advantages of home delivery accrue almost entirely to the customer. From the point of view of the e-retailer, shipping items in bulk to a network of stores is clearly more cost effective. Shipping direct to the home necessitates contracting out this part of the supply chain to third parties. Clearly, unsecured delivery provides the opportunity for crime. The extent to which such opportunity will be taken will depend on many specific factors such as: the type of buildings (suburban houses versus city apartments), friendliness and or vigilance of neighbours, the relations between delivery personnel and their clients (informal agreements to leave items in an agreed place on customer's premises), the conditions or traffic and street architecture that make the delivery vehicle more or less accessible to thieves, and the presence or absence of law enforcement. A situational prevention approach would begin with these and other questions in order to identify where opportunities arise and ways in which such opportunities could be either removed or modified.

The examples just given range over several complex topics in themselves: motivations of offenders, environments, locations and security procedures. The situational crime prevention approach provides a systematic way to identify the specific factors that will allow for modification of situations that help to reduce the opportunities for crime, while at the same time addressing the complex topics of motivation and environment. The following chapter applies this approach to the entire e-commerce environment.

Notes

1 Underhill (2000) reports an instance where the simple study of customer use of shopping bags unearthed an obvious clue to shoplifting: individuals in the store with a shopping bag that was not from a local store.
2 The following account draws heavily on Garfinkel (1997: 315–34).
3 In fact, this is a highly simplified description of an online payment system. For a detailed account see Jones (2002).
4 This applies especially to the UK where special efforts to speed up verification procedures were recently put in place. See the case study in Chapter 7.
5 Visa claims reductions of up to 20 per cent in credit card fraud since it introduced software that detects aberrant spending patterns. Maremont, M. (1995)

'A magnetic mug shot on your credit card?', *Business Week*, 24 April, Science & Technology, 3421: 58.

6 In 1999, for example, a hacker working from Eastern Europe stole 300,000 card numbers from online music store eUniverse, and posted 25,000 of them on the Internet. He demanded a ransom of $1 million or else he would publish the rest of the names (Kutler, 2000).

7 Unlike other attempts at online payment services, this company has proved very popular. See https://www.paypal.com/ and the PayPal information centre http://www.pay-pal-infocenter.com/.

8 Cybercash has recently been taken over by Verisign (https://www.verisign.com) a widely respected company that offers verification procedures (PKI) for credit cards. For a detailed account of how Cybercash works for credit cards see http://www.cis.ohio-state.edu/cgi-bin/rfc/rfc1898.html.

9 Stalder, Felix (1998) 'DigiCash: learning from failure', *Telepolis*, 11 November 1998. It is of particular interest that Digicash refused to allow accountless operation in order to guarantee the anonymity of its users, and this has been identified as one reason for its failure. See http://www.echeque.com/kong/digicash.htm. As we note in Chapters 7 and 8, however, technology is sweeping aside the anonymity of cash transactions. The huge success of PayPal, now a part of the online line auction site Ebay, demonstrates this. While PayPal offers online 'cash' payment, there is still a requirement of registration and the possibility of tracing the identities of users. The use of PayPal for payments to online gambling and pornography sites – a major source of income to PayPal – was terminated upon its acquisition by Ebay.

10 Details on how First Virtual works can be found at http://www.virtualschool. edu/mon/ElectronicProperty/klamond/Fvpymnt.htm. However, this company's web page (http://www.firstvirtual.com/) is no longer accessible in the USA.

11 http://www.commerce.net/.

12 Staff (2002) 'PayPal gambling probed', *CNN Money*, 12 July. In fact in a laudable sign of coroporate responsibility, Ebay in its agreement to take over PayPal declared that it would sever all PayPal ties with online gambling and pornography: http://money.cnn.com/2002/07/12/news/companies/paypal/index.htm.

13 US Securities and Exchange Commission (2002) 'Internet fraud: how to avoid Internet investment scams', http://www.sec.gov/investor/pubs/cyberfraud.htm.

14 Greenberg, Paul A. and Caswell, Stephen (2000) 'Online banking fraud raises more security concerns', *E-commerce Times*, Newsfactor Network, 1 February, http://www.newsfactor.com.

15 Willan, Philip (2000) 'Mafia caught attempting online fraud', *IDG News Service*, Networld.Fusion at http://www.nsfusion.com/news2000/1004mafia.html.

16 Financial Action Task Force (FATF) (2001) *Suspicious Activity Review*, No. 3, Bank Secrecy Act Advisory Group, October. France: OECD.

17 Financial Action Task Force (FATF) (2001) *Report on Money Laundering Typologies for 2000–2001*, 1 February, FATF XII. France: OECD.

18 Federal Trade Commission (1999) *Drugstores on the Net: The Benefits and Risks of Online Pharmacies*. Prepared statement of the FTC before the subcommittee on

oversight of investigations of the committee on commerce, United States House of Representatives, 30 June.

19 *Ibid.*

20 Enos, Lori (2000) 'US states target illegal online pharmacies', *E-commerce Times*, 31 March, http://www.newsfactor.com.

21 Kiefer, Francine (1999) 'Online pharmacies draw federal scrutiny', *Christian Science Monitor*, 29 December, http://www.csmonitor.com.

22 Carey, Benedict and Marsas, Linda (2001) 'Bill on online drug sales raises hope, fears', *Los Angeles Times*, 16 July.

23 *Ibid.* For a Canadian online pharmacy see http://www.canadadrugs.com.

24 As an aside, it is worth noting that items of an intimate nature are the most often stolen from regular drug stores, so there is some possibility that the shift to online purchasing of these items could decrease their rate of theft (Clarke, 1999).

25 Philippsohn, Steven (2001) 'Trends in cybercrime – an overview of current financial crimes on the Internet', *Computers and Security*, no. 20, pp. 53–69. The FBI estimated in 2000 that while overseas criminals account for up to one-third of all online fraud against US businesses, not one single prosecution had been made against any of the perpetrators.

26 Richards, Asha (2001) 'Downfall of the online pharmacy: the legal climate for online drug sales'. *Internet Law Journal*, 16 April. The House held a hearing on 'Drugstores on the Net' which was followed by the Internet Pharmacy Consumer Protection Act that initially failed to make it to the house floor. When a version of it subsequently did reach the House, it passed 324 to 101, but legislative analysts believe that it will probably not make it through the Senate. See Carey, Benedict and Marsas, Linda (2001) 'Bill on online drug sales raises hope, fears', *Los Angeles Times*, 16 July. However, the Pharmaceutical Freedom Act of 2000 did validate the online sale of prescription drugs, requiring that sites post accurate information, and offer medical consultations, the names of consulting doctors and other background information concerning licensing.

27 This table is based on Henkel, John (2000) 'Buying drugs online: it's convenient and private, but beware of rogue sites', *FDA Consumer*, January–February, online revision June 2000, http://www.fda.gov.

28 Enos, Lori (2000) 'US states target illegal online pharmacies', *E-commerce Times*, 31 March, http://www.newsfactor.com.

29 Krebs, Brian (2000) 'N.J. sues to stop online pharmacy sales', *Newsbytes*, 3 April, http://www.computeruser.com/news/00/04/03/news5.html.

30 Grossman, Mark and Hift, Allison (2001) 'Online drug sales cause legal headaches', Giglaw.com at http://www.giglaw.com. and comments@mgrossmanlaw.com.

31 http://pages.ebay.com/community/aboutebay/overview/index.html.

32 King, Julia (1999) 'Websites crack down on fraud', *Computerworld*, 31 September.

33 Internet Fraud Watch, http://www.fraud.org/internet/2001stats10mnt.htm. Internet Fraud Watch works with the FTC to maintain a database of consumer complaints against Internet fraud.

34 Federal Trade Commission (2000) 'Going, going, gone…Law enforcement efforts to combat internet auction fraud', *For the Consumer*, February.

35 Wood, Christina (1998) 'Is your software stolen?', *PC World*, December: 177–84.

36 The argument mirrored those made by the recording industry when cassette tape decks were introduced: that sales of cassettes and records would decrease. Instead, sales of records and cassettes increased considerably. The opponents of Napster have yet to demonstrate empirically that the exchange of music on Napster and like websites affects regular sales. See King, Brad (2000) 'Napster: music's friend or foe?', *Wired News*, 14 June, http://www.wired.com/news/ visited 12/10/2001.

37 Websites include KaZaa, Morpheus and Gnutella.

38 Gibney, Frank Jr (2000) 'Napster Meister', *Time*. vol. 156, no. 20, 3 November.

39 For example, one company claims to have invented a technology that can embed CD tracks with 'road bumps' that will stop uploading or copying ('ripping') of the songs. See Staff (2001) 'Sunncomm introduces Napster-proof technology', *CD Computing News*, June, vol. 15, no. 6, pp. 1–2.

40 Patrizio, Andy (2000) 'New life for peer-to-peer computing', *Informationweek.com*, 8, 3 November, http://informationweek.com/813/peer2peer.htm.

41 Koller, Mike (2001) 'Peer-to-peer picks up steam', *Internetweek*, 3 September, CMP Publications.

42 Bielski, Lauren (2001) 'Peer-to-peer technology', *ABA Banking Journal*, no. 56. Peer-to-peer architecture appears particularly suited to the online banking and brokerage communities.

43 Palletto, John and Cohn, Mike (2001) 'Jxta peer-to-peer community continues to draw adherents', *Internet World Magazine*, 2 October, http://www.internet-world.com.

44 The application of digital certificates to each participating computer may help reduce this vulnerability. See Texar Corporation (2001) *Peer-to-peer computing: issues and opportunities for information sharing*. White Paper, January.

45 There are other websites that go further than Napster. Napster provided a central register that all users had to go through in order to identify other users' files. The Gnutella network does not use a central registry yet still provides access to a file-sharing network. Similar websites and networks were set up to avoid censorship. Freenet is the best example, which lacks any central authority (http://freenetproject.org/cgi-bin/twiki/view/Main/WebHome).

46 This section is taken directly from the report of McKinnon and Tallam (2002) who interviewed senior security managers from a sample of parcel carriers, mail order companies and retailers.

47 In the UK in 2000, goods worth approximately £18.9 billion were delivered to the home. It is predicted that by 2005, the value of goods delivered to the home will have risen by 83 per cent to £34.5 billion, with much of this growth fuelled by a steep increase in online shopping. Retail Logistics Task Force – DTI Foresight (2001) *@Your Home: New Markets for Customer Service and Delivery*, DTI, London.

48 One mail-order company operating 350 trunk vehicles reported that approximately once a year a vehicle suffered a break-in through the roof, while twice in the past five years thieves had cut through the side of a vehicle and stolen merchandise. One of the major parcel carriers has had one vehicle hijacked over the past five years, another has had none stolen in the UK over the past year (McKinnon and Tallam, 2002).

49 These depots typically have a high rate of throughput with regular scanning of parcels, offering little opportunity for theft. External theft is rare with employee theft most common (McKinnon and Tallam, 2002).

Chapter 6

Reducing opportunities for e-commerce crime

In *Situational Prevention: Successful Case Studies,* Clarke (1997) outlined four main ways of reducing the opportunities for crime:

- increasing the perceived effort;
- increasing the perceived risks;
- reducing anticipated rewards;
- removing excuses.

Within each of these four ways, he also identified four 'opportunity-reducing techniques', making 16 in all. In this chapter, we use this scheme to survey techniques that can be used to prevent e-commerce crime. Our purpose is not to classify every possible technique, but to demonstrate how readily the situational prevention approach can be applied to e-commerce crime. As we have noted in our introduction, it is a characteristic of situational crime prevention that it evolves and changes in response to new environments, particularly those environments that are directly affected by changes in technology. It is therefore not surprising that we have found it necessary to make some small changes to the scheme in order to encompass the full range of opportunity reducing techniques in the e-commerce environment. By the same token, we have found that not all the 16 techniques apply with equal force to e-commerce crime. For instance, the general absence of laws – and hence punishment – governing the Internet suggest that while it may not be difficult to think of ways to increase the perceived risks of e-commerce crime, this may not at present be as effective as with other crime. Of course, this situation could change as the Internet gradually becomes more subject to control and regulation (see Chapter 7).

Wherever possible reference is made to actual attempts that have been made to reduce e-commerce crime. However, as yet, there exists little systematic research on the effectiveness of crime prevention techniques in the e-commerce environment, although there are a number of well-researched techniques to prevent intrusion into computing systems.[1] Many of those techniques are highly technical, but using an overall situational approach helps to avoid the trap of imagining that technology will solve the problems of crime prevention in e-commerce.

Before embarking on this survey, it is important to emphasise several aspects of the situational approach that guided this task:

- Situational crime prevention is not confined to physical locations, but concerns itself with all aspects of the transaction between target/victim and offender. Therefore situations must be examined in all their complexities, the 'virtual elements' such as the relationships among different users of the online environment, and the 'physical elements' such as the actual places in which individuals reside and carry out physical actions.

- The situational approach is not confined by elements of time. When a customer makes an online purchase, he does so within a certain span of time, which may be defined as a 'virtual point of sale'. But the online sale is a highly complex process as demonstrated in Table 4.2, and exists only within the context of cyberspace in which various kinds of information move rapidly and over long distances. These rapid movements can, however, leave traces or maps of their movement that may be stored. Thus, the 'virtual point of sale' can be included as part of a history of tiny fleeting electronic movements of information to become an important focus of enquiry as to what went wrong, in the case of an intrusion or theft. 'Situations' therefore can be reconstructed as slices of time in order to identify security weaknesses.

- The conception of information as a hot product, and the identification of SCAREM attributes of the information system, suggests that there are strong motivations and opportunities for individuals to commit crime on the Internet. The situational approach attends not only to the 'physical' elements of a situation but also to the motivations of offenders. The two are, of course, inextricable, as the situational approach has argued and demonstrated many times.

- The classification scheme is based on a rational choice organising principle that tries to ensure that all aspects of situations are systematically covered. The original classification had only eight categories. It was subsequently increased to 12, and then to 16. Wortley (1996, 1997) has argued that these 16 techniques need to be expanded further to take account not just of situational inducements to crime, but also of situational pressures and provocations to commit crime. His arguments are compelling and will likely lead to a further expansion of the classification. For this reason alone, the present exercise in classifying opportunity reducing techniques in the e-commerce environment must be regarded as exploratory not definitive.

The 16 opportunity-reducing techniques are summarised in Table 6.1 and discussed below under the four main situational prevention approaches listed above. For the sake of clarity, it should be noted that a particular technique might quite easily fit into more than one category. For example, some target hardening can both increase difficulty and increase risk.

Increasing perceived effort

Two of the four techniques falling under this heading – target hardening and access control – were found to apply in the e-commerce environment with relatively little modification, while two others – deflecting offenders and controlling facilitators – did not seem to be as relevant. Deflecting offenders refers to design measures that prevent the accidental convergence of likely offenders with suitable targets. For example, laying on a bus service at pub closing time would help to get drunken patrons out of a town centre and back to their homes before they could get up to mischief or into trouble. The analogy in the e-commerce environment would be somehow to discourage easy access to computers, but this would be like trying to discourage customers from entering shops. Keeping people away from valuable databases is more easily accomplished in other ways through target hardening or access controls, including firewalls. Controlling facilitators was too broad to be useful in this context. A major facilitator of crime in e-commerce is information itself, as we have seen in the previous review of the CRAVED attributes of information and the SCAREM attributes of information systems. Many of the ways to control information fall under other opportunity-reducing techniques discussed below.

Instead of controlling facilitators and deflecting offenders, we substituted 'safeguarding data integrity' and 'authenticating identity', both of which have special roles in increasing the perceived effort of crime in the e-commerce environment. The issue of authenticating identity is picked up again in the concluding chapter.

1. Target hardening

Strictly speaking, in the e-commerce environment information is the prime target (though, as we have seen in Chapters 3 and 4, it assumes many forms), but other products and services such as computers, cell phones, credit cards and bank accounts must also be considered as targets of one kind or another. In addition, loopholes in the delivery system provide many opportunities for straightforward physical theft of items purchased on the Internet.

Table 6.1: Opportunity-reducing techniques in the e-commerce environment.

INCREASING THE PERCEIVED EFFORT

1. Target hardening	2. Access control	3. Safeguarding data integrity	4. Authenticating identity
• Firewalls	*Merchants:*	• Check attributes of critical files	• Accept only credit card payments and require PINs
• Design security into operating languages	• Require passwords and PINs	• Use public-key cryptography and other digital identification methods to verify files	• Use digital cash and digital certificates
• Design-out security holes in software	• Differentiated access control		• Promote use of smart cards
• Control information about software holes	• Refuse suspect sellers (auctions)	• Governments should allow high level of cryptography to be used internationally	• Auctions: no cash payments
• Keep computing devices in physically secure place	• Vet employees	• Advise customers to keep records of all transactions with online retailers	• Install biometric authentication
• Use robust packaging for home delivery	*Customers:*		
• Keyless entry and ignition for delivery vehicles	• Do not open suspect e-mail or files		
	• Only give credit card information on secure sites		
	• Query requests for personal data		
	• Do not use public access computers (e.g. Internet cafés) to purchase		
	• Be wary of grey market websites		

Table 6.1: Opportunity-reducing techniques in the e-commerce environment (continued).

INCREASING THE PERCEIVED RISKS

5. Detecting intrusions	6. Formal surveillance	7. Surveillance by employees	8. Natural surveillance
• Establish audit trails	• Publicise use of encryption and strong security surveillance	• Include regular employees in security team	• Establish community watch on auction sites
• Analyse user patterns to detect deviant use	• Electronic tracking of delivery vehicles and products	• Train all employees in correct security procedures	• Monitor for illegal sales
• Check for 'sniffers' and remove	• Maintain hidden presence on news groups and bulletin boards	• Offer incentives for employee vigilance	• Provide customer feedback on auction transactions
• Check for rogue files			• Encourage reporting to Internet service provider (ISP) of suspect e-mails and information requests
• Minimise 'cookies'			

REDUCING ANTICIPATED REWARDS

9. Target removal	10. Identifying property	11. Reducing temptation	12. Denying benefits
• Keep valuable databases offline	• Copyright web pages	• Immediately repair damage to system	• Encrypt valuable databases
• No dial-up access to databases	• Prominently display copyright material on software and other electronic products	• Limit publicity about new security	• Make software inoperable if user not authenticated
• Refuse auction of stolen, counterfeit or unethical items	• Use RFID tags for home delivery merchandise	• Regulate fraudulent advertising and scam websites	
• Discourage payment in cash for auction items		• Adopt filtering software	
		• Advise customers to resist too-good-to-be-true offers	

Table 6.1: Opportunity-reducing techniques in the ecommerce environment (continued).

REDUCING ANTICIPATED REWARDS *CONTINUED*

- Provide third-party escrow services and card acceptance for auction customers
- Use anonymous packaging for home delivery items
- Avoid unattended home delivery

REMOVING EXCUSES

13. Rule setting	14. Alerting conscience and controlling disinhibitors	15. Assigning responsibility	16. Facilitating compliance
• Develop security policy and procedures for employees	• Responsible use agreements	• Penalise customers for breaches of security	• Devise easy back-up and restoration for customers' software
• Adopt secure transaction protocol	• Customer education: 'Copying software is stealing'	• Hold auction websites responsible for illegal sales	• Easy access to information about copyright holders
• International agreements for copyright law, grey market commerce	• 'Authors deserve remuneration'	• Hold Internet service providers responsible for fraudulent websites	• Publish names and links to trusted online merchants and professionals
• Promulgate best practice guides	• Campaign against Internet 'culture', e.g. 'Hackers are vandals'	• Hold college campuses responsible for hackers	• Provide links to organisations that rate online businesses and survey online fraud
• Rights and responsibilities policy for organisations facilitating Internet access	• 'Hackers hurt innocent people'	• Insist that merchants acknowledge security errors	
• Require proof of delivery for merchandise		• Remove user rights if rules of use not followed	

Firewalls

Bandit screens introduced to London post offices in the 1980s reduced robberies by some 40 per cent (Ekblom, 1988). 'Firewalls' fulfil a similar function in the online environment. Firewalls may be installed as either hardware or software, and their function is to stop unauthorised users from another network, usually from the Internet, gaining entry to valuable databases. Because the Internet is such an open system, anyone theoretically can attempt to gain entry into a company's closed network (intranet). While merchants may want Internet users to enter their websites, they certainly do not want the common user to enter their valuable databases. An important function of the firewall is also to control any transmission of information out of the intranet to the Internet. The firewall intercepts all messages and transmissions and checks for their authenticity. There are many different versions and arrangements of firewalls, and many highly technical factors that need not concern us here (Ahuja, 1996). Suffice it to say that all firewalls intercept all transmissions to and from a company's private network and the Internet. They intercept e-mail and web browsing, filter unwanted transmissions and check and filter files that are sent back and forth.

A major problem is where to locate the merchant's website in respect to the firewall, behind it or outside it. A website is more likely to be attacked than files behind the firewall. However, if the website is attacked, it could result in embarrassment (such as happened to the US Department of Justice when its website was attacked and reconfigured with pornographic images) or expensive downtime. On the other hand if the website is behind the firewall, the firewall will have to be carefully configured in order to allow the verified customers to pass through. This is very difficult and some claim that in this situation two firewalls may be needed (Garfinkel, 1997: 20–4).

Securing computers

In any event, the computer and accompanying network hardware must be maintained in a physically secure location, usually in a locked room, with access limited only to those so authorised. Highly valuable databases such as customer credit information etc. should also be maintained in this secure location, and certainly behind a firewall. However, problems of security remain with the many workstations and computers in a typical business office, and these workstations may have several different users. Since these workstations are most likely behind the firewall, special security procedures are necessary to make sure that employees do not compromise the system either purposely or inadvertently. This is achieved by various procedures such as disallowing employees to download files without proper authorisation, disallowing employees to take home work on disks and not allowing or limiting dial-up access to the Internet. The latter is most important because the most serious intrusions into networks (especially telecommunications and government agencies) have occurred through dial-up entry. Finally, screen locks that switch the screen off after a period of inactivity and require a password to switch it back on should be used to avoid unauthorised persons picking up information from the computer screen. It bears repeating that many of the cases of hacking described throughout this book have been carried out by those who were not computer sophisticates, but who obtained necessary information from employees or others inside the merchant's network.

Eliminating security holes in software

Many products would be less amenable to criminals if they had been designed differently. For example, the early design of credit cards made them easy to counterfeit and eminently usable by those unauthorised to do so (Clarke, 1999). The introduction of picture ID for credit cards and other design changes has made them much more difficult to use for fraud (Levi, 2000). And in respect to software, when new operating system languages are written, especially those for the Internet (and surely more will be written), they should also be designed to include security concerns from the outset. Unfortunately, because of the structure of computer languages, it is far more difficult and mostly impossible to rewrite them to correct the errors that cause security holes.[2] Software manufacturers must therefore convey information concerning these bugs to security managers and the computing world generally. For example, Microsoft uses 'Black Hat Briefings' for this purpose. Unfortunately, because the Internet is an open system, it is especially difficult to limit this information to the intended audience. In fact, many Internet newsgroups and bulletin boards are devoted to disseminating information concerning these holes and how to fix them. Hackers can benefit from this dissemination as much as legitimate users and can learn how to use the holes to break through firewalls. Some have argued that the Black Hat Briefings should not be open to the public [3] and that, more generally, guidelines for the disclosure of such information are badly needed.[4]

Securing home delivery

Where a consumer product is the target during home delivery, hardening may be achieved by the use of robust packaging that prevents goods being stolen when the package bursts or comes undone, and by distributing smaller items in 'letter box size' packages. This permits greater use of the postal system, which is cheaper, more convenient and avoids the need to use less secure forms of unattended delivery (McKinnon and Tallam, 2002). Many items are stolen while the driver is away from the van depositing articles with the customer. In the United States, FedEx has tested the use of RFID (Remote Frequency ID tags) transponders embedded in driver wristbands to replace the keys on 200 of its delivery vehicles (D'Hont, 2000). This permits automatic keyless entry and ignition. When the driver moves more than a short distance from the vehicle the doors automatically lock and automatically reopen upon return. Ignition is achieved by pressing a button, but will only happen when the vehicle 'recognises' the driver's RFID tag. This illustrates how RFID technology can be used to address the problem of van drivers inadvertently leaving their vehicles open when they go off to make a delivery.

2. Access control

This technique is one of the most widely used and well developed in the computing environment. It can be traced to the use of moats and draw-bridges of medieval times, and the design of apartment buildings as they relate to 'defensible space'.

PINs and passwords

Passwords and PINs, of course, are the most common technique for controlling access in the computing environment.[5] Since the wide adoption of bank cards and debit cards many more people now use PINs to gain access to their accounts. Multi-user workstations in business offices depend on user IDs and passwords to allow different users to log on to the same machine. Because of the valuable (and vulnerable) nature of business databases, different levels of access must be set up, and employees differentiated on the need-to-know basis. All web e-commerce sites require passwords and user IDs for access to the purchasing step in the shopping program. Because these PINs provide access to vital data, the merchant databases that contain the passwords represent extremely high value to merchants and to customers, and thus make attractive targets. Thus, although passwords are created in order to protect the computing environment, the passwords themselves become targets for criminals. Auction websites have a special responsibility to refuse to register sellers who have a poor or suspect transaction record (usually available for inspection on an auction's website). However, in the case of auctions, requiring a user ID and password to register as a seller does not guarantee the identity of the individual who has registered. Some argue that this is the way it should be, since after all this is the way it is at garage sales or even in shops. If one pays cash, one's identity is irrelevant to the purchase. The authentication of identity continues to be a major issue in the online environment, and will be discussed further in Chapter 8.

Employee vetting

Much retail theft occurs as a result of employee theft.[6] Access to valuable information is also made possible by collusion between employees and thieves who may be provided with passwords by dishonest (or negligent)

employees. There is a wide variety of techniques available, both technological and managerial, to reduce or prevent employee dishonesty.[7] One way is
to vet new recruits more closely and exclude people with a previous record
of stealing. In the study by McKinnon and Tallam (2002), security managers
in several of the parcel carriers consulted identified more effective screening
of employees as the measure most likely to cut the level of theft within their
organisations. In the UK some companies make a policy of requiring appli-
cants to obtain a 'subject access form' from their local police, listing any
previous convictions. The onus is on the applicant to obtain this documenta-
tion. There also appear to be quite wide variations in the amount of time
taken by local police authorities to provide these forms. A view was
expressed by some managers interviewed by McKinnon and Tallam that a
past conviction for theft did not necessarily give an accurate indication of an
employee's future behaviour and, besides, new recruits with an unblem-
ished record could have stolen goods in the past without being caught.
Several managers argued, however, that there was a 'hard core' of persistent
offenders who moved between companies and warehouses. To identify such
individuals they would like to pool information on staff caught stealing, but
this is prohibited by data protection rules.

Controlling access to customers' computers
Criminals can obtain information about individual online users or customers when individuals fail to maintain proper security procedures with
their own personal computer. Web browsers can be set up to record the
history of web pages visited and can also retain passwords and user IDs.
And if an individual user is not using a firewall, such information can be
accessed from a remote location.

Customers should also be discouraged from opening e-mail or program
files sent over the Internet from unknown sources, as these may contain
hidden programs that can embed themselves in one's computer. While
viruses certainly do damage, other programs may search the computer for
passwords, bank accounts, etc. and send them to a criminal who is connected to the Internet on the other side of the world. Peer-to-peer
programs such as those that are downloaded for music exchange (e.g.
KaZaa, Morpheus) are especially prone to this. In January 2002, for example, it became known that these and other companies were embedding
programs with the download of their software (which is free) on the user's
computer, which then monitored the previous two days' web browsing, in
order to target the user with advertisements. Finally, the usual security
procedures should be taken in regard to credit card use online: one should
never give out credit card information unless on a secure e-commerce site
and one should always query requests for personal information.

Customers must also be taught to be constantly vigilant for deceptions that
are used by savvy operators who imitate legitimate online retailer web pages

and purchase systems, and ask users to input their credit and other personal information. Examples of these scams were described in Chapter 5. Customers should be warned to check out the authenticity of websites if buying grey market products such as pornography, prescription drugs, investment and tax avoidance services online. It is clear from the review of such sites in Chapter 5 that deception is more likely at such sites, and this includes as well the utilisation and theft of the customer's credit and other personal information.

3. Safeguarding data integrity

It is important to ensure that files have not been moved, changed or deleted while in transit, especially in regard to online transactions. Performing standard verification procedures on file integrity makes it harder for those who would either change the files for nefarious purposes or deny that they had done so. The following measures should be considered:

- Periodically verify attributes of critical files by using check-sum[8] operations, and comparing them to their originals. To guard against repudiation (when customer claims a transaction never took place), use public-key cryptography and other digital identification methods to verify files (see technique 10, 'Identifying property').

- Allow commercial use of the highest level of cryptography. The US government strictly controls the levels of cryptography allowed on products and services whose destination is abroad. This means that the civilian sphere (that is commerce) is far less protected by cryptography than is the military sphere. Governments must allow the use of high-level cryptography in the civilian sphere and internationally to guard against terrorism, because terrorism is in fact a commercial threat. Since September 11, there can no longer be a clear distinction between commercial and military spheres when it comes to terrorism.[9] The terrorist act of September 11 had direct and severe impact on the US economy and commerce generally. There are also many cases on record of foreign nationals hacking into commercial networks of the USA. Furthermore, because commerce now widely uses the Internet, any attack on one part of the Internet must have an effect on commercial activity.

- Customers should keep records of transactions for all online purchases, including receipts, transaction numbers, etc.

4. Authenticating identity

The anonymity afforded users of the telephone when electronic switching was introduced in the 1960s facilitated the use of the telephone to make obscene or harassing calls. The introduction of caller-ID in the early 1990s, which effectively removed the anonymity of phone calls, was found to reduce the number of obscene and harassing calls (Clarke, 1997). Some argue that anonymity is an essential element of open markets (although it is never stated just how widely this belief is held, nor why it is so essential.) This poses a fascinating paradox for e-commerce. On the one hand, users on the Internet demand privacy in the extreme to be able to interact not only anonymously but deceptively using 'virtual' identities. On the other hand, the e-commerce merchant must establish with some certainty that the user really is who he says he is before releasing the product.

To this end merchants are advised to favour only credit cards as payment, because the opportunities for credit card fraud are rapidly decreasing as a result of procedures that essentially add significantly to knowledge of the customer's identity (Jones and Levi, 2000).[10] This trend can only continue as PINs are required with their use and new 'smart cards' are introduced.[11] A basic smart card contains a computer chip embedded in the card itself. It may be either exposed so that it may be read on contact with the card reader, or embedded inside the plastic of the card, and read by means of remote electronics (some phone cards are like this). There are several advantages to the smart card over the regular card with a magnetic stripe. These and other promising attributes of the smart card are outlined in the following chapter when we recount a case study of the reduction in credit card fraud.

The future promises new ways to authenticate the cardholder, such as biometric authentication of identity (see Chapter 7),[12] but already special authentication procedures employ digital signatures, digital certificates or other software to establish the 'identity' of the consumer, i.e. that the consumers have legitimate accounts with the payment system and are who they say they are. These systems are highly sophisticated technologically, and have an excellent record for securing payments. Digital signatures also have other important benefits: not only do they establish clearly the identity of the consumer to the vendor, but they also establish a clear audit trail. In the case of repudiation,[13] for example, a situation in which the consumer claims that he did not order a particular item, the digital signature will reveal whether in fact he did so. In other words, it takes the place of the traditional personal handwritten signature. This technology has spawned a flurry of legislative activity that has passed laws (or is in the process of doing so) regulating encryption in the business environment, its use by law enforcement,[14] and defining and giving legal recognition to digital signatures and certificates.[15] National and international legislation (Bell et al., 2001) has been very active in recent years, much of it based on this technology.[16]

Box 6.1 Digital certificates

The use of digital certificates in consumer electronic payments is relatively new, but has been extensively researched over the past few years, especially in regard to electronic transactions between businesses, where the amounts or value of the exchange are very high.[17] However, recently there has been an increasing willingness to apply this technology to consumer purchases. Visa International has published extensive information concerning its recommended security standards, with particular reference to PKI infrastructure (see below) that uses digital certificates for authentication.[18] The work of the SEMPER project for the EU, for example, has established a model electronic payment system[19] that also anticipates the use of digital certificates, and has used the PKI concept extensively in designing its legislation concerning e-commerce and security, although different countries are at different stages in acknowledging the legality of digital certificates and signatures.[20] In the USA, the Electronic Signatures in the Global and National Commerce Act (E-SIGN) was passed into law in 2001, and affords electronic signatures the same legal status as a written signature.[21] Digital certificates and signatures offer several advantages over any other method of electronic authentication. While the topic is far too complex to deal with in any depth in this book, briefly the way this technology works is as follows.

The system is based on a simple principle, still used by Western Union when it wires money for a client. The client in London gives cash to Western Union and the name or other identifier of the recipient in New York. The client is asked by Western Union to provide a question and its answer that only the recipient could know. The recipient goes to the Western Union desk in New York, gives his or her name, answers the question correctly, and receives the money. The authentication process depends on both the sender and the receiver knowing the 'key' to the message (which 'unlocks' the money which is conveyed by a trusted third party). Obviously this method would be very cumbersome if it were to be used by an online retailer with thousands, perhaps millions of customers. Every customer would have to have a question that only he and the retailer knew. In addition, the customer would have to convey somehow either by e-mail or phone what the question was, which would defeat the whole purpose of the exercise! Instead, a complicated system called 'Public Key Infrastructure' (PKI) is established.

PKI works by establishing encrypted keys at each end of the transaction. The sender uses one key to encrypt the message, and the other key is used to decrypt the message by the recipient. These keys are mathematically related, but one of the keys can be 'public' or shared with others. These keys are used along with a digital signature, a cryptographic mechanism that guarantees sender verification, which provides a unique 'fingerprint' of the digital environment from which the message is sent. These signatures can be combined with the message itself and again encrypted so that a unique 'fingerprint' of the document itself is produced. Thus the recipient, using this key, can not only verify the authenticity of the sender, but also of the document itself, and can be sure that the message was not intercepted and changed or that it has been sent by an individual who is pretending to be the sender.[22] This very oversimplified description nevertheless demonstrates that this system is highly complex. Estimates are that it costs between $500,000 to $1,000,000 per company to establish. Nevertheless, Visa International has already incorporated aspects of PKI into its verification procedures for credit card payments[23] and many other major e-commerce websites have introduced the system.

Increasing perceived risks

As noted above, the absence of laws regulating the Internet make the set of opportunity-reducing techniques falling under this heading of less application in the e-commerce environment than elsewhere. To have any force, risks of detection have to be matched by threats of punishment. Nevertheless, three of the four techniques falling under this heading – formal surveillance, surveillance by employees and natural surveillance – all have some role in increasing the risks of e-commerce crime. The fourth, entry/exit screening, has less application because it is more difficult to distinguish from access control in the computing environment. The purpose of entry screening in the everyday environment is to ensure that people entering a place – a country, a transport system, a place of entertainment – are in compliance with the regulations about things they may bring into that place, have the correct credentials or have paid entry dues. The main purpose of exit screening is to ensure that people leaving places such as libraries or shops have not stolen things or, more generally, have complied with regulations about exiting (such as stamping a time card at work). In the e-commerce environment, however, exit screening would seem to be redundant if entry screening/access control is working efficiently. In place of exit screening, therefore, we propose a new category of detecting intrusions.

5. Detecting intrusions

Merchants can monitor every keystroke made by customers from entry to website to exit after sale. They can also monitor the keystrokes of all employee users. The collection of this information provides audit trails that can be analysed for regular patterns and individual profiles. This technique has been used to flag deviant or unusual credit card use, and can also be used to flag any unusual computer use that does not fit with past profiles. Security engineers may check for 'sniffers' which are hidden programs that can record all 'packets' of information as they are transmitted through various points of a network or networks. These sniffers are widely available on the Internet along with instructions on how to install them (Schultz and Longstaff, 1998). Those who place the sniffer can collect all passwords and user IDs that pass through the sniffing point. These sniffers exploit weaknesses or errors in operating system languages, as well as the decentralised structure of the Internet itself. Sun operating systems have been the favourite targets. Two fixes are possible: (a) security managers should frequently run software (made available by Sun) that checks for these error states and can detect possible operation of rogue programs; and (b) all transmissions should be encrypted using one of the many systems now available.

6. Formal surveillance

Formal surveillance, whether undertaken by personnel such as security guards and police, or through the use of surveillance aids such as CCTV, speed cameras and burglar alarms, has a well-recognised place in situational crime prevention. In the retail environment, Electronic Article Surveillance (EAS) systems have been installed in many retail outlets, particularly selling DIY products and clothing. These use 'tags' or foil strips which, if not de-activated at the checkout, trigger an alarm when the goods pass through an acoustic wave at the door. These tags cost less than one pence each and have a proven record in preventing retail theft in the UK and USA (DiLonardo, 1996; DiLonardo and Clarke, 1996).[24] In the computing environment formal surveillance might be conducted in the following ways.

Where information is the target
Advertise clearly on the e-commerce website, especially on pages in the purchasing process, that high-level encryption is used and that databases are protected by a trusted name-authentication company (e.g. Verisign). Surveillance may be especially effective at certain times of the day,

depending on the e-commerce site's customers. If the majority of purchases are made during the day, the chances are that attacks on the computing environment from hackers will occur late at night, when few if any systems operators are on duty. Thus it is necessary to monitor user activity and assess what time of day intrusion attempts are more likely.

Where consumer products are the targets

Tracking technology considerably enhances the scope for surveillance.[25] According to McKinnon and Tallam (2000):

> The tracking of cases, of pallets, roll cages and tote boxes is now widespread across the retail supply chain. This almost invariably involves the scanning of bar codes, either manually or automatically as the unit loads pass a sensor. The scanning of inbound supplies is common in mail-order warehouses. Downstream of the order picking operation, however, there was until recently limited use of track and trace. One large UK mail-order firm only introduced a bar-coding and a scanning system for picked orders two years ago. These orders, in most cases comprising several products, are generally put into bags or parcels for onward distribution to local depots. The implementation of this track and trace system, which cost £8 million, dramatically reduced shrinkage (loss of product for unknown reasons) by some 50 per cent.

Analysis of the tracking data can also help to pinpoint where packages are lost along the supply chain. Track and trace systems are generating large quantities of data on the movement of vehicles, packages and products that can be analysed at a disaggregated level to discover where and how most of the shrinkage occurs. New software packages are being developed to help companies find patterns in the occurrence of theft and detect criminal behaviour among employees and customers. Pattern analyses of various kinds are now extensively used by accountants as part of CAATT (Computer Assisted Audit Tools and Techniques) (Coderre, 1999).

Tracking of home delivery vehicles

The tracking of home delivery vehicles could be enhanced by RFID tags. The main security benefits would accrue at the local level where most vehicle theft currently takes place. McKinnon and Tallam (2002) report that a manufacturer of GSM-based vehicle tracking devices is planning to launch a new low-cost system catering mainly for the needs of small vans. It should be noted that vehicle-tracking systems are not designed to act as a deterrent to vehicle crime. There is usually nothing visible on the vehicle to advertise the fact that a tracking device has been installed. If there were, a thief would naturally try to find it and remove or disable it, reducing the chances of the vehicle being recovered.

Box 6.2 Tracking delivery vehicles (McKinnon and Tallam, 2002)

The lone operator of a delivery vehicle is an easy target for thieves who may steal the entire vehicle along with its consignment. Vehicle tracking systems significantly increase the risk for offenders. Satellite or terrestrial tracking of vehicles allows their position to be monitored on a continuous basis at any point on the road network and at any time.[26] Companies install tracking and communication devices in commercial vehicles primarily to assist fleet management and achieve higher levels of operating efficiency. This technology offers the added benefit of increasing security and making it much easier to recover a stolen vehicle. No general statistics are available on the numbers and types of vehicles with GPS. It was estimated in early 2001 that around 50 companies in the UK were offering vehicle tracking services. One of the largest of these companies, MinorPlanet (www.minorplanet.co.uk), has installed tracking devices in over 200,000 vehicles in the UK. This fleet comprises company cars, hired cars, vans, trucks and public service vehicles. Isotrak, on the other hand, specialises in the tracking of commercial vehicles (www.isotrak.co.uk). Its equipment is installed in over a thousand trucks in the UK. Another major player in this sector is Thales Telematics whose satellite-based Orchid tracking system is quite widely used in the UK (www.global-telematics.com). The Tracker Network (www.tracker-network.co.uk) markets tracking devices as a means of recovering stolen vehicles. They have been installed in around 350,000 vehicles in the UK, the vast majority of which are cars.[27] So far the Tracker Network has made around 7,000 successful vehicle retrievals and recovered over £50 million in stolen property.

A survey reported by Isotrak in early 2000 suggested that only 0.3 per cent of commercial vehicle fleets in the UK contained one or more trucks that were 'technology-enabled'. This study predicted that by 2005 around 5 per cent of lorry fleets would have at least some intelligent vehicles. The rate of adoption of this technology is likely to accelerate as the real cost of installing the equipment and subscribing to road information networks steadily declines. Some vehicle manufacturers (e.g. Schmit-Cargobull, the trailer manufacturer) are already installing much of this equipment as standard. This will further depress the unit cost. Operators of commercial vehicles are being encouraged to adopt this technology by, on the one hand, the growth of traffic congestion and, on the other, the continued tightening of customer delivery requirements. By giving operators full 'visibility' of their fleets at all times, the new GPS-based road information systems are helping them to adapt their logistical operations to an increasingly congested road network. Another stimulus to the growth of vehicle tracking will be the introduction of distance-based taxation for trucks, for which the UK government is proposing to use GPS-based tracking.

More generally, it is an easy matter for law enforcement to monitor the content of newsgroups and bulletin boards that exchange crime-facilitating information. At the same time public announcements of fraud investigations, their frequency and their successful prosecution should be made.

7. Surveillance by employees

Regular employees in various positions such as doormen, parking lot attendants and shop assistants, all assume some informal, if not formal, responsibility for monitoring conduct in their workplaces. Substantial reductions in crime have been found as a result of enhancing this vigilance. It is a well-established principle of retailing security to train employees in security procedures, and even to encourage them to be actually part of the formal security programme (Nalla and Newman, 1990). This principle could easily be extended to all those working in e-commerce positions. For example, they could be trained in security procedures, they could be rewarded for vigilance, and they could be invited to contribute ideas for improving security.

8. Natural surveillance

Natural surveillance operates through people going about their everyday business, such as trimming bushes in front of their homes, and through such practices as banks and retailing stores lighting the interiors of their businesses, and even staying open for much longer hours, which keeps more people around and in the store. The Internet is an open system that fosters aliases and anonymity. This creates an environment of natural surveillance in which all virtual actions are constantly observable, even though identities cannot be assured. One could characterise the Internet as the extreme result of the 'open society' in which everyone gets the chance to observe the interactions of everyone else, but it also means that each person may be 'watched' by everyone else. This may be an exaggeration, but it is certain that there is little privacy on the Internet. True, the very idea of many newsgroups and bulletin boards is to allow mutual surveillance as participants exchange information. Many participants in such programs just 'hang out' and watch what is happening rather than contribute to discussion (Mann and Sutton, 1998). We will return to this issue in the final chapter when we discuss the broader implications of surveillance and privacy in the information age, as they relate to e-commerce in modern democracies.

Customer service could be used to educate consumers about maintaining vigilance and security procedures, and to encourage them to report any suspicious e-mails or website requests for information to the respective e-commerce website or to the Internet service provider (ISP). Some venues of online trading also offer excellent opportunities for natural surveillance. Auction sites provide 'community watch' forums where buyers and sellers can leave feedback concerning their transactions and report suspicious activity, whether fraudulent, possibly stolen items, etc. Auction sites should do whatever they can to provide incentives for customers to participate in these online community watch sites, and make freely available all the feedback made concerning the records of all individual buyers and sellers.

Reducing anticipated rewards

All four of the techniques under this head – target removal, identifying property, reducing temptation and denying benefits – have a role in preventing e-commerce crime.

9. Target removal

In describing this technique, Clarke (1997) reports the case of a church in Northern Spain that installed a machine at its entrance so people could use their bank or credit cards to make donations. Thus the main target of thieves – cash donations – was removed. The targets that have to be removed in e-commerce are the valuable databases and computing systems needed to run day-to-day operations. As noted in Chapter 4, the selling of consumer products on the Internet actually removes these items from stores where they are available to thieves. There is also an advantage to the customer because comparison shopping is made much easier and obtaining information about the product is facilitated. Thus, e-commerce itself has removed the targets, though, as we have seen in Chapter 3, other valuable targets have replaced consumer products: the computing system and customer databases. The obvious solution to this threat is to keep valuable databases offline, eliminate dial-up access and maintain them in a physically secure facility.

Auction sites should refuse auction of stolen, counterfeit or unethical items and those participating in online auctions should be taught never to pay for an item with cash, because the highest cause of loss in online auctions is non-receipt of items that have been paid for with cash. Credit cards are the most secure form of payment both for the seller and buyer – even though surveys show that the majority of people believe that credit cards are an insecure form of payment online. The truth is that credit cards are far more secure online than offline. Online auctions also provide third-party escrow and card acceptance services so that the seller can accept credit card payment via the trusted third party, and the buyer can submit credit card information to a trusted third party without fear of fraud. Utilisation of a trusted third party to pay for auction items ensures that the intended fraudster has to produce the goods first before receiving payment, which also makes clear that the benefits cannot be enjoyed unless the contract is fulfilled.

10. Identifying property

Writing one's name in a book is a basic form of identifying ownership. Similarly, the registration of motor vehicles denotes ownership and when first introduced dramatically reduced vehicle thefts (Clarke, 1997). Copyright information should be prominently displayed on websites, on software and on other electronic products. RFID tags (see Box 6.3) offer a means of solving the POD (proof of delivery) problem of home delivery. By incorporating an RFID reader in the reception box that is in communication with a central server, it is possible to confirm the delivery of an order containing an RFID tag. The unique tag would match the record of the order on a central file, confirming the delivery has been made.

Box 6.3 Smart labels

Smart labels or radio frequency identification tags (RFID) (DiLonardo, 1997) provide a wireless connection to local receivers and can uniquely identify objects or people. They communicate by radio signals in either one or two directions with the receiver, which is in turn connected to a computer. The tags can either be read only and used solely for data capture, or read and write for recording information about the object's movement and handling.

Smart labels have several advantages over bar codes (Prophet, 2000: 26):

- They do not require line-of-sight with a scanning device. Packages do not therefore need to be oriented in a particular direction, reducing the need for human intervention.

- They can be embedded in packaging and products and therefore hidden from view. They are readable through wood, plastic and cardboard, though not metal.

- They can hold much more information than the standard bar code and are reprogrammable at point of use.

Different types of RFID tags can be used at different points in the value chain, from vehicle, through pallet/roll cages to cases and individual products, thus contributing to supply chain efficiencies (Herbert, 2001: 8). In 2001 in the UK the standard tag currently used on pallets and roll-cages had a 1-metre range and cost around £3. Product-based smart labels normally have a range of about 60 cm and cost in the range 50–90 pence depending on the number purchased. This price has dropped by roughly 50 per cent over the past two years and is predicted to continue falling. The range of the tags is also expected to rapidly widen, as is their size expected to decrease to that of a grain of rice or smaller. The tags are already used on expensive fashion clothing products. Within the next 5–10 years they are likely to become standard

---

on many of the non-food items currently distributed through mail-order and online shopping networks to the home.

11. Reducing temptation

The mere presence of a weapon, such as a gun, can induce aggression in some people (Clarke, 1997). Cars that are popular for joyriding, if parked on certain streets, tempt delinquent joyriders. Failure to deal promptly with minor signs of decay tempts people to commit vandalism. The equivalent to this situation in the computing environment is the Internet itself. Hackers find the mere existence of the Internet a temptation. Indeed, some have even claimed that people can become addicted to surfing the web. The problem e-commerce retailers face, therefore, is how to strike the right balance between demonstrating to potential vandals that all computing systems of the e-commerce website are under constant surveillance and intrusions dealt with immediately, and at the same time not announcing this important information in such a way that it offers a challenge to hackers to overcome the site's security system.

Where information systems are the target

Repair system damage immediately, especially if caused by vandalism. Note on the website that the system is closely monitored for intruders and announce this on the purchasing web pages. Citibank's security statement may be taken as a model.[28] It is displayed without fanfare, but is there for those who want to find it. Use customer service and every chance there is to educate customers about the security systems in place. Filtering software that removes spam and fraudulent messages from known sources can also be installed by users and, increasingly, by ISPs.

Where home delivery of a consumer product is the target

The high-value, branded products, targeted by thieves at all levels in the home delivery channel, can be easily identified by their packaging. Anonymous packaging makes it harder for employees to identify the contents and removes the temptation induced by the promotional images. The labels on packages and parcels can also identify contents. Ironically, in the case of international airfreight shipments, the tightening of security following September 11 now requires shippers to provide more information about contents in the waybill and on the package. The conflicting pressures of security and sales could be reconciled if an outer layer of packaging were added while the products were in transit through the supply chain.[29] Using alternatives to unattended home delivery (see Box 6.4) would remove the temptation for doorstep thefts.

Box 6.4 Alternatives to unattended delivery (McKinnon and Tallam (2000)

- *Home access systems.* These systems give the delivery company access to the customer's premises, normally the garage, shed or other outhouse. One system, which is currently being tried in 50 homes in the Midlands, UK uses a telephone-linked electronic keypad to control the opening and shutting of the door by both the delivery person and the customer.[30]

- *Home reception boxes.* Several types of reception (or 'drop') box are currently being marketed in the UK. One security concern common to all of these boxes is their inability to provide a POD, confirming that the goods have been physically transferred from the delivery driver to the customer or some other member of the household. The absence of this confirmation creates an opportunity for dishonest behaviour on the part of the driver and/or household member.

- *Mobile reception box.* Mobile reception boxes are filled by the supplier at its premises, delivered to the customer's home and secured to an outside wall by means of a cable.[31]

- *Communal reception boxes.* Individual drop boxes are clearly inappropriate for apartment blocks. For such residences, communal reception facilities comprising banks of lockers have been developed. These employ luggage locker technology that has been extensively used in railway stations and airports around the world.[32]

- *Collection points.* A collection (or 'pick up') point has a different address from the purchaser's home. It can be very close to the residence (e.g. next-door neighbour), be within walking distance (e.g. local post office) or far enough away to require a separate car or bus journey (e.g. purpose-built collection centre). Surveys suggest that leaving goods with neighbours is by far the most popular form of unattended delivery, preferred by around two-thirds of consumers.

- *Other mechanisms.* These include workplace collection, use of existing retail outlets,[33] mechanised storage and retrieval,[34] purpose-built collection centres[35], and local collection and delivery services.[36]

12. Denying benefits

This technique is similar to reducing temptation. A typical example is the attachment of a PIN to car radios rendering them useless if stolen unless the PIN is entered. New versions are immobilisers that render the car inoperable unless a PIN or digital signature is received from a keyless entry system. The obvious technique to achieve this on the Internet is to encrypt all databases and messages so that, if stolen, they are rendered useless. At a minimum, owners and users of valuable databases should use encryption technology to secure all transmissions and make software inoperable if no authentication of the user is made.

Removing excuses

Most ordinary people, and perhaps hardened offenders as well, make excuses for the crimes they commit. Making it harder to make these excuses, particularly for everyday offences such as drunk driving or tax evasion, has been found to be an effective approach to preventing crime. The four techniques falling under this approach are rule setting, facilitating compliance, alerting conscience and controlling disinhibitors (such as alcohol or peer pressure). In the e-commerce environment, the first two apply directly, but the latter two are difficult to distinguish from each other. They were therefore combined into one category and a fourth category, 'assigning responsibility', was added.

13. Rule setting

If there are no clear, unambiguous standards, rules and procedures for the handling of cash or electronic transactions, or if the rules are unclear or not visibly enforced, individuals will take advantage of the ambiguities. The Internet culture would prefer no rules – paradoxically, considering that computer languages tolerate absolutely no deviation from their grammatical structure. In e-commerce, there is of course the necessity for procedures for implementing secure transactions and these have already been outlined. However, there are areas of great ambiguity on the Internet where there is no clear way to apply rules or set clear standards. The first of these areas is that of cross-border commerce where the laws of different countries (and in the US different laws of each state) compete for status, and even agencies of enforcement compete with each other for jurisdiction. The second area is the commerce in grey-market products and services such as prescription drugs, gambling and certain tax avoidance schemes in investment services. The application of laws and regulations is often unclear, and also varies from jurisdiction to jurisdiction. The third area concerns intellectual property and the application of copyright law, which, although frequently revisited by legislatures, remains very different from country to country. At the level below legislation, however, clear rules are needed as follows:

- All merchant websites should publish a clear security policy and specific security procedures to be followed by all employees, and adopt a secure transaction online protocol. These rules should be posted clearly on the website.

- International bodies must develop international agreements for consistent application of copyright law, grey-market commerce and cross-border crime.[37]

- Best-practice security guides should be promulgated for e-commerce. There have been several initiatives over the past two years to establish codes of practice for home delivery operations. The Direct Marketing Association has drawn up guidelines for companies selling direct to the home. The Freight Transport Association has a Best Practice Programme for urban deliveries, while the BBC's *Watchdog* programme invited retailers and carriers to sign on to its 'Delivery Charter'.

- Places and organisations such as public libraries, Internet cafés, and college campuses should develop a computer use rights and responsibilities policy, educate all users and require all users to indicate agreement with the policy.

- Electronic proof of delivery (POD) should be required for all merchandise purchased via home delivery. The recipient's signature can be downloaded to a terminal on the vehicle or back at base. Only then is the credit card account debited. This minimises the risk of a customer fraudulently denying receipt of the goods and repudiating a credit card payment (McKinnon and Tallam, 2000).

14. Alerting conscience and controlling disinhibitors

When Clarke (1997) refers to alerting conscience, he is not referring to the 'general sense of guilt' that individuals may feel when they do something wrong, a sense that derives from a multiplicity of society's socialisation processes. Rather, he is concerned to link conscience to a specific act. The idea of this technique is to stimulate conscience at the specific point at which the offender may be contemplating action. For example, the common sign 'Shoplifting is stealing' at the entrance to a shop serves to prick the conscience of would-be shoplifters. The battle on the Internet is the battle for conscience that has been 'neutralised' by the culture of the Internet and it is the culture of the Internet that may act as the disinhibitor to committing computer crime, rather than the drugs or alcohol that serve as the most common disinhibitors for other crimes. The potential offender on the Internet has to be reminded that the hacker's ethic that 'everything on the Internet should be free' does not make everything free, and to treat other people's property as one's own is wrong. Nor does it justify damaging information systems since innocent people suffer.

A concerted educational effort will be needed to counteract the hacker's ethic. As commerce gradually comes to dominate the Internet, new generations of computer users may come to see that the Internet cannot be, and perhaps should not be, free to all. Campaigns and posters (hard copy and electronic) that display these messages are recommended, such as:

'Copying software is stealing.'
'Hackers are vandals.'
'Authors deserve remuneration for their work.'
'Copying software is punishable by prison.'
'Hackers cause serious personal and financial damage.'
'Hackers violate privacy rights.'

15. Assigning responsibility

The relationship between law and the Internet is opaque. This is largely because the Internet is popularly thought of as a kind of frontier, something like the mythical Wild West. This idea in turn derives from the Internet's highly decentralised architecture that is pictured as 'anti-law' because there is no central authority that 'runs' the network.[38] The next step in this argument, which is questionable, is to argue that it is therefore not possible to assign responsibility to any particular individual or organisation for bad things that happen. It is the picture of 'every man for himself', a kind of cooperative anarchy. While it may be true that there is no single authority that 'runs' the Internet, it is also certainly true that one could direct an attack at certain features of the Internet and almost bring it down – as some hackers have done. However, it is also necessary to recognise that there are very clear rules about how the network operates: rules about the structure of messages (how they are moved from one place to another, how Internet addresses are organised, how files are recognised) and strict procedures that must be followed in order for individuals to log on to the network. So, lying beneath the apparent chaos of millions of people connected together through different devices and different operating systems, there is a 'backbone' of strict rules that keeps the Internet running. Attacks that violate these rules – and most unauthorised intrusions certainly do that – should therefore be viewed harshly, and individuals assigned full responsibility for these acts. So also should those organisations be held responsible that allow hackers to operate through their services. Finally, organisations that allow criminal activity to exploit their otherwise legal services should be held responsible for doing so. This issue will be discussed further in the following chapter on policing the Internet. For those in authority to do so, the following may be appropriate:

- Penalise customers for breaches of security.

- Hold auction websites responsible for illegal sales.

- Hold Internet service providers (ISPs) responsible for fraudulent websites.

- Hold college campuses responsible for hackers who obtain unauthorised entry into other systems by exploiting the college computing system.

- Insist that merchants acknowledge security errors and report fraudulent activity.

- Remove user rights if rules of use are not followed.

16. Facilitating compliance

The provision of public urinals in Italy in the nineteenth century made it much easier for citizens to comply with a ban on urinating in public (Clarke, 1997). Perhaps nothing quite as striking could be managed in the e-commerce environment, although there is a clear need to make it easier to comply with prohibitions against illegal copying of software. One way is through easy back-up and restoration of customers' software. Compliance with copyright restrictions may be aided by providing ample information to customers about security procedures and other information that authenticates the company's identity and status in the business world. The publication and dissemination of names and other information of trusted and authentic online merchants and professionals (e.g. pharmacies, investment services) may assist individuals in choosing their merchants wisely. Websites and links to organisations that publish and rate online businesses should also help compliance. Information and links to organisations that survey the web for fraudulent websites and other aspects of online fraud are becoming more common (e.g. Internet Fraud Watch,[39] the National Fraud Information Center,[40] the Internet Fraud Complaint Center[41] and many more).

Displacement

It is clear from this review that there are many different ways of reducing opportunities for e-commerce crime and that a wide range of organisations, individuals and authorities must be involved in implementation. Little research exists on the effectiveness of these techniques in the computing environment, but, in the everyday environment, one result of opportunity reduction is to displace a proportion of the crime to some other target, place or time rather than to eliminate it entirely. In fact, there is often less displacement than expected by critics of opportunity reduction and in some cases there is also a 'diffusion of the benefits' so that targets and places outside the immediate focus of the opportunity-reducing measures also gain some protection (Clarke, 1997). However, it is quite possible that closing off a particular opportunity to commit a specific crime in e-commerce may have the effect of maximising the attraction of other criminal opportunities presented by the information environment. In the absence of research on this issue we can only speculate what may happen when situational interventions are introduced. Table 6.2 provides some examples of possible displacement effects resulting from the implementation of the situational techniques presented in Table 6.1. Clearly, future evaluations of situational crime prevention in the e-commerce environment must take account of these possible displacement effects and also, we would add, of possible diffusion of benefits.

Conclusions

Bringing about the changes demanded by situational intervention means that the parties involved must be convinced that the problem warrants such change. In the e-commerce environment the need for change in response to the threat of crime is rarely as clear as it is in traditional policing. When confronted with a crime threat, it is almost automatic for police to respond to eliminate it (though in practice, of course, the police cannot afford to try to eliminate all crime, and do place priorities upon certain kinds of crime and disorder). However, in the e-commerce environment, the extent to which any organisation should work alone or with others to prevent crime requires much more consideration. In the business world, the first question that is always asked is whether the cost of prevention is higher than the losses incurred, or whether the prevention techniques interfere with aggressive marketing practices. In general, research suggests that it is usually possible to incorporate security techniques with effective marketing principles, and that in fact it is possible to present security in many situations as an enhancement to a product (Clarke and Newman,

Table 6.2 *Possible displacement resulting from situational techniques applied to e-commerce.*

Crime prevention measure	Preventive technique	Displacement possibilities
Increasing the perceived effort		
Target hardening	Firewalls	Bribery/coercion of IT staff
Access control	Passwords	Bribery/coercion of IT staff; extraction of passwords by duress
Safeguarding data integrity	Public key cryptography	Identification of new targets
Authenticating identity	No cash payments, credit card payments only	Identity deception or theft
Increasing the perceived risks		
Detecting intrusions	Maintain audit trails	Mail bombs to destroy databases
Formal surveillance	Analysis of usage patterns using neural networks	Destruction of mainfame computers and virus attacks on Internet servers
Surveillance by employees	Incentives for employee vigilance	Collusion between employee and outsider
Natural surveillance	Community watch on auction sites	Falsification of transaction records and customer comments

Table 6.2 Possible displacement resulting from situational techniques applied to e-commerce (continued).

Reducing anticipated rewards

Target removal	Refuse auction of stolen or illegal goods	Increase in illegal sales in chat rooms and bulletin boards
Identifying property	RFID tags	Theft of tags, arms race to neutralise RFID tags
Reducing temptation	Immediately repair damage to system	Hackers shift to easier targets
Denying benefits	Make software inoperable if user not authenticated	Arms race to defeat encoding system; theft of easier targets

Removing excuses

Rule setting	International copyright agreements	Crime relocated to non-complying countries
Alerting conscience and controlling disinhibitors	Campaign against 'Internet culture'	May incite more resentment, shift hacking from universities to targeted ISPs or Internet cafés
Facilitating compliance	Publish names and links of trusted online merchants	Fraudsters may construct false websites that are identical to trusted merchant sites

Adapted from Smith, Wolanin and Worthington (2003).

2002b). This is an issue, however, that lies behind all decisions by businesses concerning the implementation of crime prevention techniques that cost money – especially if they perceive that some aspects of crime prevention ought to be dealt with by police agencies whose mission, at least as popularly defined, is to fight crime.

In any event, the next step in applying situational crime prevention is to identify the parties involved in preventing e-commerce crime, and to suggest ways in which these parties may be brought together to develop an effective strategy to police crime in the e-commerce environment. As it turns out, much of the infrastructure for policing the online environment is already in place, as we shall see in the next chapter.

Notes

1 An exception to this observation is the excellent book by Ross Anderson (2001). Anderson brings together research from several different disciplines and fields to present a coherent, encyclopaedic review of research concerning all security issues in e-commerce and beyond. For an excellent overview of crime prevention techniques that generally apply the routine activities approach of capable guardian, suitable target and motivated offender to electronic theft, see Grabosky, Smith and Dempsey (2001).

2 Although much improvement has occurred over the years, particularly in regard to UNIX, arguably the backbone of the Internet operating languages.

3 Keeling, James E. (2001) 'Social engineering – for the good guys', 16 July, http://www.sans.org/infosecFAQ/policy/social_good.htm.

4 Clark, Don (2001) 'Microsoft's conference on security flaws yields proposal for disclosure guidelines', WSJ.com, 9 November, Wall Street Journal archives.

5 For an excellent review of the many technical (computer-driven) methods of access control, see Anderson (2001: 35–71)

6 There are various estimates of the extent of the cost of employee theft. The US Department of Justice reports that the cost of employee theft is $60 billion annually, and the US Chamber of Commerce estimates that employee theft accounts for one-third of all business failures: http://retailernews.com/tfs698.html. In the US a recent national survey of retail stores in 2000 found that employee theft accounted for 44.5 per cent of loss, and shoplifting for 32.5 per cent. See Staff (2002) 'Theft: retail's real grinch', http://retailindustry.about.com/library/weekly/aa001122a.htm. Perhaps the biggest threat is now through collusion of data security employees and outside hackers. A ring of thieves recently stole 30,000 credit histories made possible by information given them by a low-level

employee. See Weiser, Benjamin (2002) 'Identity ring said to victimise 30,000', *New York Times*, 26 November, front page.

7 Case, John (2002) 'Employee theft: the profit killer', http://www.employeetheft.com/.

8 This is a computation that summarises a number of characteristics of a file, and should be identical to the check-sum performed on the original file (Ahuja, 1996: 164–6).

9 In fact, Anderson (2001) argues that the functions of law enforcement and spying (intelligence) are rapidly merging together.

10 From the e-commerce merchant's point of view, it is essential that not only information concerning the customer's credit information is obtained, but also as much information about the customer's buying habits and online interests as possible. This new approach was outlined in the discussion of the e-commerce value chains (Chapter 2). Credit card payment provides far more information about the customer than any other popular form of payment.

11 For a concise description of the types and functions of smart cards see Clarke, Roger (2001) http://www.anu.edu.au/people/Roger.Clarke/EC/ChipIntro.html, November. The rapid and widespread application of smart card technology to enhance credit and debit card transactions, process payments for entry into transportation systems, sporting and entertainment events, and in many other settings is usefully surveyed by Schwartz (2002/3).

12 The difficulties of authenticating the identity of individuals cannot be understated, especially given the comparatively recent increases in theft of identity. It is speculated that the increase in identity theft is a direct result of the successful steps taken in controlling credit card transaction fraud, especially introducing smart cards in the UK. The only way to overcome smart cards with PINs is to assume the complete identity of an individual, which would include knowing the PIN of that individual's card and the password for the online bank account etc. Ways to counteract this are also in progress, such as using a biometric device to match the card with the individual (Jones and Levi, 2000).

13 The 'five pillars' of classical data security are: authorisation, authentication, integrity, confidentiality and non-repudiation (Hurley, 2001: 42–7).

14 Law enforcement is very involved in encryption technology because of the perceived need for law enforcement to be able to intercept encrypted messages by criminals or enemies of the state. See Cabinet Office, UK (1999) *Encryption and Law Enforcement: A Performance and Innovation Unit Report*, May.

15 Such legislation was passed in the US 106th Congress (Nunno, 2001: 395–401).

16 See, for example, the Digital Millenium Copyright Act 1998 (DMCA) which proposes a maximum $500,000 fine and five years' prison for copyright violations, among a number of other highly restrictive standards. Also Zielinski, Dave (2001) 'Stop thief! The great web copyright crackdown', *Presentations*, July, http://www.presentations.com.

17 Traders in electric power have been the earlier significant users of this technology.

Power companies traded more than $30 billion in electric power by 2000. Greenberg, Eric (2000) 'Real-world security', *PC Magazine*, vol. 19, no. 15, pp. 106–9.

18 Visa International (2000) 'Account Information Security Best Practices Guide', 15 November, at https://www.visa.com/nt/gds/pdf/AcctInfoSecBestPractices Guide. pdf; 'Account Information Security Standards Manual', 15 November, at https://www.visa.com/nt/gds/pdf/AcctInfoSecStandardsManual.pdf.

19 Lacoste, Gerard, Pfitzmann, Birgit, Steiner, Michael and Waidner Michael (eds) (2000) 'SEMPER Secure Electronic Marketplace for Europe, Final Report of Project SEMPER', 19 June, http://www.semper.org.

20 Staff (2000) 'E-commerce and security – a European view', *International Security Review*, March/April, no. 115, pp. 10–13.

21 Holmes, Johnson (2001) 'E-SIGN: guidelines for signatures on the electronic highway information strategy', *The Executive Journal*, Spring, vol. 17, no. 3, pp. 40–3.

22 This is a highly simplified rendition of PKI. For a concise explanation see Kalakota and Whinston (1997: 135–45).

23 'Account Information Security Standards Manual', 15 November 2000, at https://www. visa.com/nt/gds/pdf/AcctInfoSecStandardsManual.pdf.

24 The scanning of bar codes on packages/bags has several shortcomings:

- Staff can fail to scan packages and try to steal them.
- Bar codes can be accidentally misaligned and rejected by automatic reading devices. Manual intervention is then required, giving staff an opportunity to steal the package.
- The handling units can be opened and individual products removed or other items substituted. As these products are not separately scanned, this loss may not be noticed until after the final delivery is made.

25 The following material on tracking is taken directly from McKinnon and Tallam (2002).

26 Many vehicles have two-way communication with an operating centre (or 'hub') and can be equipped with numerous on-board sensors to monitor various aspects of vehicle and driver performance. The operational and performance data can either be transmitted on a real-time basis to the hub using 'in-cab mobile data communications' or recorded for downloading into the company computer when the vehicle returns to its base. This latter system is much cheaper as the localised downloading of data by radio transmission is virtually free (McKinnon and Tallam, 2002).

27 The stolen vehicle recovery systems work like an electronic homing device. A covert transmitter is hidden discreetly in one of several dozen places around the vehicle. There is no visible aerial or other identifying feature so the thief can't see it and won't know it's there. When the vehicle is stolen and reported to the police, TRACKER activates the system, which sends out a unique silent radio signal across a dedicated nationwide transmission network. With TRACKER Monitor, a sophisticated sensor detects any unauthorised movement of the vehicle, even if it is

towed or lifted away. It then sends a warning signal to TRACKER's 24-hour monitoring centre who will call you to alert you of the possible theft. Once activated, the TRACKER signal is picked up by special detection equipment fitted in patrol cars and helicopters of every police force in the country, allowing them to locate the stolen vehicle to the exact spot. Because TRACKER works via land-based radio transmission, it is virtually impossible to interrupt or block the signal, by hiding the vehicle in a steel crate or concrete building for example, as may happen with some satellite systems (McKinnon and Tallam, 2002).

28 https://www.c2it.com/SUV/privacypromise.jsp.

29 This, however, would increase packaging costs, reduce space-efficiency in vehicles and warehouses and run counter to the main objective of the UK Packaging Waste Regulations which is to minimise the use of packaging material.

30 The key pads communicate with a central server allowing the 'home access' agency to alter the PIN codes after each delivery. The PIN code can be transmitted to the delivery driver by mobile phone shortly before he arrives at the home. The customer can also control the issuing of the access code by entering it in the online order and sending it via the web to their keypad. When the driver closes the door, the wall-mounted keypad device issues another code number which can be used to confirm that the delivery has been made. Upon receipt of the order a confirmation message is sent to the customer's mobile phone or e-mail address. In the marketing of these home access systems, it is claimed that they can also be used by repair men, cleaners, etc. The lack of a POD still remains, however. While the keypad records the opening and closing of the door and relates to a particular driver and company, there is no guarantee that the order is actually delivered (McKinnon and Tallam 2002).

31 The main example of such a system in the UK is provided by Homeport. This employs an electronic device resembling an intercom (called the 'Homeport') that is attached to the wall into which the cable is inserted. The cable is connected to the reception box and looped through the lid to keep it shut. Homeports have slots for three cables allowing three separate boxes to be left at the one address. They are activated by the customer's smart card and handheld devices operated by delivery drivers (McKinnon and Tallam, 2002).

32 The main provider of this type of box is a company called Bybox. They have adapted a particular type of luggage locker (manufactured by the French firm Logibag) for the collection of remotely purchased items. On entering the 'single-use' PIN-code allocated for a particular order, the appropriate locker door opens automatically (McKinnon and Tallam, 2002).

33 Small shops, garages and post offices have been identified as the most suitable existing outlets to assume the role of collection points. Their high density, particularly in urban areas, will minimise the distance that the average home shopper has to travel to collect an order. Serving as a local collection point will also generate an additional revenue stream for these outlets helping them to remain economically viable. In 2000, a company called DropZone1 formed a

network of collection points comprising existing petrol stations and small grocery stores (McKinnon and Tallam, 2002).

34 The mechanised storage/retrieval (MSR) devices could be installed within existing retail outlets if sufficient space were available. This would greatly enhance the security of the operation. More localised outlets, at a shorter average distance from the online shopper's home, would be unlikely to have the space, capital resources and throughput to permit investment in an internal MSR system. They are much more likely to be found in freestanding locations in areas open to the public such as railway station concourses, bus terminals or shopping centres. The security of these systems in a public location has therefore yet to be tested (McKinnon and Tallam, 2002).

35 No dedicated collection centres have so far been constructed in the UK. A company called Modus Properties has developed an ambitious plan to set up a network of around 50 purpose-built collection points called 'e-stops' in major population centres around the UK. The level of security at a purpose-built collection would be partly a function of its location. Modus Properties were planning to locate many of their e-stops in cheaper inner urban locations, where the level of crime would often be above average. This strengthens the case for incorporating a range of security measures into the basic design of the collection centre. The additional cost of these measures, however, further weakens the economic case for their development. It seems unlikely that this plan for a network of purpose-built collection points will come to fruition in the foreseeable future (McKinnon and Tallam, 2002).

36 This represents an extension to a collection point service, where the company not only receives the order on the customer's behalf but also delivers it to their home at a convenient time. At the time of ordering the customer gives the retailer the address of the collection company. When the goods arrive, the customer is notified by e-mail, phone or mobile text message and asked to specify a narrow time-window when the goods can be delivered. The final delivery is then made on an attended basis over a short distance, usually within 24–48 hours. The person receiving the goods at the home can sign for them, providing a POD. Customers pay an additional charge for this 'last mile' service (of around £4 per order). A service of this type is provided by a company called Beck and Call across an area of 25 square km in Central and West London. In the two years that they have been operating they have not experienced any thefts, either from their depots or vehicles (McKinnon and Tallam, 2002).

37 An excellent overview of attempts by international bodies such as the OECD, UNCTAD, WTO, UNESCO, ITU, World Bank, UNCITRAL and the EU to regulate cross-border e-commerce is found in Mann, Eckert and Knight (2000).

38 This belief that 'nobody runs the network' is probably right. The organisation that comes closest to 'running' the Internet is the Internet Corporation for Assigned Names and Numbers (ICANN). This is the organisation left over from the original organisation that first started the Internet, financed by the US

government. The funding future of this organisation is currently uncertain. See http://www.icann.org. Abolishing the organisation, however, would not terminate the Internet. It would probably go unnoticed. However, it does set certain rules, especially address protocols.

39 http://www.fraud.org/internet/intinfo.htm.
40 http://www.fraud.org/internet/intinfo.htm.
41 http://www.ifccfbi.gov/.

Chapter 7

Policing e-commerce

The previous chapter described many techniques that could be used in reducing the opportunity for crime in the e-commerce environment. It did not, however, address perhaps the most important issue: who will apply these techniques, and how will they be implemented? We propose in this chapter to answer this question by identifying (a) the mechanisms of policing that operate in the e-commerce environment, and (b) the social organisations that support and apply these mechanisms. By mechanisms of policing we mean any element, whether physical, social or cultural, that serves to control the behaviour of individuals and groups with the effect of reducing or preventing crime – in other words, what sociologists call social control. To prepare the groundwork for this analysis we will present the case of the successful reduction in credit card fraud in the UK, since it contains both the broad and narrow approaches of situational crime prevention and concerns the prototypical online payment system that dates back some 30 years. In presenting this case we will detail the situations that make credit card fraud possible – an extension of the analysis we began in Chapter 5 concerning the risks of online payment systems. We will see that the identification of the specific situations that make credit card fraud possible – the narrow approach of situational prevention – naturally leads to the mechanisms needed to control them. And these in turn point to the organisations and individuals needed to contribute to the modification or elimination of these situations.

Reducing credit card fraud: a case study

What is credit card fraud?

Credit card fraud forms a part of bank services fraud that includes cheque fraud and the fraudulent use of bank (ATM) cards and cheque cashing cards. For reasons to be described shortly, credit card fraud accounts for the largest proportion of bank services fraud. Credit cards are convertible targets for criminals, since they have no value in themselves, but rather, once obtained, provide access to a very valuable service that makes stealing the card as good or better than stealing cash. In fact, there is one way in which counterfeit cards do have intrinsic value, which is when they are sold in bulk by organised crime to other criminals who then convert them into cash or goods of value. However, even in this case, the cards' value lies in their ready convertibility.

Analysing the opportunity structure of credit card fraud

Credit cards are a product that delivers a service of great value to customers: the possibility to purchase goods or cash without having the money to do so. They also make the sale of goods a smoother, easier transaction for merchants (especially online sales as we saw in Chapter 5), and make the decision to buy for the customer easier by avoiding the necessity to have money in hand to pay for the item. The issuers of the cards benefit in many tangible and intangible ways: they earn income from the fees or interest they charge their customers, and in the case of bank cards, they bring their banking service to the customer 24 hours a day through ATMs. All in all, everyone benefits. However, since credit cards are both a physical product (i.e. a piece of plastic) and a service, both those features of the card present a variety of opportunities for fraud. The cards can be counterfeited, and the service corrupted in a variety of ways. Thus if credit card fraud is to be reduced or prevented, the first step is to identify each opportunity for fraud that criminals can exploit. These opportunities may be broken down into roughly two groups: those that arise because of the technological attributes of the plastic card itself, and those that arise as a result of the transactional situations that occur during the use of the card's service, that is in converting the card into valuable goods or services.

Opportunities offered by technology
There are two challenges to the physical design of the plastic credit card in order to eliminate the opportunity for fraud:

- to design and manufacture a card that ensures that it is a genuine card of the issuer and not a counterfeit;
- to design a card that contains features that ensure that the person who is using the card is in fact the legitimate cardholder.

The story of the development of cards designed to achieve these very difficult goals is a classic story of the 'arms race'(Ekblom, 2000) that occurs between society and criminals in a rapidly changing world of technology, and the necessity of trying to keep one step ahead of the fraudsters (Steel, 1995: 16). Not surprisingly, counterfeiters manufacture credit cards by copying the legitimate process. They can engage in three processes: primary, secondary and tertiary manufacture.

Primary manufacture
The credit card is constructed of a white plastic base easily obtainable from legitimate sources.[1] In early counterfeit cards, a silk-screen process was used to add colour to the card and, when dry, identification features of the bank or

other issuing company were added. The card was finally embossed with the name, account number and other details that are defined according to the requirements of the system used by the card issuer and then laminated. These cards were relatively easy to detect as counterfeit, although up to the early 1980s they were very successfully used by fraudsters. That point-of-sales (POS) staff often failed to detect them is related to the actual situation in which the card was used (see below). It was not long, however, before counterfeiters were able to apply high-quality micro-printing or thermal dye printing, such as that used by American Express or Visa. The industry responded by introducing cards that contained ultraviolet identification marks, and signature panels placed over the base colour, but counterfeiters quickly learned how to reproduce these, adding their own signature panels. In the early 1990s, business responded by introducing unique holograms, thus making the cards 'impossible' to copy (Arend, 1993). At first counterfeiters used cheap foil in an attempt to make rough copies of holograms which were easily detectable. They were successful none the less. However, counterfeiters soon found sources of hologram manufacture, and by the mid-1990s counterfeit cards appeared with holograms of high quality, virtually indistinguishable from legitimate cards. At this time police agencies and industry investigators discovered that the majority of these high-quality counterfeit cards were manufactured in the Asia Pacific Rim area, and sold or marketed both in Asia and Europe (Newton, 1994; Bury, 1999:7; Steel, 1995:16).

Secondary and tertiary manufacture

The industry response to the counterfeiters was to introduce the magnetic stripe on the back of the card, which contains information about the account number and the address of account holder. At first, this presented a challenge to counterfeiters whose only way around this was to paste on a strip (Iannacci, 1994: 83) that looked like a magnetic stripe, then at the POS have the salesperson key in the information manually (again, this point of vulnerability is intimately related to the situation in which the card is used). However, counterfeiters discovered that they could purchase (in some countries legitimately[2]) machines that could encode and decode the magnetic stripes, so they were able to re-encode their credit cards so that these were undetectable by computers at POS. Thus counterfeiters obtained pre-printed base cards (secondary manufacture) from either a legitimate or illegitimate source and added their own embossing, holograms and logos of their choice, and encoded them depending on what delivery system they intended to target. Or they obtained finished laminated cards complete with logos and holograms to which they added their own embossing and encoded information. There are many variations of the above, including obtaining stolen credit cards that may be re-encoded (tertiary manufacture). The industry responded with a number of initiatives with varying success including holomagnetics (Crocket, 1993: 19), 'watermark magnetics'

(Steel, 1995: 16), micro-dots, special embossed characters and tamper-evident signature pads (Lisker, 1994: 14), 'electronic fingerprints'[3] and indent printing (Newton, 1994). These have been either tried and subsequently copied by counterfeiters or considered but rejected by card issuers because they were not cost-effective. Recent innovations promise to raise the stakes for the criminals, but before examining these we need to touch briefly on the second of the problems faced by card designers, and that is the design features that will tie the card to the legitimate cardholder. This has proved a most difficult task.

Authenticating the cardholder

The most basic method of linking the card to the cardholder has been the signature required on the back of the card, but it is well established that POS staff cannot be depended on to carefully validate the customer's signature.[4] To overcome this problem (a problem clearly related to the situation in which the card is used) some card issuers have introduced laser engraved signatures and photographs. Citibank in the USA and the Royal Bank of Scotland in the UK have introduced photo cards, which have proved very popular with customers, and have also demonstrated considerable reductions in credit card fraud. However, it remains doubtful whether inspection of photographs made at the POS is a more reliable way of linking the card to the cardholder than inspection of signatures (Newton, 1994). The industry has also resisted photographs because of their expense. Thus the overall trend in the industry has been to look for ways to remove the responsibility of merchants for authenticating cardholders and replace this with various forms of electronic verification, as follows:

- *Biometrics*. These cards incorporate some physical attribute that is unique to the cardholder, such as facial characteristics, iris scans, finger or hand print (Polding, 1996: 23). These features have been used only experimentally, and their wide-scale introduction is probably a long way off, largely because of the expense both of manufacture of the card and of upgrading terminals to recognise them.[5]

- *Card validation code (CVC)* – increasingly adopted in the United States (Lisker, 1994: 14). This technique ties the account number to the magnetic stripe on the card through a code that must be validated by the issuer each time the card is used. It appears as a number printed in reverse italic (difficult to copy) on or near the signature panel.[6] A simpler version of this is the addition of a four-digit non-embossed card identification number (CID) on the face of the card that is not reproduced on the printed credit slip. This is used especially for telephone orders when the sales person requests the cardholder to read out this number (Colacecchi, 1993: 8).

- *Smart cards.*[7] These cards appear to offer the most promise, though their introduction may take a long time and their actual application is complex. A basic smart card (see previous chapter) contains a computer chip embedded in the card itself. It may be either exposed so that it may be read on contact with the card reader, or embedded inside the plastic of the card, and read by means of remote electronics (many phone cards are like this). There are several advantages to the smart card over the regular card with a magnetic stripe. First, it actually can process information on the card and can store a record of its use. It is therefore possible for the card to contain several levels of security, to be able to conduct security checks within its own microprocessor, so that, in the more sophisticated cards, they do not need to be constantly checked by a central system that contains a database of the usual information, such as credit limits etc. The card also can require a PIN number to be entered (much as is already required for bank cards for ATMs which incidentally have a very low fraud rate), or it may contain its own means of identification using a special messaging algorithm (Marrinan, 1995: 46). The smart card has been used in France since the late 1980s, and that country has a very low credit card fraud rate (Demery, 1998).[8] Trials of the smart card have been undertaken on many university campuses in the USA (Marrinan, 1995), as well as in selected regions through the world, in particular Switzerland and Australia[9] (including at the Olympic Games in Sydney), New Zealand (Pamatatau, 1997), South Africa (Polding, 1996) and Taiwan,[10] all with promising results in so far as user acceptability is concerned, though there are no measures of fraud available. The UK began to phase in smart cards with PIN numbers in November of 2000.[11] Experts claim that the level of investment that fraudsters would need to make in order to hack through a smart card (sometimes called a chip card) will far outweigh the reward, and in addition the chips can more easily be updated and changed, making it easier to remain one step ahead of even the most sophisticated fraudster (Bury, 1999: 48), though admittedly staying one step ahead is something like an 'arms race' as each side tries to go one better than the other. In fact at the time of writing, researchers at the Cambridge Computer Laboratory have discovered a vulnerability of smart cards.[12]

One may ask: if the smart card is so superior (and it has been available since the early 1980s[13]), why has it taken so long to be introduced, particularly when credit card fraud is increasing at such a rapid rate? Part of the answer no doubt lies in the expense that is entailed in producing the cards and probably the even greater expense of upgrading terminals at POS that can read them, especially for small-volume merchants for whom this would simply not be cost-effective. There is also little incentive for merchants to do so, since they stand to lose much less from this type of fraud than do banks (Fitch, 1984: 15). This latter point suggests that the other part of the answer to reducing credit card fraud lies with the delivery systems employed in conjunction with credit cards because, in truth, as far as crime prevention is concerned – and perhaps also from a business point of view – the two cannot and should not be separated (Marrinan, 1995).

Opportunities for fraud offered by the delivery system of credit cards
The intricate relationship between card design and service design is portrayed in Table 7.1, which shows the stages of service delivery, the transactions that occur along the way, and the points of vulnerability revealed by the Home Office study upon which this table is based (Levi, 2000; Levi and Handley, 1998a, 1998b; Levi, Bissell and Richardson, 1991). The Home Office study produced a dramatic reduction in cheque fraud along with considerable reductions in credit card fraud, as we will see below. The table identifies the four situations in which opportunities for fraud occur in the delivery of credit card service: primary issuance of the card, card acquisition, point of sale and card-not-present. Analysis of these situations by the Home Office study led to the following conclusion with regard to situational prevention measures:

- Redesign or improved design of service in addition to the card itself is essential if fraud is to be reduced because of the situations in which counterfeit or stolen cards are used. Eliminating counterfeit cards would not prevent an offender from using a stolen card. Careful checking procedures at the POS may.

- The motivations of participants in delivery of the service differ. Merchants do not stand to lose substantially from credit card fraud, so efforts to modify situations that require their active participation may be unsuccessful. In contrast, the card issuers and banks stand to lose significantly.

- Similarly, the users of credit cards are well protected by loss. Most credit card issuers in the US guarantee that the maximum loss a cardholder may incur is $50, and most issuers do not even charge that amount for losses from illegal use of a card. Similar rules operate in the UK. Thus getting the cardholder to take preventive actions, such as not leaving one's purse in an automobile, may also be difficult.

- The role of regular police in preventing credit card fraud is unclear. Their role in tracking down counterfeiting by organised crime fits more closely their traditional image, but their role in tracking down fraudulent use of a card at the POS, or online purchase, is less clear.

Thus the challenge to modify the situations in which credit cards were used was to obtain the cooperation among different organisations and individuals with different stakes in the outcome. In this case, this was facilitated by the Home Office, which took a number of concrete steps, the first of which was to get the parties concerned to recognise that there was a problem, the solution of which would benefit all parties concerned.

Table 7.1 The delivery system of credit cards with points of vulnerability.

Stages of delivery	Transaction	Points of vulnerability
Card issuance	Banks and building societies, specialist card issuers (First Direct and MBNA), retail-store card issuers, global card networks (Visa/MC, American Express, Diners Club) market their services and acquire subscribers.	(a) Organised counterfeiters manufacture their own cards. (b) Criminals 'skim' cards they obtain through theft.
Card acquisition	Card mailed to cardholder's address or cardholder collects card from issuer.	(a) Cards purchased from counterfeiters. (b) Cards stolen through other crimes such as burglary, theft or robbery. (c) Postal delivery of cards intercepted through corruption of postal workers, bogus mail forwarding requests. (d) Opportunists use cards delivered to old or incorrect addresses. (e) Fraudsters pose as telemarketers to obtain card information.
Point of sale (POS)	Salesperson verifies card account, signature or other identifying features, and amount.	(a) Floor limit may be set too high.[a] (b) Verification by signature inadequate. (c) Diversity and competition between card issuers hampers establishment of central database of hot cards. (d) Premium of speed of transaction places pressure on staff to ignore signs of card fraud. (e) Salesperson may collude with fraudulent customer.

Card-not-present (CNP) sale	Sale transacted over phone or on Internet. Sales person verifies card account and owner by reference to large databases of personal and card information of customer.	(a) Visual verification not possible. (b) Databases of identity verification are vulnerable to hacking. (c) Impossible to guarantee identity of purchaser. (d) Information used for identity may reside on customer's personal computer which is also not secure.
After the sale	(a) Items delivered to customer's home or collected at local store. (b) Items downloaded to customer's computer. (c) Items are returned.	(a) Fraudster may attempt to return items for cash. (b) If by mail or Internet order, customer may claim did not receive item or may claim never placed order.

[a] Visa claims that 59 per cent of all fraudulent transactions are for less than the common floor limit of $50. Lowering the floor limit, therefore could be the most immediate way to reduce fraud. However, speedy and cheap telecommunications are needed for increasing the number of online card verifications (Fitch, 1984: 15).

The problem recognised

Almost from their inception, credit cards, and their cousins bank cards and cheque cashing cards, created fraudulent opportunities for criminals, but these risks or losses were seen as relatively small costs of conducting a business (Fitch, 1984: 15). Nor was the problem given much attention by the police. In fact in 1991 Levi *et al.*, the authors of the Home Office study, described the situation of bank services fraud as one of a 'stand-off' between the police and business, each waiting or expecting the other to solve the problem (Levi, Bissell and Richardson, 1991).

The Home Office Report that Levi and his colleagues prepared served to identify and bring to public notice the extent of bank services fraud. It argued persuasively that, even if the losses from credit card fraud were tiny in comparison to the gross turnovers in sales, it was nevertheless possible to reduce that loss which would in turn contribute to the bottom line. It also argued that fraud reduction should be seen as an indirect profit-enhancing activity and therefore worth pursuing. At the end of the 1980s, competition among credit card issuers and merchants had become intense, so any initiatives that could increase the bottom line were seen as providing business opportunities. The time therefore was ripe for obtaining the cooperation of all parties concerned. A series of meetings, and the sharing of the information collected by the Home Office, served to convince the parties concerned that there was a problem and that practical steps could be taken to solve it.

Coordinated interventions

The preventive measures that resulted from the Home Office initiative are summarised in Table 7.2 according to the particular stages in service delivery. Almost all these measures were applied to some degree. The Home Office obtained the cooperation of the major parties affected by credit card fraud (the card manufacturers, the card issuers, the banks, the merchants and trade associations) not only in collecting information but also in disseminating the findings. It also brought these groups together with police agencies at joint meetings at every stage. The efforts to obtain coordinated changes in banking services also addressed cheque-cashing fraud and bankcard (ATM card) frauds as well as credit card fraud. It should be added that, once the Home Office had convinced the parties concerned that the problem was severe and that its solution would help the bottom line, businesses developed their own ways to cooperate, even while remaining fiercely competitive. Joint initiatives introduced at this point were (Levi and Handley, 1998a):

- the Credit Industry Fraud Avoidance System (CIFAS) was set up to merge data sets and maintain hot card files;

- APACS (Association for Payment Clearing Services) began to collect extensive data and information on the credit card industry and disseminate this through its website and through sponsoring customer and merchant education;[14]

- reduction in costs of telecommunications to facilitate more online card verification occurred as a result of industrial action and union bargaining;[15]

- introduction of hot cheque files occured;

- sharing of information concerning counterfeit cheques and suspect bank accounts took place;

- police cheque fraud squads were set up to work in concert with banks;

- advanced anti-counterfeiting technology was introduced into cheque printing and plastic card manufacture;

- the requirement of PIN numbers for cheque and debit cards was introduced.

Table 7.2 Points of intervention and preventive measures.

Stages of delivery	Preventive measures
Card issuance	(a) Addition of magnetic stripe, followed by holograms, biometric identification devices, laser engraved signatures, photo cards. (b) Police action against organised counterfeiters. (c) Encouragement of bank–police liaison. (d) Customer education about reporting lost or stolen cards.
Card acquisition	(a) Tighter controls over requests to redirect mail, including re-checking of customer requests. (b) Identification of insecure addresses and regions of delivery through crime pattern analysis. (c) Customer collection of cards from bank required for those living in insecure regions. (d) Customer education concerning risks and costs of card loss through theft, and encouragement of personal preventive habits. (e) Customer education concerning risks of telemarketing fraud. (f) Police coordination with postal service.
Point of sale (POS)	(a) Reduce telecommunications costs and increase speed of connection so that online verification of amount and card account information may be done so that floor limit may be kept as low as possible, with most transactions actually verified online. (b) Introduce laser-engraved signatures with photos for verification. (c) Improve staff training and offer rewards for vigilant employees. (d) Allow customers to choose Personal Identification Numbers (PIN). (e) Introduce smart cards with chips that process PINs and offer several layers of security. (f) Card issuers and merchants pool resources to establish central database of hot cards (Credit Industry Fraud Avoidance System – CIFAS).[a] (g) Use pattern analysis to develop individual profiles of card use and predict possible fraudulent use.[b]
Card-not-present (CNP) sale	(a) Smart cards with terminals on home computer may eliminate necessity for extensive databases for verification. (b) Use encryption, firewalls and separate computers unconnected to the Internet for large databases of card information. (c) Customer education concerning risks of storing private information on personal computer, especially when connected to Internet. (d) Customer education concerning Internet scam companies, checking out Internet companies for reputation.

After the sale	(a) Never issue cash for return of items bought with credit card.
	(b) Use tracking of delivery services to verify actual delivery.
	(c) Use secure order processing Internet software which also provides forensic information such as audit trails, location of computer from which order is made.
	(d) Reverify customer order before shipping.
	(e) Require customer to report the card validation code (CVC) at time of order to ensure that customer is legitimate cardholder.
	(f) Use secure electronic delivery software for customer downloading of software, music, etc. that also provides forensic information to verify download took place and was completed.
	(g) Have a clearly stated and publicised shipping and returns policy and procedure.

a   CIFAS has an extensive website that covers many areas of fraud and consumer education: http://www.cifas.org.uk/.
b   Visa claims reductions of up to 20 per cent in credit card fraud since it introduced software that detects aberrant spending patterns (Maremont, 1995: 58).

The effects of intervention

Figure 7.1 displays the points of intervention and the probable effects of these interventions on the levels of credit card fraud. In 1991–93, cheque card fraud accounted for roughly one-quarter of losses, with debit cards accounting for another quarter and credit cards the remaining half. This distribution continued roughly until 1995 as the three major forms of bank services fraud progressively decreased. This decrease was most likely the result of the new security features designed into cards at the beginning of 1993, and the targeting of bank services delivery systems towards the end of that year. In 1993–4 concerted efforts were made to improve the design of plastic card services. This included the sharing of information concerning fraudulent cards and fraudulent cheques, suspect bank accounts and closed bank accounts, so that databases merging all this information could be checked each time a credit card or cheque cashing card was used at the POS. This worked much better for cheque fraud because merchants generally must shoulder more of the loss from cheque fraud whereas the card companies bear more of the loss from credit card fraud (Levi, Bissell and Richardson, 1991).

The work of the Home Office did not stop with the original report. It was followed up by periodic updates (Levi and Handley, 1998a, 1998b; Levi, 2000) and initiatives that clearly contributed to a substantial reduction in credit card fraud in the years that immediately followed the report. The actions taken to change the delivery system are described in Table 7.2. By the end of 1995 bank services fraud had dropped to an all time low, and cheque fraud in particular remained at a very low level and became even lower with the introduction of additional security designs into cheque printing in 1998. We should also note that we have been discussing in this section *proportions* of loss, not total losses which are also reported in Figure 7.1. An accurate portrayal of the extent of plastic card fraud could not be made without taking into account the actual turnover, since the actual number of transactions each year involving plastic cards has increased tremendously. This would also contribute to the tiny portion of cheque fraud of total fraud loss, since the actual number of cheques used for payments has been declining over the past few years in the UK (though not in the US), and is expected to continue to decline. Thus fraud losses against turnover were 0.145 per cent of all transactions in 2000 compared to 0.33 per cent in 1991. It is reasonable to conclude, therefore, that fraud prevention technology and intervention in the service delivery system have been quite successful. However, in terms of total losses, it is a different story.

Figure 7.1 Plastic card fraud losses 1991–2000, showing security design interventions.

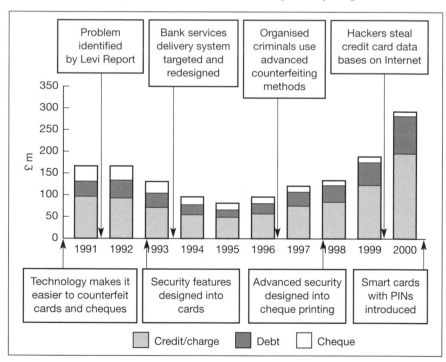

Statistical data adapted from APACS Cardwatch: http://www.cardwatch.org.uk.[19]

Unfortunately, as foreseen by Levi, the decrease in credit card fraud did not last. After falling some 50 per cent between 1991 and 1995, plastic card fraud losses rose by an average of 14 per cent per annum from 1995 to 1999.[16] The areas in which the losses occurred are informative. It can be seen from Figure 7.2 that the three main types of loss from credit card fraud in 1999 were from lost and stolen cards, counterfeit cards and card not present. These numbers reflect quite accurately the preventive measures that were taken after the original Levi Report, and the changes that occurred after those preventive measures had been so effective. It is most likely that the lost and stolen category could be folded into the counterfeit category, when we consider the modus operandi of organised crime groups in counterfeiting cards. Secondary or tertiary production of cards – skimming off actual cards, re-encoding stolen cards– would suggest that organised groups were taking advantage of a market in stolen credit cards.

Figure 7.2 Types of credit card fraud (%) UK, 1999.

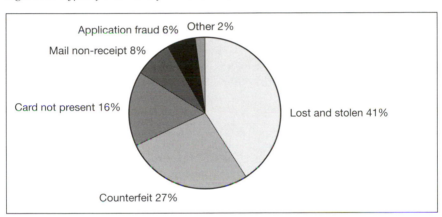

In sum, there are probably four reasons for the rise in credit card fraud since 1996:

1. Confronted with more stringent security checking at the POS, criminals invested more effort into producing high-quality counterfeit credit cards, or stealing credit cards that could easily be 'skimmed'.

2. Organised crime entered the scene. As the economies of the Pacific Rim grew rapidly through the 1990s, organised crime operating out of East Asia turned its attention to credit cards as a source of revenue (Steel, 1995:

16). The Levi Report reviewed data that demonstrated a meteoric increase in losses of major retail banks from credit card fraud for the period of 1988 to 1990 of almost 150 per cent (Levi, Bissell and Richardson, 1991) which policing sources attributed to organised crime activity.

3. It is likely that there has been a more concerted effort on the part of police–bank–merchant cooperation in regard to cheque fraud than there has in credit card fraud (Levi and Handley, 1998b).

4. Increases in card-not-present transactions via the telephone and Internet have taken place.

Thus we can see that the successful reduction in credit card fraud brought about by the changes that followed the Levi Report may have shifted criminal attention to other points of opportunity in the credit card delivery system. That point of weakness was clearly in the poorly protected link between the card user and the user's identity. This speculation is also borne out by the increase in 'card-not-present' credit card fraud. This type of fraud appears as a significant type of fraud largely because of the increase in the late 1990s in the acceptability of telephone ordering by credit card, and the rapid increase in ordering via the Internet using a credit card. These vulnerabilities have been outlined in Chapter 5, and additional ways of counteracting them described in Chapter 6.

The dynamics of change

We have shown that considerable changes in patterns of credit card fraud followed the publication of the Levi Report in 1991, and have suggested that those changes occurred as a result of initiatives urged by that report and also steps taken by the Home Office to develop cooperative efforts among the major parties concerned that focused on identifiable points of risk. The elements of those initiatives were summarised in Table 7.2. The ways in which the recommendations of Table 7.2 were put into practice are worthy of additional consideration. The changes occurred as a result of the following principles promulgated by the Levi Report and the managerial and organisational efforts that followed it:

1. Make a convincing case that the problem is a real one. A careful review of all data and research on the problem of credit card fraud was conducted, including the direct collection of information from the major 'players' in the credit card delivery system, including the criminals.

2. Involve the major organisations and individuals that are directly affected by credit card fraud in the collection and sharing of the information. This includes banks and other card issuers, merchants, database specialists, trade associations, customer advocacy groups and police.

3. Make recommendations for practical changes in the delivery system that will identify points of vulnerability, and demonstrate quickly the financial advantages of minimising fraud.

4. Bring together the major participants in order to effect these changes.

5. Involve law enforcement at operational and senior level at every stage of the research and collaboration for change.

6. Maintain vigilance for identifying indications of displacement of one kind of credit card fraud to another or to another type of crime.

It is remarkable that the degree of cooperation in sharing information and databases was reached so quickly among businesses whose main mission is to compete with each other. It is even more remarkable that the widespread introduction of smart cards, began in 2000 and expected to be completed throughout the UK by 2003, has been managed in the face of the enormous cost of their production and especially of the updating of card readers and cash registers at POS. Whether this change will be cost effective for the industry remains to be seen. That the banks and card issuers and merchants have gone along with this suggests that there was more involved than cost. One suspects that looming in the background was the possibility of tighter government regulation of the banking and financial services industry. The establishment of the Financial Services Authority (FSA) may have had something to do with this.[17] In sum, the necessity for broad cooperation among different parties with diverse and sometimes competing interests is well demonstrated by this case study of credit card fraud, seen within the context of banking services fraud in general.

It must be clear from this case study that modifying even one small situation, such as the purchase of an item with a credit card at the POS, requires the input of a wide variety of parties, individuals and organisations. It is certainly not a problem that could be (or ever has been) solved by the police acting alone – that is, in the traditional action of police, by arresting an individual who attempts to make a fraudulent purchase. The problem, if it is to be solved, goes far beyond the single situation of one fraudulent purchase or purchaser. The implications for situational crime prevention and for policing are therefore clear: a narrow focus on analysing a situation or situations is needed in order to uncover the extent of the problem and identify points of intervention. A broad approach that involves partnerships and coordinated efforts is needed in order to modify those situations. This broad approach must make use of the mechanisms of control that are available in the e-commerce environment, and it is to those mechanisms that we now turn.

Mechanisms of control in the e-commerce environment

As David Wall notes, there is the belief that 'Internet users go on some sort of moral holiday when they enter cyberspace' (Wall, 2001: 160). It is a world, so it seems, very different from the offline world where police patrol the freeways and give tickets to law violators. The media also do their best to identify rule-breakers by demonising the world of the Internet by focusing on the activities of paedophiles, stalkers, pornographers, gamblers and fraudsters, or turn hackers into heroic outlaws – even when they are tracked down and prosecuted (Levi, 2001). In a world where there appears to be no law and order, 'who ya gonna call' when you observe a crime or are victimised by one? There is no highway patrol on the Internet superhighway.

Yet there are electronic highways on the Internet, and vast amounts of traffic for the most part travel smoothly from one place to another, and there are rules and protocols that ensure that information flows smoothly throughout vast networks. And perpetrators of fraud and computer viruses have been tracked down and caught. This fact seems to contradict our portrayal in the earlier chapters of this book, of the world of e-commerce as a world overcome by the Internet, whose basic fibre is criminogenic – the CRAVED of information and the SCAREM of information systems – a place where there is no law and little order. Which is right? To answer to this question we need to specify more clearly what mechanisms of control operate in the e-commerce environment, and follow this by identifying the types of organisations that implement these mechanisms of control. In doing so, it is helpful to think of the mechanisms of control as of two kinds: active and passive.

Active control requires the imposition of rules, regulations and laws upon individuals and groups by persons and technologies that have the authority to do so. These mechanisms are concerned to search out rule-breakers and apply whatever sanction is deemed to work in that particular case. Obviously, the enforcement of criminal laws is a prime example of active control, but there are also many other aspects of such control such as red light cameras at intersections which impose technology on the behaviour of individual motorists, identify rule-breakers and transmit the appropriate fine or punishment. Speed traps of various kinds also fall under this category, as do penalties for workers who show up late for work. In sum, active control focuses on rule-breakers.

Passive control seeks to arrange activities of everyday life so that the behaviour of individuals and groups is shaped or modified without active imposition upon them, and in many respects so that individuals conform their behaviour willingly to the 'rules' or conform without active awareness of their conformity. This form of passive control is best demonstrated by the design of roads to achieve traffic control. Freeways, for example, have one major rule that all motorists obey mostly without thinking: they are designed so that all cars going in one direction do so in concert and only on one pre-appointed side of the freeway. On such freeways, cars are guided over up-ramps, intersections, etc. in order to avoid collisions. Much of our everyday behaviour is guided by this kind of passive control, and much of this control may be designated as 'beneficial' since it prevents all sorts of possible accidents. In the online world, passive control is embedded in the ways in which e-mail messages are processed and forwarded to their intended recipient. There are details and strict protocols embedded in the Internet technology and software that ensures that e-mail messages get to their destination without running off the 'superhighway'. The user is mostly unaware of these protocols, and becomes aware of them only when a disaster occurs, such as a virus or worm that grinds the electronic freeway to a halt.

Many mechanisms of control – perhaps most – are hybrids of these two types of control. For example, when a customer pays for an item at the POS in a retail store, he or she hands over the credit card, and after roughly six to ten seconds, signs the credit slip. In those ten seconds, the card information is transmitted to the bank's database and authenticated. The database contains all kinds of information about the cardholder, and the purchase is checked against it. If approved, the shopper continues merrily on. If not approved, the purchaser is confronted with the problem of explaining why the card was not approved, and is potentially flagged as a rule-breaker. Of course it is unlikely that the card user will be arrested, since there may be many reasons for the failure to verify the card (it may be an expired card that the user had forgotten to renew for example). However, in the vast majority of instances, the user's card is approved, and nothing further is thought of the exchange. That is to say, once we become familiar with new technologies and their absorption into everyday life, we become controlled by them – most often happily because of the convenience and benefits they afford. This applies to a diverse range of behavioural settings from traffic control to credit control. And it is worth noting that the instances in which rule-breakers are flagged (active control) are extremely rare compared to the almost infinite number of instances in which individuals are passively controlled. In the sociological literature, the terms used for these types of control are generally 'policing' for active control and 'surveillance' for passive control. However, this characterisation doesn't quite fit since surveillance can be both active and passive, as can policing. Undercover surveillance by police, for example, may be highly intrusive, but the object of surveillance is unaware of the intrusion. Thus it may be more useful to think of control in terms of its visibility, as depicted in Table 7.3.

Sources of control in the e-commerce environment

Wall has argued that, contrary to the popular view, there is a wealth of opportunity to control crime on the Internet and that beneath the seemingly disorganised nature of cyberspace there exists an extensive governance structure (Wall, 2001). Drawing in part on Wall's classification of levels of governance on the Internet, we suggest that there are several identifiable types of organisations and groups that contribute considerably to control in the online environment, some more and some less inclined to either active or passive control.

Table 7.3 Matrix of 'policing'.

	Active control	Passive control
High visibility	• Policeman gives motorist ticket for speeding. • Picture or other ID required to use credit card or cash cheque. • Alarm triggered when item taken from store without payment.	• Traffic lights and signs. • Obligatory filing of income tax returns. • Registration of births, deaths, marriages, automobiles, etc. • Credit check to obtain bank loan. • Credit card checked against database for approval.
Low visibility	• Hidden red light cameras give tickets for infractions. • Undercover stakeout, police wiretapping. • CCTV on street corner.	• Freeway overpass. • Shopping mall design. • Wireless Internet or phone connections. • Government and corporate databases of personal and credit information.

Active controllers

• *The Internet users themselves.* We briefly described the situational techniques of natural surveillance and surveillance by employees in Chapter 6, and we noted the mutual surveillance by users of online auctions and other peer-to-peer venues on the Internet. The extent of natural surveillance and how it works on the Internet is unknown. Its essential feature, however, is that because it blends in with everyday activities and surroundings, it is functionally secretive and therefore akin to spying (see below). Much surveillance of this type, however, is concerned with identifying and flagging rule-breakers. The classic analogue to this type of surveillance is that thought to operate in the traditional puritan villages of New England, portrayed so graphically in Hawthorne's *The Scarlet Letter.*

- *Corporate security organisations* (e.g. the computer security departments of corporations) whose function it is to protect corporate databases and computing infrastructure and monitor access to and transmission of electronic transactions. Corporations vary considerably in the extent to which they integrate their computer security procedures with the broader needs of security engineering and also those of situational crime prevention. The tendency is, though, for computer security to be split off as a separate function in the same way that auditing is often set apart from other loss prevention functions of corporate departments (Kalakota and Whinston, 1997). And in most text books on computer security or security on the Internet, attention is paid predominantly to arcane and technical details of computer security, not to the broader situational issues (significant exceptions are Anderson, 2001, and Grabosky, Smith and Dempsey, 2001). While the emphasis is generally on prevention, the focus is on identifying rule-breakers, especially hackers of any kind.

- *State-funded public/private policing organisations*. In the USA, the Department of Justice and the FBI created the National Infrastructure Protection Center (NIPC) in 1998 as a partnership between government and industry. It is designed to protect critical infrastructure of the Internet.[18]

- *State-funded public police organisations*. State and local police agencies may set up their own computer crime units. National governments have extensive intelligence collecting units that monitor Internet activity (e.g. the National Criminal Intelligence Service, NCIS, in the UK). However, as Anderson (2001) notes, there is a continuing trend to blur the distinction between law enforcement and intelligence-gathering. The intelligence-gathering function of public policing utilises hidden formal surveillance, in contrast to the type of formal surveillance described in Chapter 6 that is highly visible and used mainly for deterrent purposes. In this case we would call it formal spying which in the information society includes such activities as wiretapping, traffic analysis, communications intelligence and crypto control (Anderson, 2001: 455–69). The entire issue of surveillance is currently a hot topic in regard to situational crime prevention, particularly as it relates to privacy, and is discussed further in the following chapter.

- *Law and regulation*. The role for national governments in the information society is complex, and the extent to which national governments can coordinate and apply legislation to actively control e-commerce crime remains to be seen. For example, in the case of the 'Love Bug' virus that was traced to a perpetrator in the Philippines, prosecution was not possible because at the time the Philippines had no law against any form of cybercrime. For this reason, the Philippines would not allow extradition either. Thus the perpetrator went free, even though he had caused untold millions of dollars worth of damage around the world, including to NASA and the CIA (Goodman and Brenner, 2002).

The modern history of laws enacted to deal with cybercrime begins in the 1970s. The first wave of legislation was directed at the protection of privacy rather than to fighting the various forms of computer-related crime. As a result of such major events as the Watergate scandal where the taping of conversations ran rampant, and the civil rights movement in the USA where the FBI indulged extensively in wiretapping, legislation concerning various aspects of privacy emerged. Legislation concerning privacy followed in a majority of western countries and even constitutional amendments.[19] The United States still does not have one single piece of legislation that deals with the privacy online issue. US law does not view the right to privacy as a human right, rather it is treated as a property right. The US Constitution is largely silent on the privacy issue, although the Supreme Court has managed to come up with some claims to the right to privacy in the fields of search and seizure and abortion (DeCew, 1997). However, there are several different acts that concern different aspects of protection such as protection of financial data (Gramm-Leach-Bliley Act), health information (Health Information Portability and Accountability Act) and children's information (Children's Online Privacy Protection Act).

A second line of legislation occurred in regard to economic crimes committed in the computing environment. These laws were directed largely against the stealing of software, hacking into bank accounts, and crimes facilitated by computer systems and networks. These legislative reforms began mostly in the 1980s and continue through to the present.[20] The third area of legislative reform, which began in the 1980s and continues to the present, was directed at protection of intellectual property and copyright. Finally, the fourth area of legislative activity, which has proliferated in the 1990s, is directed against illegal and/or harmful content on the Internet, such as the dissemination of pornography and paedophilia, hate speech and defamation (Goodman and Brenner, 2002). It also targeted the responsibility of Internet service and access providers for controlling content. Obviously, there are major differences in regard to such legislation in many countries depending on political and cultural factors.

Passive controllers

- *The Internet service providers* (ISPs, e.g. AOL and MSN). ISPs have been the targets of regulation and law suits trying to hold them responsible for the material and activities that flow through their portals. National governments, such as those of China and Singapore, have made it a condition for ISPs to do business in their country that they abide by regulations concerning content and marketing practices (Norman, 2001). However, these commercial enterprises are mainly concerned to make sure that information travels through their portals unhampered and smoothly, much as automobile traffic flows through a significant interchange between two freeways. Users of these ISPs pay money for this service that makes their Internet usage trouble free. Users are also bombarded with advertising and other kinds of information designed to affect their everyday life.

- *Decentralised or 'distributed' command and control on the Internet.* There are at least two organisations that really do govern the Internet, though this kind of governance is called these days 'distributed systems' (Anderson, 2001). These are: the IAB (Internet Architecture Board) which in turn oversees the Internet Engineering Task Force (IETF[21]). The IAB is composed of both public and private representatives, and sets standards and protocols for the Internet worldwide.[22] The other is the IANA (Internet Assigned Numbers Authority), which is the organisation responsible for assigning Internet addresses, protocol identifiers and Internet port numbers. Its motto is: 'Dedicated to preserving the central coordinating functions of the global Internet for the public good.'[23] While it is obvious that there is no direct centralised 'command structure' as there is in a traditional military organisation, nevertheless these organisations, though not nationally based, do set standards and rules for Internet and network communication, without which the Internet could not operate. Their control is similar to that exercised by the designers and lawmakers who 'govern' our freeways and streets. Traffic in cities and freeways would grind to a halt if there were no protocols concerning speed, stop lights, giving way, where overpasses and bridges should be built, and so on. Yet the cities and freeways have police patrolling them and enforcing the laws and regulations. Their equivalent does not exist on the Internet. However, this is more than made up for by other already established patterns of organisation and control in modern society that have been quick to recognise the power provided them by the information age.

Hybrids of active and passive control

- *Bureaucracies, government and corporate.* These have become a major source of the social control of individuals and organisations in modern society. Because bureaucracies function by establishing and promulgating rules of many different kinds, but especially of procedures to enhance efficiency, they actively promote conformity. Thus they are accurately identified as active controllers. As Dandeker has argued, there has been a massive rise in bureaucracies over the past two centuries, both in regard to government with the rise of the nation-state and the private sector with the early application of military organisation to factories and later scientific management of labour based on productivity studies and the 'science of discipline' (Dandeker, 1990).[24] However, another key function of bureaucracies – perhaps their prime function in modern society – is the keeping of records, which results in the amassing of huge databases. This activity existed long before the Internet, but it has been given new impetus and greater effectiveness by the electronic age. Two major facilitators of the Internet add power to the databases of bureaucracies: the enormous capabilities of the storage of information afforded by the computer, and the ease at which the information can be accessed and transmitted from place to place.[25] The amassing of databases essentially contributes to passive control, the unseen hand that checks our credit card when we make a purchase.

- *The marketplace.* Corporate bureaucracies, like government bureaucracies, are concerned internally with identifying rule-breakers and enforcing conformity with their rules. However, in dealing with the marketplace, corporate bureaucracies apply their new-found bureaucratic power to help control it in an active way, not through punishments as is most common in identifying rule-breakers, but through enticements. In these respects, they are active controllers. As one drives through a city, reads a magazine, watches television, surfs the web, one is inundated with marketing ploys of merchants and corporations. They will do what they can to entice an individual into their store or website, to buy their wares. These enticements have probably existed for as long as humans have been exchanging goods and services. Merchants have discovered that the Internet provides unique opportunities to tailor their inducements to individual tastes. Using sophisticated tracking software, they are able to collect detailed, individualised information concerning their customers' buying habits and preferences on their websites. Each time an individual is attracted into a store or website and buys an item, that situation is one in which the merchant has exerted some control over that individual, even though that individual may have made rational choices based on personal desires (O'Shaughnessy, 1987). Through their effective marketing merchants can collect enormous amounts of information from their customers. Records about individuals are, however, a significant source of passive control, as we have already noted above. We should also understand that the 'marketplace' is not a one-way affair from seller to buyer (or even seller to middleman to buyer). Negotiation, bargaining and all the rest of the practices and even rituals are involved in the marketplace. Furthermore, as we noted in Chapter 5, on the Internet individuals can be both buyers and sellers at the same time when they visit online auctions, and may exert influence in terms of posting their satisfaction or dissatisfaction with vendors or sellers on the feedback notice board provided by auction sites. Sellers, even when they have enormous facilities at their disposal – the power of mass advertising for example – can be notoriously wrong in their estimates of whether people will buy their wares. The not infrequent box office flops of highly promoted Hollywood movies are testimony to this. As we noted at the beginning of Chapter 2, it is the element of trust that is required for buying and selling in the marketplace to proceed efficiently. So we could say that trust is an important source of passive control that lies behind the practices of the marketplace.[26]

Having outlined the general sources and mechanisms of control in the e-commerce environment, we are now able to look more closely at the specific organisations and individuals that might be enlisted to implement the many prevention techniques described in the previous chapter. The case study gave us a brief introduction to this topic: bankers, merchants, customers, card manufacturers, trade organisations and even criminals were enlisted to reduce credit card fraud. Ideally, partnerships must be formed among these organisations and individuals in order to carry out a successful situational crime prevention programme. There is more to the idea of developing partnerships for 'policing' the environment than meets the eye.

Partnerships for crime control in the e-commerce environment

In his influential book, *The Culture of Control*, David Garland has argued that the government move towards establishing crime control partnerships in the UK is an indication, or perhaps more accurately a 'symptom', of late modernity, in which the amount of crime has increased exponentially. Partnerships, he says, are a symptom of a deeper problem of modern society because they reveal that both academic criminology and applied criminal justice have more or less admitted that 'nothing has worked' and that the problem is too big for any of the professional arms of criminal justice to solve on its own (Garland, 2001). Whether or not the shift away from consigning all problems of crime to the police and the criminal justice system is a good or bad thing, we leave to the concluding chapter. Whether it has actually happened on a large scale, though, is an open question. To give Garland the benefit of the doubt, we note that the tenor of his book is more towards a kind of 'history of the future', an attempt to outline the way the world of late modern society will be, by delineating the forms of policing and control that have emerged in the last 30 years or so. We are inclined to think that the world of e-commerce represents the future, so that if we were to find any signs of the kinds of spread of policing beyond the traditional confines of criminal justice we would find it here. Our case study on credit card fraud has suggested that this is so. Our delineation of the mechanisms of control in e-commerce and the sources of that control in various organisations and groups certainly supports Garland's contention. We have seen so far that active control, the type of control most widely applied by criminal justice agencies, plays a minimal part in the 'policing' of e-commerce. And even though we identify law and regulation as one mechanism of active control in policing e-commerce, it is apparent that it has had minimal impact on the prevention or control of the kinds of crimes we outlined in Chapter 3. In fact, its preoccupation appears to have been more to do with regulating the practice of e-commerce, especially in regard to 'privacy rights', instead of identifying opportunities for crime and legislating ways to eliminate them.

What are partnerships?

Partnerships are collaborations among individuals and organisations that:

- pursue a common goal or interest;
- assume common responsibility for the task;
- bring together persons or organisations with diverse competencies, cultures and authorities;
- exchange information freely and openly;
- meet either online or in physical places on a continuous basis.

In the world of e-commerce, there are many organisations and individuals that may be called on to help modify criminogenic situations (Grabosky, Smith and Dempsey, 2001: 179–207). In the online world partnerships may take on a special form. The extent to which partnerships necessarily involve direct collaborative organisation and action is difficult to determine, since the core of online partnerships may be characterised more in terms of information exchange. In fact, there is extensive information exchange provided throughout the online world via websites that advocate various causes (Internet security for example[27]) or the more informal newsgroups such as alt.comp.virus. Both these kinds of information exchange can range from the very helpful and cooperative to the antagonistic revelation of so-called fiascos of security by ISPs and other companies with an online presence. In regard to the techniques of crime prevention outlined in the previous chapter, the range of partners that would be needed to implement crime prevention strategies would include many different people, organisations and groups, few of them policing organisations, most of them with missions other than policing, but whose functions nevertheless serve to contribute to control of the e-commerce environment. The list below, based on Clarke and Newman (2002a and 2002b), describes such groups. It is of course not exhaustive, but does serve to demonstrate the broad approach needed for situational crime prevention to develop strategies of crime prevention. While the list does repeat some of the sources of control listed above, we have provided more specific suggestions concerning their roles in applying some of the techniques of crime prevention recommended in the previous chapter.

Partners for crime prevention

- *Regular police*, i.e. uniformed, beat police and detectives, whose function in the world of e-commerce is still emerging. Currently, their activities seem to be confined mostly to active types of control: arresting individuals for cheque fraud, identity theft, paedophilia, stalking, and at the federal and state levels, con games and scams on the Internet. However, the introduction of mapping systems to analysing police data has led to a considerable broadening of police data collection. The renowned COMP-STAT programme of the New York City Police Department that pioneered the use of mapping software in management of policing has now broadened its scope. It now collects an enormous breadth of information that it integrates into its mapping analysis. This requires cooperation with many local and regional departments not directly related to traditional crime data collection such as departments of energy, engineering, city planning and transportation.[28] As this activity expands, the databases maintained by the police lead them more towards the mechanism of passive control, slowly breaking down the traditional distinction between law enforcement and intelligence-gathering.

- *Merchants* who may be able to help themselves by extending the use of passive control: displaying their products in ways that reduce the opportunity for theft, using appropriate security procedures to protect their data files, checking for credit card or cheque fraud and tracking their merchandise for inventory control. However, their relationship with law enforcement remains uncertain. Retailers are reticent to involve law enforcement directly in their affairs for fears that arrests performed on their premises will negatively affect business. This problem often arises in the case of shoplifting. However, the fact that it does arise suggests that partnerships need to be formed between the retailer and law enforcement to devise a strategy that will reduce shoplifting without necessitating highly visible arrests. Situational prevention provides ways to reduce or prevent shoplifting without the necessity of direct law enforcement involvement by arrest, but nevertheless with the close cooperation of police. For example, the study by Poyner and Webb (1997) which reduced considerably thefts from shopping bags in crowded marketplaces solved the problem by (a) working with the police to collect data and observe the situations in which thefts occurred, (b) modifying the layout of the markets so that they were less conducive to thieves: better lighting, wider aisles between stalls and so on, and (c) working with market management to bring about the needed changes in design and practice.[29]

- *Trade associations* can provide education, establish standards and facilitate data collection. They play an important role of passive control by educating customers and merchants about steps to take in order to prevent their victimisation, such as how to protect PINs, how to protect against theft of credit cards, how to secure personal computers. They also play an important part in developing standards and guidelines for security procedures in their respective industries. For example, trade bodies representing companies involved in home delivery, such as the Freight Transport Association, British Retail Consortium, Mail Order Traders Association and Direct Marketing Association, could more closely monitor criminal activity in this sector and provide more guidance to members on security measures. They could also encourage the benchmarking of companies' security systems and provide a forum for the exchange of ideas and experiences in this field. Trade associations concerned with home delivery could also work with member companies to establish more formal systems for registering neighbours' addresses as alternative delivery points and making this information available in a central database. These activities seek to structure the everyday environment, enhancing passive control.

- *Consumer groups* raise demand for more secure products. Higher levels of security can be built into the hardware and software of the computing environment, thus enhancing passive control. Lessons can be learned here from the case of product tampering, which is, after all, not altogether different from the tampering with computer files or software. Both need to be securely packaged. In 1982, seven people died in the Chicago area as a result of swallowing cyanide-tainted Tylenol. This catastrophic event, followed by a series of copycat incidents (some 300), spawned widespread public, governmental and business concern. Each of these parties had a strong interest in bringing about changes that would prevent the future occurrence of this tragedy. This brought about an unusual level of cooperation in effecting legislation, which resulted in regulations enacted by the FDA in 1983 to require tamper-resistant packaging. There was also eagerness on the part of business to produce and demonstrate tamper-resistant packaging, reassuring their customers (whose voice has been widely heard through the leadership of Ralph Nader) that their safety and trust were of prime importance. The result has been the continued spread of tamper-resistant packaging across product types (from cosmetics, medicines, beverages, frozen foods, toys and even original works of art, multimedia and of course credit cards) over the 20 years since the Tylenol event. The equivalent of consumer associations and groups in e-commerce are the many newsgroups formed to promote a variety of causes. For example, the alt.comp.virus newsgroup has campaigned for many years concerning the inadequate software design of Windows by Microsoft, which makes it easily vulnerable to viruses.[30] However, the role of newsgroups is largely through exchange of information on the Internet medium, and does not appear, to date, to have led to the kind of extensive organisational cooperation between software and hardware companies and consumer groups and government agencies that occurred in the case of product tampering. Perhaps this is because in the case of product tampering people were killed. So far, there appears to be no case on record where software tampering resulted in loss of life.

- *Corporate security staff and private policing organisations* whose explicit responsibility is to prevent loss to companies and businesses caused by crime. In contrast to formal policing organisations, modern private security organisations are usually not oriented to arrests, but rather to introducing security procedures that prevent loss (Nalla and Newman, 1990); in other words, their emphasis is on passive control. In recent years collaboration between corporate security organisations, the security departments of companies and regular police departments has been increasing. For example, the Edmonton police meet on a regular basis with a variety of security firms to coordinate their operations, and similar arrangements occur in New York City, Vancouver and elsewhere. In Amarillo, Texas, Allstate has assumed responsibility for responding city wide to alarm calls (Law Commission of Canada, 2002). Of particular relevance to e-commerce, many companies that specialise in computing facilities, both hardware and software, have worked in collaboration with police on investigations searching for missing or wanted persons, and in developing surveillance operations using CCTV and other technologies (Law Commission of Canada, 2002). The latter are probably hybrids of both passive and active control, and represent perhaps a reverse trend in which private policing organisations adopt traditional policing tactics.

- *Human relations and management* staff whose function may be expanded to include training line personnel in security procedures such as natural and informal surveillance, tracking products, secure use of computers, secure procedures in dealing with customers (passive control). Security functions are increasingly included as part of the normal responsibilities of any job. The use of staff as part of the overall surveillance and control of crowds has been long established by Disney in its theme parks (Shearing, Clifford and Stenning, 1997). Supermarket POS staff are routinely trained to detect shoplifting scams (Nalla and Newman, 1990).

- *Internet service providers (ISPs)* such as AOL and MSN, as well as universities that provide Internet access for their students and staff, form a significant part in the structure of Internet governance, as outlined above. While much of the language used by these service providers is suggestive of active control (e.g. helping track down spoofers, pornographers, viruses) in fact most of this control is exerted by requests to customers to be vigilant and report rule infractions, and offering services to customers (e.g. pornography filtering options, parental control options) to customers. Consumer groups have targeted ISPs (again, via newsgroups and publication of embarrassing information on the Internet) to ensure the integrity of their systems.[31] The relationships between consumer groups as represented on the Internet newsgroups and chat rooms and ISPs and software companies continues to be a rocky one. In these cases it is probably more accurate to term them as 'antagonistic partnerships'. There are, however, private companies that promise total security packages that include 'forensic accounting'.[32] In general, the role of ISPs in control seems ambiguous, a hybrid of active and passive control.

- *Accounting organisations and staff* whose explicit function is to track buying, selling and all financial transactions. Recent events concerning Enron and WorldCom have focused attention on accounting as a significant means to prevent crime and fraud. CAATT (Computer Assisted Audit Tools and Techniques) have long been an important aspect of fraud prevention and detection (Crowder, 1997: 17–20).[33] To date, however, the communication between accounting departments in companies and security departments has not been well developed, each seeing the other as working on problems completely separate from each other. However, some companies have managed successfully to combine the two.[34] Accounting systems are excellent examples of passive control, since they rely so heavily on the collection and tracking of data and exchanges of information. However, the CAATT systems are very much active controllers, since they are oriented to identifying departures from standard accounting practices and thus in identifying rule-breakers.

- *Managers and designers of public spaces* such as hospitals, public housing projects, mass transit, shopping malls, entertainment and sporting complexes, where effective design and management of space may affect opportunities for crime[35] and represent the prototype of passive control, as we have indicated earlier. Designers of the public space on the Internet such as Cisco systems[36] pay special attention to the secure design of their networks and conduct extensive training and education with customers, many of which are Internet or intranet service providers. They also develop partnerships with other businesses that are focused directly on security issues.[37] The same may be said for the other major network developer and designer, Sun Microsystems, a company that emphasises partnerships and provides extensive training and educational services for customers.[38]

- *Designers of products and services* (Clarke and Newman, 2002a, 2002b) who may be able to design their products with security against crime built into them, such as tamper-proof products, anti-theft devices built into automobiles, counterfeit-proof banknotes, theft-proof credit cards (smart cards), and computer operating system programs. Cisco systems has attempted to design security into its computing systems, although companies such as Microsoft and Sun Microsystems have been criticised for failing in this regard. Eliminating crime from the design of products is of course an example of passive control.

- *Collectors and guardians of records* whose function, both in companies and in government, is to collect information about products and people and maintain it in large databases. On the government side these may include car registrations, drivers' licence information, social security numbers, tax returns, births, deaths and marriages and in the UK health cards. On the business side these may include credit information, buying preferences, personal income and address information, past purchasing habits and many more. As noted above, this kind of information is fast becoming incorporated into the mapping and collection of information by policing agencies. It is an example of passive control that helps shape the interactions of everyday life in e-commerce, making financial payments more efficient, a supreme example of passive control.

Conclusions

We have demonstrated in this chapter that the broad approach of situational crime prevention draws heavily on a wide variety of sources of 'policing' in the e-commerce environment – though in truth, it is not clear what policing means in the e-commerce environment itself and increasingly in society in general. If we think of policing in its traditional sense – searching out criminals, catching them, arresting them and turning them over to the criminal justice system for processing – then there appears to be little room for this kind of policing in the e-commerce environment, or if there is, such activities have to be carried out by traditional police in partnership with other agencies, often private agencies. The expansion of policing into private sectors of society, the gradual blurring of the line between law enforcement and intelligence, and the wide variety of sources of control necessarily drawn upon by the broad approach of situational crime prevention present to some a frightening vision of the future brought home, the 'big brother' society. They charge that this is a prime symptom of a society where control over individuals' lives is becoming pervasive and endemic: they see a 'culture of control' (Garland, 2001) or a 'culture of surveillance' (Staples, 1997). It is to these issues that we turn in the final chapter, in responding to the charge that situational crime prevention ushers in a new era where personal privacy is sacrificed for commerce, among other things.

Notes

1 The following outline draws heavily on: Newton (1994: section 6). See also for a review of this study: Staff (1994) 'Beating the counterfeiters'. *Cards International*, 12 July, p. 7.
2 These machines are freely advertised in *Byte* magazine for example. *Business Week* (1984) 'A magnetic tape that foils bank-card fraud', Technology, 15 October, p. 108; www.businessweek.com/index.html.
3 Staff (1994) 'Preventing credit card forgery; use of electronic fingerprints', *USA Today Magazine*, April, 122(2587): 7.
4 Sales personnel have a high turnover rate, so training, if it is conducted at all, has to be constantly repeated, which it is difficult for businesses to maintain and is also expensive. Furthermore, it is not at all clear that even the most conscientious salesperson can make reliable judgments as to the similarity of each signature (Levi, Bissell and Richardson, 1991).
5 Depending on the type of smart card, it has been estimated in the USA that it would cost around $300–400 or more per terminal to upgrade (Fitch, 1984: 15).
6 It may be noted that the successful use of this technique will depend on the POS having a quick link to the issuer so that it can be checked without holding up the well-oiled POS process. The extent to which such high speed (and cheap) telecommunications are available depends considerably on the country and region. No doubt this method has become popular in the United States because of the cheap and efficient telecommunications available. Another big advantage is that it does not require expensive retooling of POS card processors.
7 For a concise description of the types and functions of smart cards see Roger Clarke's comprehensive website at http://www.anu.edu.au/people/Roger.Clarke/EC/ChipIntro.html, November 2001.

8   There are 25 million smart cards in circulation in France, where credit card fraud has decreased dramatically since 1987 when they were first introduced (Demery, 1998). See also Staff (1994) 'Fighting the war against fraud', *Banking World*, March, 12(3): 28.

9   Clarke, Roger, http://www.anu.edu.au/people/Roger.Clarke/EC/SCBF.html, November 2001.

10 Taiwan Economic News (2001) 'Credit cards with chips to help fight fraud in Taiwan', *China Economic News Service*, 8 January.

11 Ungoed-Thomas, John (2000) 'Pin numbers to replace credit signatures', *Sunday Times*, 26 November, p. 4. See also the APACS website that reviews the history and planned introduction of smart cards: http://www.apacs.org.uk/.

12 Markoff, John (2002) 'Vulnerability is discovered in security for smart cards', *New York Times*, 13 May.

13 *Business Week* (1984) 'How "Smart" cards can outwit the credit crooks', Technology, 15 October, p. 105. www.businessweek.com/index.html

14 44 http://www.apacs.org.uk/.

15 Cooperation among the different players has been much slower in coming in the USA, perhaps because of the larger and more diverse market, but also because there has been no clearly focused campaign by any US government agency to attack credit card fraud in the same way as was accomplished by the Home Office. However, recent steps towards cooperative efforts have emerged largely as a result of perceived threats occurring on the Internet. MerchanFraudSquad.com was set up as a network to share ideas and best practices in combating credit card fraud and other types of fraud on the Internet (Clark, 2000: 116–17).

16 Patterns of credit card fraud vary somewhat from country to country. For example, Canada experienced a very high rate of credit card fraud in 1993 (Ballard, 1994: 26). It is possible that preventive measures applied in one country or region could displace credit card fraudulent activity to other countries. Much more research and data would be needed, however, in order to verify this. The credit card fraud rate in France is considerably lower than in other countries, largely because of its long established use of smart cards and PIN numbers. However, France has a high rate of foreign card fraud, since those foreigners who use their regular credit cards must have information manually input at the POS, thus exposing the cards to regular conditions of vulnerability (Demery, 1998: 72–6).

17 Staff (2001) 'Too big for its suits? Britain's super-regulator opens fully for business on December 1st', *The Economist*, 17, November, p. 67.

18 NIPC (2002) Mission statement. The National Infrastructure Protection Centre: http://www.nipc.gov/.

19 Legislation was enacted in: Sweden (1973); the United States of America (1974); the Federal Republic of Germany (1977); Austria, Denmark, France and Norway (1978); Luxembourg (1979 and 1982); Iceland and Israel (1981); Australia and Canada (1982); the United Kingdom (1984); Finland (1987); Ireland, Japan and the Netherlands (1988); Portugal (1991); Belgium, Spain and Switzerland (1992); Spain (1995); Italy and Greece (1997). Constitutional amendments occurred in Brazil, the Netherlands, Portugal and Spain (Goodman and Brenner, 2002).

20 The following countries enacted new laws against computer-related economic crimes: Italy 1978; Australia state law, 1979; United Kingdom 1981, 1990; United States of America federal and state legislation in the 1980s; Canada and Denmark 1985; the Federal Republic of Germany and Sweden, Austria, Japan and Norway 1987; France and Greece 1988; Finland 1990, 1995; the Netherlands 1992; Luxembourg 1993; Switzerland 1994; Spain 1995; and Malaysia 1997 (Goodman and Brenner, 2002).

21 http://www.ietf.org/. Other important 'governing' organisations are: the IRTF (http://www.irtf.org/), a research group working under the IAB; the Internet Society: 'a professional membership society with more than 150 organisational and 6,000 individual members in over 100 countries. It provides leadership in addressing issues that confront the future of the Internet, and is the organisation home for the groups responsible for Internet infrastructure standards, including the Internet Engineering Task Force (IETF) and the Internet Architecture Board (IAB)': http://www.isoc.org/isoc/; finally the RFC (Request for Comments): 'The Requests for Comments (RFC) document series is a set of technical and organisational notes about the Internet (originally the ARPANET), beginning in 1969,' which provides considerable input into the work of IETF: http://www.rfc-editor.org/.

22 See for a review of its functions, mission and organisation the Charter of the Internet Architecture Board (IAB) at http://www.cis.ohio-state.edu/cgi-bin/rfc/rfc1358.html.

23 http://www.iana.org/.

24 Dandeker's (1990) argument closely follows the classic works of Max Weber on bureaucracies and the rationalisation of society.

25 Dandeker (1990) provides a fascinating account of the tremendous importance of swift transmission of information in the winning of many major military battles since at least early Greek history.

26 This important element of the marketplace has rarely been spotlighted so strongly as on 9 July 2002 with President Bush's speech on corporate ethics (*Wall Street Journal*, p. 1) responding to corporate accounting scandals and reports of high-profile individuals with insider information who disposed of stock days before they became worthless.

27 The Computer Security Resource Centre, for example http://csrc.ncsl.nist.gov/.

28 Rashbaum, William K. (2002) 'Crime-fighting by computer: scope widens', *New York Times*, late edition – final, section 1, p. 43, col. 5.

33 It has been recently argued that corporations have a social responsibility to prevent crime when they are in a position to do so. Thus corporations have been pressured to redesign their products when it was clear that the design of these products actually contributed to crime (for example, automobiles without security systems). Voluntary partnerships with government (especially at the local level) have successfully managed to reduce assaults relating to alcohol use, vandalism and assaults in retail areas. See Clarke and Newman (2002b); Hardie and Hobbs (2002).

30 In May 2000, for example, this newsgroup was very active in criticising Microsoft about the 'I Love you' virus that was released in the Philippines:

> That Microsoft fails to provide anything but a useless general warning in even the easiest cases (as with the 'Love Bug' script) and fails to protect the user's system and resources shows its disdain for computer security and borders on negligence.

Carolino, Rey Q. (2000) 'Love letter virus – a simple program that rocks the world', *Philippine Headline News Online*, http://www.newsflash.org/2000/05/hl/hl012106.htm.

31 See for example (among many): *Internet Security Newsletter* (1998) 'World online ISP security fiasco', Posting by Paul van Keep, Tuesday, 23 June 1998. This ISP had used inadequate methods of password protection. Widespread publicity forced the company to respond by improving the security design of their operations: http://www.landfield.com/isn/mail-archive/1998/Jun/0120.html.

32 Total Investigation Services Ltd: http://www.totalinvestigations.ca/.

33 Staff (2002) 'Accounting for change', *The Economist*, 29 June, pp. 13–14.

34 Cisco Systems has developed extensive security and accounting procedures and standards. See: 'Security and accounting solutions', http://www.dtr.com.br/cdrom/cc/sol/mkt/ent/dial/ref/dlp8_st.htm.

35 There are many examples of this. For a brief overview see the case studies in Clarke (1997), cases 2, 3, 4, 9, 10, 11, 12, 14, 16, 21, 22, 23.

36 http://www.cisco.com.

37 Cisco has an extensive network of companies that they accredit as 'partners for their expertise, experience, and high customer satisfaction in delivery of planning, design and implementation services related to network security, in general...': http://www.cisco.com/warp/public/765/partner_programs/specialisation/services/vpnsecurity/

38 http://www.sun.com.

Chapter 8

Situational prevention and the 'society of control'

The 2002 movie *Minority Report* imagined a future, only 50 years hence, in which 'pre-crime' police arrest people for the crime they are about to commit. It is a world where all individuals – criminals and law-abiding citizens alike – can be identified by iris scans. A voice calls out to shoppers as they pass each storefront, calling them by name, reminding them of past purchases. Those who have shopped on the web know that already merchants are able to remind customers of past purchases, and try to suggest other items that are consistent with their tastes. But the movie goes much further. The pre-crime police send little iris-scanning robots into apartment buildings to identify marked pre-criminals. Of course, Hollywood could not make a policing movie without violence and chase scenes, so it retained the idea of pursuit and arrest as the central element of its pre-crime policing model. However, the underlying concept of late modern society painted by this movie – and by critics of situational crime prevention – is to intervene at any cost in the course of events so that the crime is stopped before it can be committed. The movie adopts a 'big brother' model, portraying surveillance as visible and openly intrusive, whereas critics of the 'culture of control' that encompasses situational crime prevention claim that surveillance occurs 'behind the scenes', hidden and obligingly submitted to by unthinking, unknowing citizens.

In this chapter, we will examine whether the portent of the future painted by these critics is consistent with the current ideas and practices of situational prevention. In doing so we will also address the question posed at the beginning of this book: is situational prevention the cause or the result of the supposed shifts in policing and control that have occurred in late modern society? We shall also explore whether situational crime prevention is an ideology of control as charged by some of its critics. And our answers to these questions will lead us to assess where the future lies for situational prevention *vis à vis* the field of criminology, or rather, where the future lies for criminology *vis à vis* situational prevention.

Our route into these issues is to revisit some of the techniques of situational crime prevention discussed throughout the book, especially in Chapters 6 and 7. While all the techniques of situational prevention are by definition also techniques of control (whether passive or active as outlined in the previous chapter), some techniques are more visible and active in the e-commerce environment. Perhaps the most important of these fall under the general heading of surveillance, which we have recommended should be undertaken by individuals other than the police as a preventive technique. And we have argued that the Internet is a perfect place to carry out surveillance because of its criminogenic properties of stealth, deception and anonymity. We have also reviewed with some satisfaction the new technologies that make the tracking and identification of products and people almost as powerful as depicted in *Minority Report*.

So we are not surprised that the issue of surveillance has been the focus of criticism directed at situational prevention,[1] even if the criticisms are derived from broader critiques of late modern society in general – the 'panoptic society' – or from critiques of 'state capitalism', of which surveillance is presumed to be an end product (Staples, 1997; see also Rule, 1973; Gandy, 1993; Lyon, 1994; Lyon and Zureik, 1996; Curry, 1997). The idea of the 'panoptic society', first popularised by Michel Foucault (1995), derives from the prison advocated by Jeremy Bentham, 'The Panopticon', which was designed so that one guard from one location in the prison could observe all prisoners. Thus its application to society assumes a complete centralised system of surveillance, synonymous with a totalitarian society. We will argue below that there is little prospect in a modern democracy of surveillance technology creating the conditions for the emergence of such a society, but our quick response to these criticisms is that, for the most part, citizens benefit greatly from surveillance. It is the balance between the benefits of surveillance and its costs that presents the problem. The greatest cost is that of personal privacy, and in larger terms, the loss of freedom. To respond to these criticisms we must address three related issues: the concept of privacy, the question of identity, and the issue that combines these two: the tracking of people and products.

Surveillance and privacy

As Alan Westin (1967) noted in *Privacy and Freedom* (and de Toqueville before him) democracies are especially suited to the surveillance of all citizens (sometimes referred to as the tyranny of the majority), because of their open structure. Staples (1997: 4) articulates the same point when he notes that 'surveillance and discipline have become oddly democratic, everyone is watched, and *no one* is trusted'.[2] This makes for a puzzling contradiction in democracies since they are so devoted to the pursuit of individualism and the defence of privacy. The Internet represents this contradiction most clearly, perhaps even in exaggerated form. The ethos of the Internet has been from its popular inception (in contrast to its actual beginnings as a military solution to efficient communications) a place where the promise of democracy is truly kept: all knowledge becomes available to all people, no filters, no power structure and no censors. All individuals may publish their own material at virtually no cost. The power of capitalist (or nationalist) media is subverted and knowledge is democratised.[3]

However, we argued in the previous chapter that the idea of privacy or anonymity on the Internet is a myth. We have described many ways to monitor activity on the web that are highly intrusive yet are managed without the user's knowledge. Furthermore, even though users can adopt any username they like on the Internet, and create several different names through various e-mail service providers, their messages can usually be traced back to them (or at least to the computing device they use) if a concerted effort is made. This is because the architecture of the Internet keeps a record of where a message goes from one Internet portal to another on its way to its final destination. Thus messages are often never erased from one's personal computer or from another computer somewhere on another network. The chances are that copies of them remain somewhere in a back-up system, or even on a hard drive that does not actually erase the bits on the disk that represent the message, but simply rearranges the naming of files and their locations. Experts, therefore, can often retrieve messages and other documents that users think they have erased. We have also noted that the criminogenic properties of the information society not only make it possible for individuals to spy on each other through chat rooms, but also make it possible for government agencies to spy on individuals.[4] Indeed, not only government agencies but also merchants can spy on their customers, and even their competitors' customers, so long as they keep up with new technologies. So it would seem that individual privacy is under attack, and that situational prevention is partly responsible.

A key element of privacy is anonymity, which is also commonly regarded as a criminogenic characteristic of modern democracies.[5] But anonymity is in decline. The last institution to preserve anonymity in late modern society is the postal service, where senders can protect their identities by not putting return addresses on envelopes.[6] However, this is likely to change. The competitors to government postal services all require individual identification of both sender and receiver, though the level of authentication varies with the level of security the shipper is prepared to purchase. And following the recent anthrax case in the United States, it is to be expected that the extent of anonymity in the US mail service will also decline.[7] Another protection for anonymity is also well on the way to extinction: paying for items or services by cash. As we noted in Chapter 5, credit cards are the major form of payment in online shopping, and in fact for payment everywhere.

After reviewing the massive expansion in information collection and processing undertaken by governments (see Box 8.1), Westin (1967) concluded in *Privacy and Freedom* that there is a continuing battle between surveillance and privacy and that at particular times in the histories of modern democracies crises occur in which the balance of surveillance against privacy tilts one way or another. For example, he argues that the McCarthyism of the 1950s in the USA was a crisis of privacy where government overruled individual privacy rights in order to combat the red scare. But this eventually tilted back, partly as a result of the Watergate excesses, and new laws and regulations were brought into force requiring public disclosure of information and preservation of individual privacy rights. In the current period of terrorist threats, the USA and other western democracies may be entering a new era in which the necessities for surveillance of citizens is favoured by governments and people alike in order to protect against terrorist attacks. A number of the terrorists who attacked the World Trade Center were travelling with fake passports, while others had obtained driving licences under false pretences. When it became apparent that there were Al-Qaida cells throughout the US and other countries, the immediate question that arose was, how is this possible? Why can't we identify people more carefully? Why are such people allowed to enter the country and why are they allowed to stay there, unidentified? When the idea of a national identity card was raised (as it has been from time to time in the history of both the USA and the UK – Laudon, 1986) it was briefly debated, but quickly fell from public view. This is of particular interest when one considers that proving one's identity is so essential to managing one's life in modern society. In the US, driving licences do serve for want of anything better as an ID card. While most of them now include photographs, these are generally a poor form of identification and it is not difficult to obtain a false licence.[8] Each state issues licences according to different criteria and on 16 July 2002 President Bush announced a plan to introduce national standards for the issue of driving licences – a tentative first step towards transforming these licences into a national ID card[9] – and once again met with howls of protest by civil libertarians.

It is to the issue of establishing identity that we now turn, for paradoxically identity is a product of surveillance since it depends on the databases and records of governments and corporations to establish its authenticity. This has significant implications both for the prevention of crime (especially identity theft – see Box 8.2) and for the lives of private citizens.

Box 8.1

In *Privacy and Freedom* Alan Westin (1967) outlines the recent history in American society of the precursor to Internet surveillance – passive surveillance – which he identifies as largely a revolution in information collection and processing. The following are the steps he outlines (bearing in mind that he was writing in 1967):

1. Massive expansion of information-gathering was spawned by the growth of large governmental and private organisations. These files about individuals include, just to mention a sample: social security numbers, births, deaths and marriages, school records, employment records, financial records, public and private health records, automobile registrations, tax records, and licences of many kinds.

2. The increased mobility of individuals has led to the accumulation of dossiers by government and private agencies, in order to keep track of individuals for a number of purposes, such as granting passports and granting credit. Westin notes that in the 1960s the Retail Credit Association maintained dossiers on 43 million people. Imagine the numbers today!

3. The advent of the electronic digital computer accelerated the collection and analysis of these enormous collections of individual records.

4. The development of new public programmes produced the requirement for the collection of much more individual information, for example the Civil Rights Act of 1964.

5. Advances in computing have rapidly enhanced the ability to share information across agencies and organisations. (This is still a goal of today's government agencies, but a goal still largely out of reach, given the events of September 11 in which the FBI, the CIA and other law enforcement and intelligence agencies failed to share crucial information.)

6. Replacement of cash transactions with credit card and other types of transactions that require individual identification of the participants has created the possibility and the need for massive data collection concerning individual transactions.

Box 8.2 Identity as a hot product

The *Foresight* study by Jones and Levi showed that there has been a dramatic increase in recent years in identity theft in the UK (Jones and Levi, 2000). And in the US of the 10,000 financial crime arrests made by the United States Secret Service in 1997, 94 per cent involved identity theft (Willox, Regan and O'Connor, 2002). It has been further estimated that there were between 500,000 and 700,000 cases of identity theft in the first six months of 2000.[10] Extensive investigations and legislative work concerning privacy have been undertaken in the wake of spectacular criminal cases of identity theft,[11] spawning a number of interest groups[12] and government agencies that campaign for online privacy rights, such as the Privacy Rights Clearinghouse.[13] The problem was considered sufficiently severe in the US that President Clinton signed into law the Identity Theft and Assumption Deterrence Act[14] on 30 October 1998.[15]

Of course, the impersonations and deceptions that are used in traditional frauds have existed long before e-commerce and the computing environment. However, we have argued that the SCAREM attributes of the computing environment throw the whole idea of identity into a quandary. As we have noted many times, the Internet allows for – even fosters – deceptions, anonymity, aliases and 'virtual identities'. In the case study of credit card fraud described in Chapter 7, we noted that this crime has been reduced considerably in the UK by the adoption of several situational techniques. These included improved technology in making the cards, requiring PIN numbers for users and the utilisation of large databases against which a card can be checked for usage deviating from the cardholder's established pattern. However, there is a good possibility that criminals have redirected their attention to other points in the e-commerce transaction offering more value or vulnerability. If the card itself cannot be easily counterfeited, a better solution is to assume the identity of the user. Thus online retailers' databases of credit card and other personal information become the target, or the cards themselves become the target in theft from cars, burglary and muggings.

The problem of identity

The issue of identity translates into three perplexing problems: (a) the authentication of identity (which presents itself mainly to merchants and other officials who need to be assured that their customers are who they say they are); (b) the tracking of identities; and (c) the protection of consumers' privacy, since it is impossible to verify identity without obtaining private information about an individual's personal history.

Authenticating identity

Identity is composed of two attributes: what we are and who we are. What we are is determined by 'accidents' of birth, that is biology. Who we are is determined by life events. Until recently, all ways of authenticating identity drew upon *who* we are, not *what* we are, with the exception of fingerprints. The recent development of DNA files has begun to add to the biological method of identification. Picture IDs also attempt to use biological data for purposes of identification, though this is a very crude method compared with DNA and the other new biometric methods such as voice patterns, retinal scans, hand scans, facial scans and iris scans.[16] However, these approaches only do half the job. They do establish that this is an individual who is unique in certain ways, but they do not attach a name or other features to the person. This has to be done by using the person's life history data which come from basically four sources: (a) public records of birth, marriage, taxes paid, etc.; (b) commercial databases (energy or telephone bills, mortgage papers); (c) professional and employment history (school or university, educational degrees); and (d) family records (family referees, parents or guardians). A shortlist of documents deriving from these sources includes (Jones and Levi, 2000):

- electoral register entries;
- mortgage account information;
- property ownership and leasehold;
- credit account and other financial facilities information;
- insurance policies;
- marriage and financial associations;
- previous addresses;
- telephone numbers – fixed and mobile;
- employment information from applications for financial services;
- library cards and other memberships;
- satisfied court judgments;
- e-mail address(es);
- higher educational qualifications;
- forwarding addresses – redirections;
- previous address linking;

- previous authentication events;
- payment systems facilities – debit/credit/cheque/charge cards, virtual wallets, etc.

In order to obtain a new passport in the US, for example, an individual typically has to produce a selection of two or more of the above documents or sources of identity. It is also apparent that the older the person, the more evidence there is to establish his or her identity. A national database containing these sources of identity verification would be extremely powerful. Another possibility would be to link the many existing databases together by developing a search engine that would pull out the required information from each database. Many of the search engines used on the Internet do something similar and there are specialised services on the Internet that promise, with varying degrees of success, to do just that. And these are not government websites, but private, interest group or commercial websites.[17]

In fact, large databases are not needed in order to process smart cards. This is because much individual information can be stored, certainly all the information listed above, on a smart card. It can also be categorised into different levels of security right on the card, so that depending on the level of verification needed, say to purchase an item or to enter a country, only the appropriate level of information is accessed on the card.[18] Smart cards already exist with this capacity.[19] They do not require a central database, or any database at all for their authentication, once the original authentication data have been entered. There is no need for the agent, say an immigration officer inspecting a passport, to check with a database of passports. The needed information is on the card itself. And if the card also contains biological data that link the life event contents of the card to the cardholder, then there is a high probability that the person is who he or she claims to be. Of course, if there were a list of outlaws, the agent would have to consult it. But this would be a highly specialised list of suspects, not a broad list of the kind that the opponents of national ID cards envisage.

The wide application of such super smart identification cards is probably a long way off. But if technology continues to force change at the rate it did during the twentieth century, we may expect that it will come about. The fact that American Express has recently introduced its Private Payments system, which creates a one-time credit card number for every transaction, while keeping the customer's account number private, is a small step in this direction.[20] Another such step is represented by Microsoft's introduction of its Passport and Hailstorm services that can be accessed by merchants promises to provide explicit links between individuals and their personal histories in order to make the convenience of online shopping even greater. Hailstorm will offer a range of services made possible by a massive directory of personal information including an individual's address, social and economic profile, location both electronic and geographic, notifications (e-mail alerts to other devices) and 'myWallet' payment information and electronic coupons.[21] That Microsoft envisages a database that contains both geographic and electronic location of individuals raises additional issues about tracking people's movements – an issue closely related to tracking the objects that people own and use.

Tracking identities

A discussion of personal identity, privacy and surveillance would not be complete without recognising the possibilities that technology provides in establishing and tracking the identity of products throughout their life cycles. In fact, it is the ability to track identities that contributes to the power of twenty-first century surveillance. Most products end up being owned by individuals and many are tied to the individual identity of the owner. Products also move from place to place, and owner to owner, as they proceed through their life cycle. This means they also have a life history. Tracking products, therefore, is often an indirect way of tracking individuals. There are three technologies that serve this purpose:

1. In Chapter 6, we noted the new technology of radio frequency identification (RFID) that makes it possible to track products through much of their life cycle. As these tags become less expensive to produce (soon just pence a tag) and become smaller and therefore easier to conceal they will become more widely used. They are currently on record as tracking cured hams, clothing of all kinds, airport luggage handling,[22] automated fare collection systems,[23] lab coats, pets and cattle.[24] There are even reports of attaching RFIDs to land mines so that they can be more easily traced if unexploded.[25] RFIDs are a great improvement on ordinary bar code tags that contain a limited amount of information, and that require actual physical proximity if not handling in order to be read (DiLonardo, 1997a: 64–71). Furthermore, RFIDs are fast becoming more sophisticated, able to record and transmit consumer preferences and buying habits,[26] and have been reduced to the size of a pinhead.[27] In fact, they can 'combine pricing, merchandising, data collection and protection in a single step' (DiLonardo, 1997b). The Gap, for example recently completed a three-month trial of embedding an RFID chip in every piece of denim it sells. Coca-Cola, Proctor & Gamble, Walmart and Home Depot have joined to create standards for future tags and readers so that they will be universally compatible.[28]

2. In Chapter 6 we also reviewed the increasing use of global positioning systems (GPS) to track cars and trucks. GPS makes it possible for rental car operators to track the location, speed and use of their vehicles by

customers. In theory, it may soon be possible for merchants to track the location of all major products they sell, even as they move from one owner to another. Merchants and manufacturers have tried to do this for a long time – achieved, for example, each time a buyer of a new product fills out the registration card and sends it in to the manufacturer. It is obvious, though, that once products can be effectively tracked, they also may provide a link to the owners, offering a way to monitor the activity of private individuals. The use of automatic number plate readers, speed and red light cameras and E-ZPass on toll roads (see below) already makes it possible to locate vehicles at particular places and particular times.

3. Television sets are increasingly connected to the Internet via digital cable services or satellite services, and the use of personal video cameras linked to the web provides considerably more access to the home by merchandisers and manufacturers. The advent of satellite radio via the web will also provide increasing access to automobiles and permit collection of information on the physical location of vehicles. There are already many security devices linked to the web that can provide various levels of monitoring and surveillance of the home or office.[29] New appliances and other gadgets are currently under development, some already marketed to the public, which are embedded Linux (a common Internet operating system) devices. For example, one can now purchase a networked refrigerator that can be accessed via the web. And since wireless access to the web is now widely available on handheld devices of various kinds, there exists the possibility of accessing one's refrigerator from the supermarket to check what needs to be purchased.[30] Presumably hand tools, video cameras and a host of other common devices could contain RFID chips with embedded Linux programming to connect them to the web, and thus theoretically could be traceable almost anywhere.[31]

Technology promises to merge the above three technologies into one device. Tiny GPS antennae have already been invented and attached to RFID chips. There are also versions that can be embedded under the skin. Variations on these devices could therefore be used to track not only products such as cell phones and bank notes, but also pets, livestock, criminals, people with Alzheimer's, adolescents and other loved ones.[32] These uses are obviously attractive and offer considerable convenience and security when one is concerned about a loved one getting lost, for example. But they also come at the obvious cost of the privacy of the person (or owner of an object) who is being tracked.

Personal privacy and consumerism

It is clear that the issue of privacy in the twenty-first century becomes one of defence against intrusions, not so much by governments, but by private enterprise. Consumers, especially those plugged into the information society, give up their private and personal details to merchants and other credit assessing organisations in order to establish a valid commercial identity. Without this, they cannot exploit all the benefits that the online world has to offer. And one of those major benefits, if not *the* major benefit, is to be able to move freely about the open society – the real society and the virtual one. This is a new version of the old idea of freedom of movement that is a cornerstone of western political thought. The harsh restrictions on movement of individuals within and across borders of the communist countries of the twentieth century are held up as an example of the loss of freedom in totalitarian societies. But in the information society, it is not only freedom of physical movement that is crucial for a free life, but also freedom to move through the information systems of cyberspace, essential for the economic empowerment of each individual. Technology – the Internet and the lowly fax machine – was credited with having facilitated the fall of the Soviet Union and other communist regimes of Eastern Europe. Information crossed borders, uncensored. At that time, the commercial use of the Internet was in its infancy. Today e-commerce increasingly depends on the free flow of information, and ultimately on the willingness of its participants to give up a portion of their privacy for the increased freedom of movement that technology offers.

Against surrendering privacy in order to maintain a personal (though increasingly public) identity is the philosophical notion, deriving from the Enlightenment thinkers of seventeenth- and eighteenth-century Europe, that humans should remain free from external constraints of any kind,[33] to be able to form and protect their own personal identities, especially to be able to keep these apart, unsullied by the demands of others, whether they be governments or private organisations. However, this battle has already been fought and lost. Privacy advocates lost that battle when governments first began keeping national depositories of the births and deaths of their citizens, and when town planners drew maps to identify the locations and eventually addresses of individual abodes. The postal service locked down the idea of locating individuals in specific places. Indeed, what other meaning could there be to 'getting away from it all' but that one goes on holiday without phone and contact address? But who wants that except on very rare occasions? The incredibly fast take-up of mobile phones suggests that many people do not want to be private, that they *want* to be tracked down.[34]

We suggest that the vague and idealistic notion of personal or individual identity as propagated in western thought is being replaced by a new idea, that of one's commercial identity. And this identity will be forged, not out of dealings with government, as was the great concern of Enlightenment thinkers such as Rousseau and Montesquieu, or even from those fears described by Westin in the twentieth century. Rather, they will emerge out of dealings with open markets, an idea almost realised by Adam Smith in the seventeenth century, perhaps leading sooner than we think to privacy becoming a commodity that citizens and businesses alike can trade according to needs and demands (Grabosky, Smith and Dempsey, 2001: 177; Davies, 1997). This is clearly a highly sensitive point, but one that online retailers have quickly recognised. Thus on all websites of major online retailers there is a privacy statement, and many also guarantee additional options to preserve privacy, such as electing not to have one's personal details shared with other merchants. It is not clear whether online retailers have taken these protective steps in response to what they see as economic or business concerns, or whether in response to the pressure brought upon them by governments, especially those international organisations that have been quite forward in delivering directives.[35] In any event, in the market economies of modern democracies it is customers – citizens – who will 'decide' how much of their privacy they will trade for convenience. And if they do not decide, maybe the government will?

National ID cards

National ID cards are common in European and Asian countries[36] and there are surrogate national ID cards in the US and UK – including driving licences, the social security number issued to all citizens in the US, and the national health number in the UK – but these 'IDs' are widely considered to be extremely unreliable and easy to falsify. In the US in the late 1960s it took an act of Congress to allow the Internal Revenue Service to use social security numbers as taxpayer identifiers (Westin, 1967: 196). The arguments against national IDs revolve around the notion of the 'free society' (and arguably the Internet is its extreme form), which recognises the right of people to move about freely without interference and live their lives without the intrusion of outsiders – especially the government.[37] This belief has been the foundation for the attack on the government's claim on cryptography, a claim that assumes the right of the government, in the last resort, to have the right to monitor an individual's Internet transactions. It is significant to note that the US Congress considerably loosened the wiretap laws – which previously had been highly restrictive – in its anti-terrorism legislation passed in the aftermath of the September 11 attack.

Will the information society create the impetus for such a card? It would certainly make everyday life in the post-9/11 world much easier. It would simplify greatly the process of getting through checkpoints at airports and other venues of mass transportation or sporting events. Even if there were no national ID, at a minimum 'smart' passports would greatly simplify international travel.[38]

Technology may be creating the groundwork for something like a national ID, though it is impossible to predict precisely what form this will take. The transformation of credit cards into smart cards in the UK and elsewhere is a small but significant start to nailing down an individual's ID on a card (see below). The increasingly widespread introduction of digital certificates and signatures also puts a premium on being able to claim authentication of one's transaction, and with increasing technological progress, the possibility of also being able to attach this authentication process to a smart card (and even to products as well, as we will examine below). The analysis in this book of the e-commerce environment suggests that these forms of authentication are essential to reliable and successful e-commerce transactions. And if the public continues to use the Internet to do more and more of its daily business, then these authentication procedures will become more common, and more accepted.

The movement to some kind of smart identification is well under way. How many passwords and user IDs do ordinary people have these days compared to just ten years ago? Identifying ourselves has already become 'an integral part of everyday life' (Smith, 1999). If the history of the introduction of credit cards is any indication, these new forms of smart identification, because they make life easier and more secure for the ordinary person, will surely overtake us. In 1967, Westin predicted in respect of credit cards:

> The life of the individual would be almost wholly recorded and observed through analysis of daily 'transactions' of Credit Card No. 172,348,400, Humphrey, Stanley, M. Whoever ran the computers would know when the individual entered the highway and where he got off, how many bottles of scotch or vermouth he purchased...who paid the rent for the girl in Apartment 4B...who went to the movies on a working day at the office...who was at lunch at Luigi's...there would be few areas in which anyone could move about in anonymity that would not be fully documented for government examination.
>
> (Westin, 1967: 165)

Events have not quite come about as predicted, but in some respects they have come close. The spectre that 'the government' would have direct access to all the information related above, and that all the databases would be integrated into one massive dossier on each individual, has not occurred. Westin relates the attempt in the late 1960s and early 1970s by Governor Rockefeller's administration in New York State to integrate the databases of all criminal justice agencies in that state. It was thought even then to be technologically feasible, but it never happened largely because of political opposition and competition among the various bureaucracies. Today, even though an agency exists in New York State (the NYS Division of Criminal Justice Services) whose mission is to bring together the activities of the state's criminal justice agencies, there is little sign of integrating all the criminal justice databases. Technologically, of course, it is even more feasible to do this, but at the same time there are many, many more agencies and databases to integrate compared to the 1960s. On the other hand, travellers' movements through tollways can now be tracked. The advent of 'E-ZPass' in the US provides citizens with the convenience of paying their highway tolls by allowing their vehicles to be scanned electronically and having the money automatically deducted from their credit card account. However, what was not recognised in the 1967 scenario is that today individuals have several credit cards, and that the number of the credit card is not a personal ID but an account number. And as we noted previously, establishing the link between the credit card and the actual identity of the user is no simple task. The point we must recognise is that credit cards have increasingly become entrenched as a most convenient means of making financial transactions. Technology has made this possible, convenience has made it acceptable.

The issue, then, is not so much that a national ID card may emerge from these significant changes, but that the ability to verify one's identity will most likely be driven by commercial rather than national security, ethical or privacy interests. A verifiable or 'true' identity will increasingly be established for those with the means and education to conduct their business using the facilities and convenience offered by the information society. These conveniences are not confined to desktop computers any more, but to telephones and PDAs, devices of mass communication such as the television and radio, global positioning systems, and who knows what other devices that will emerge during the technological revolution. It is conceivable that consumers will be unable to exploit these services to the full without establishing their identities to the satisfaction of those who provide these services. And in most cases, those who provide these services will be (and are) private enterprises. Thus if smart cards become widespread, they will most likely be dominated by a few major corporations, just as is the case with credit cards now. There are already companies that provide 'premium' identification, such as Verisign, which guarantees the digital verification of many online transactions conducted on major e-commerce websites. Thus it is conceivable that individuals could pay to obtain premium identity smart cards, cards whose authentication is beyond reproach. In contrast, the homeless, or poorly educated and unemployed, or illegal aliens, may, in the future, have no acceptable means of authenticating their identities.[39] To critics of the 'surveillance society' this amounts to a fascinating paradox, since it might be argued that the poor, therefore, are by definition under much less surveillance (so are more free) than are the better off.[40]

One of the main arguments raised against national ID cards is that they are the 'primary tool of totalitarian governments', to quote a former US senator, Alan Cranston (Etzioni, 1999: 71). He made this statement commenting on a proposed national database to be used for employment verification purposes. The idea of a national ID card, of course, presumes that such a database would contain the personal details of all individuals in the nation. In fact, what is emerging in the twenty-first century is the existence of multiple databases of personal information. There are websites that specialise in providing a service of searching through multiple databases to find or discover the identities of missing persons. The 'white pages' and 'yellow pages' found on many web portals are simple versions of such databases. The US government already maintains many such databases for specific purposes: taxation, handgun licensing, naturalised citizens and social security to name but a few. So also does the UK with the notable addition of the national health card, even though it is considered an unreliable indicator of identity (Jones and Levi, 2000). If one adds to that the growing number of databases of personal and credit information such as those of online retailers for credit and marketing information, and those in the health field for medical services, the amount of recorded information available on any single person in the information society is stunning, to say the least. Is it an advantage that this information is located in different places? This is difficult to evaluate. Having so many databases creates many attractive targets to criminal hackers. On the other hand, if all the information about a single person were assembled together in one database, it would become indeed a critical target and a powerful tool of government.

The slippery slope?

Does endorsing these forms of surveillance mean that we embrace the idea of a 'big brother' society? Critics complain of a fortress society (gated communities as a solution to burglary), exclusion of 'undesirables' from public spaces (access control to shopping malls), a society under constant surveillance (CCTV in public places, databases of personal information) and so on. They often assume that these examples and many others result from the unthinking application of situational prevention without regard to the broader implications for society, especially concerning privacy. Whether or not this is true of situational prevention in its 'broader' less precise meaning (i.e. when used as a synonym for any attempt to reduce crime opportunities), it is certainly not true of the academic formulation of the approach by the present authors and others. Central to this formulation is the assumption that situational crime prevention measures must be tailored to the nature of a specific problem. No single measure works everywhere and the social and ethical costs of a particular measure (such as CCTV) vary considerably with the situation in which it is employed (it is much less problematic in public car parks than in public lavatories). Moreover, there is never just one way to reduce opportunities for a particular category of crime and, in making a choice of which measures to implement, careful attention should be paid to the social acceptability of all those under consideration.

In any case, as we have just seen, the issue of privacy is not straightforward. Some scholars have even argued that part of the definition of privacy, particularly when it is seen as an offshoot to property rights (a widely recognised legal view of privacy rights), involves the right to exclude others from some property (DeCew, 1997: 54). Gated communities therefore are exercising their privacy rights and in this case situational crime prevention is not simply imposing a policy of entry control, but is assisting the privacy of a group of individuals who have chosen to live together. We make this argument simply to show that all the techniques of surveillance and other situational prevention controls clearly benefit definable sets of people. Control is not a pure negative.

Perhaps its excess is? Giddens (1990) has argued that totalitarianism is an extreme focusing of surveillance, which has prompted other critics to caution that 'the enhanced role of new technology within governmental administration and policing should give us pause' (Lyons, 1994: 11). The logic here is faulty since surveillance does not cause totalitarianism, though its excessive use by government might well be a sign of this. We have argued that surveillance occurs in many spheres of social and organisational life, not only in late modern society but also in societies long predating ours. If totalitarianism makes extreme use of surveillance it does not follow that surveillance made it so. The problem is totalitarianism, not surveillance. Furthermore, we have also argued that surveillance in late modern society is structured in what is close to the opposite form of totalitarian government: it is increasingly democratised, with power distributed across many organisations and institutions of which government is only one. In fact, situational prevention is far from becoming a massive octopus of control for several reasons:

- The literature on attempts by situational crime prevention (or its close relative, problem-oriented policing) to forge partnerships among various stakeholders to help modify situations makes it clear that getting these stakeholders to work in concert is extremely difficult, time-consuming and expensive (Laycock and Tilley, 1995). Furthermore, where such attempts have succeeded, the partnerships tend to be locally oriented and rooted. For example, the reduction of violence in and around bars in a resort town in Australia was accomplished by enlisting the assistance of local tavern keepers, local police and citizen groups (Homel et al., 1997). It was not accomplished through intervention by federal or state governments.

- Integrating all the databases that might be used to control or modify situations has also proved far out of reach in most instances, not because of technology, but because bureaucracies have proved extremely difficult to get to work in unison. The failure of various law enforcement agencies to share anti-terrorist information is a typical example.

Bureaucracies mostly do not work together, but rather compete with each other for control.[41]

- In democracies that operate market economies, there is a constant tension between government and the private sector. If there were not, private organisations and corporations would not have to spend so much time (and money) lobbying the government to do their bidding. It takes enormous effort to bring governments and private sector organisations, especially business, to work together to reduce specific types of crime – though it can be done, as in the case of credit card fraud reduction in the UK in the 1990s. However, even in cases of successful collaboration, these collaborations tend to form, achieve the mission – and then government removes itself from participation. In other words, the view that governments in capitalist democracies are in cahoots with business in order to control individuals is simply false (Hardie and Hobbs, 2002). It is true that many regulations and some legislation result from collaboration between business and government. But it is also clear that if this were not the case, regulations would often be unenforceable or worse, and would not address the relevant issues that often only business (especially e-commerce with its specialised knowledge) can identify. In the field of e-commerce especially, partnerships between government and industry are essential.

In fact, we may safely conclude that there is very little chance that 'big brother' will take over. If anything, the trends in late modern society are decidedly contrary to governments having a monopoly on crime control or indeed on other regulatory or controlling functions of society. (One large exception is income tax collection.) With the decline of the welfare state, governments have been looking for ways to divest themselves of responsibility and of spreading this to the private sector. Situational prevention can help those prepared to take on this new responsibility, and in the case of businesses, they have been doing this for many years – perhaps with some resentment that the 'police are not doing their job'. There is now a growing realisation, however, that the police cannot control crime on their own and, moreover, that many crimes may be prevented without their involvement.

An ideology of control?

So if the real benefits of situational crime prevention outweigh its negatives, what else is there to criticise? Critics argue that in its 'broad' form (see Chapter 1) – the application of opportunity-reducing measures without first having studied the nature of the specific problem is in fact an *ideology of control*, which transcends the apparent immediate benefits for a given small group of people in a particular situation. In response, advo-cates of situational prevention have, until recently, claimed to be ethically and ideologically neutral by refusing to acknowledge its broader meaning, claiming that it simply solves very small specific problems, and in so doing does not advocate or advance an overall ideology or social policy aimed at infringing personal freedoms. Critics have countered with the argument that even if situational prevention is applied narrowly, its approach nevertheless serves the interests of the powerful (the class-based ideological criticism), or in a more general sense, serves the interests of the 'culture of control' (the 'postmodern' ideological criticism).

There are really two questions here. First, is situational prevention actu-ally an ideology of control? Or is it an ideology of control by default, that is to say its proponents suffer from a kind of false consciousness by failing to acknowledge that what they are doing is advancing the dominant ideology of control in late modern society? The first question is answered by asking whether situational prevention begins with preconceptions and if so are they ideological? In its theoretical development it looks as though it does. Certainly it was promoted as an approach that contrasted with the estab-lished criminological theories, namely those focused on dispositional or social causes of crime. Unlike most current criminology, it also emphasises the role of rationality in criminal behaviour. However, the crucial difference between situational crime prevention and most other criminology is that sit-uational crime prevention is oriented to action to reduce or prevent crime, and relegates causal theory to a place of secondary importance. The contrast is rather similar to that in medicine. There are many drugs developed to treat all kinds of illnesses. How exactly these drugs work is often not com-pletely known (otherwise there would be no warnings of side effects), only that they work. What causes the illnesses in the first place is comparatively irrelevant, so long as the drug does the job. So it is with situational crime prevention. If a situation can be modified to reduce or prevent crime, that is enough. Distant causal factors (family history, social relationships, inheri-tance, etc.) may or may not have led the offender to commit the crime. It is enough to find an acceptable way to stop it – and of course to follow up to make sure that displacement does not occur.

As with medicine, of course, more complete understanding of causes might one day yield more effective preventive measurers. But action to pre-vent crime should not be postponed till then if, meanwhile, an effective point of intervention can be identified and measures be taken which will lead to a reduction of the problem. In sum, situational crime prevention is not an ideology that advocates action based upon vague and abstract con-cepts. Rather, it is a pragmatic approach that collects information that appears relevant to the crime as it is committed at that moment, then broad-ens its net to enlist the cooperation of a variety of stakeholders to modify the situation in order to make that specific crime more difficult to commit. So situational crime prevention has no disciplinary allegiance. Its assumptions veer towards a rational conception of humans, but that is hardly an assumption that places it at any particular place on the political spectrum.

The second question as to whether situational crime prevention is an ideology but fails to recognise it can most easily be answered by contrasting situational crime prevention to Marxism, the best known ideology that argued for freedom of individuals, but actually delivered a totalitarian society that was in every sense a society of control. Marx began his argument with a micro analysis of the labour used to produce a coat from a piece of linen (Marx, 1977), arguing that in this instance (situation) the amount of labour used to make the cloth was worth far more than the factory owner paid the worker. From this analysis Marx extrapolated to all labour and all owners to develop his powerful theories of exploitation of labour, labour power, surplus value and so on to his broad critique of capitalism. However, it was not enough for Marx to do an academic analysis of labour. As well, he wanted a solution, and for this he demanded action. In fact, he demanded no less than a revolution because he saw that it was impossible to get all parties concerned to work together to see the situation in the way he did, so that modifying the specific situation of the worker was impossible.[42] His theory was, therefore, turned into an ideology and a call to action that became vague (the revolution) and non-specific, advancing such abstract concepts as class consciousness, a 'class-in-itself' and 'false consciousness' with utopian promises that the state would wither away. These were powerful concepts for whipping up revolutionary fervour, but they helped little in easing the specific situations of workers trying to earn a living.

Now let us look at situational crime prevention. This takes a very narrow and specific approach in defining a problem, but a broad approach, drawing together a wide range of possible partners and resources, to modify the situations in which the problem occurs. And the implementation of this approach is multi-disciplinary – or more accurately non-disciplinary. This is why situational crime prevention is a highly adaptable theory, able to cope with the constantly changing conditions of society. It is why we have been able in this book to adapt situational crime prevention without much difficulty to a completely new set of problems presented by the information society. Its lack of an ideology makes this possible, since an ideology will force an explanation on events, blocking out a careful consideration of the relevant aspects of situations and their solutions.

Situational crime prevention therefore does not impose a preconceived solution (excepting the reduction of opportunities for crime). Rather, it encourages the collection of data and information directly impinging on that specific problem and thereby offers a solution. Both situational crime prevention and Marx claim to use science as their approaches. The difference is that Marx used 'science' to support ideological preconceptions. Situational crime prevention uses science to analyse the problem with a minimum of preconceptions – and uses elements of the situation to frame the solution. In contrast, utopian ideologies such as those of Marx, and those embedded within establishment sociology, promise the impossible: to fix the whole of society, usually aiming at eradicating 'inequality' (left deliberately vague).

Indeed, in an interesting further criticism of situational crime prevention, Hope and Sparks (2000) argue that the principal shortcoming of situational crime prevention is that it has no ideology (they say 'theory' but they really mean 'ideology'). In their criticism of situational crime prevention as too practical, they advocate a theory that they promise will save it from its poor adaptability to many situations (more on this inaccuracy below). They call it a 'sociological theory of situations', but in fact their argument is based upon the assumption that 'inequality' is somehow inherently bad, that the private sector has nothing to do with the public good and that the measure of a good criminological theory is the extent to which it adopts the utopian ideologies of the left:

> ...[situational crime prevention] does not contain a mechanism for adequate provision of public goods or safety and security. So long as this deficiency is not addressed, [situational crime prevention] will remain the hand-maiden of the private market and will respond to, and reinforce, inequalities in the means of private protection, leaving the public good of security underprovided.
>
> (p. 183)

We find this puzzling on two counts. First, compared to any other extant theory in criminology, situational prevention (and its close cousin routine activity theory) is the only theory that incorporates social change into its approach to reduce crime. Of course, this statement is self-evident, since there are no current criminological theories whose prime purpose is to prevent any kind of crime. Rather, they still pursue the 'causes of crime' whether they are of the traditional kind or of the white-collar variety, or they pursue its eradication in utopian expressions couched in Marxist derived ideological language of class warfare. Second, the examples given by Hope and Sparks (2000:183–5) of the poor adaptability of situational crime prevention are misleading. They argue, for example, that situational crime prevention cannot help solve problems in prisons because it fails to take account of the institutional setting. Apart from the fact that such a question would never be asked of other extant theories in criminology (e.g. 'theories of the life course'), it is surely evident that institutional settings would *have* to be considered when searching for solutions. Wortley's (2002) book, *Situational Prison Control*, in fact does just this.

Hope and Sparks also recount other instances where players in various settings, such as for example credit card fraud, are not motivated to contribute to changing a criminogenic situation. But not every single party involved in the situation has to cooperate. Crucial changes can sometimes be made without the cooperation of every party. This is because there is never just one way to disrupt the opportunity structure for a particular category of crime. Rather, there are multiple ways that need to be assessed for their economic costs, administrative feasibility and social acceptability before implementation of the selected measure (or measures). This is what helps to make situational crime prevention so adaptable. In fact, there are numerous cases where situational crime prevention has succeeded through forging partnerships among the crucial players. We saw this in the previous chapter in the case study of the reduction of credit card fraud. Effective situational prevention was achieved through partnerships among important players in the situation that included those (the merchants) who appeared to lack motivation to reduce credit card fraud (the banks lost the money, not the merchants).

Another recent attempt to cast situational crime prevention as an ideology of control is made by Garland (2001) who argues that situational crime prevention is a product of late modern society (p. 162) riding on the coat-tails of social change, which includes not only technological innovations, but also crime control policies. He argues that situational prevention is one of the conservative 'criminologies of control', which include those theories in criminology or criminal justice that have advocated punishment over treatment (the just deserts movement of the 1970s and 1980s), and a variety of 'hard' approaches to solving crime problems such as 'zero tolerance' and 'three strikes' legislation. These criminologies are also, he says, 'criminologies of exclusion'. This exclusion is of two kinds. People considered dangerous or otherwise a nuisance are rounded up and put in prison as a result of get-tough legislation and zero tolerance law enforcement. Or, rich people get together and live in gated communities, which excludes lots of others. Situational crime prevention is judged 'guilty' on both counts.

Earlier in his book, and in many other writings, Garland is careful to distinguish situational crime prevention from the parallel development in the 1980s and 1990s of more punitive, reactionary policies of control. However, not all readers of his book will be equally careful[43] and it is important to show precisely how situational crime prevention differs from these other criminologies of control. First, the get-tough legislation. Garland acknowledges that much of this legislation resulted in part from the 'just deserts' arguments (which were based, by the way, on demands for equal justice). There is no connection to situational crime prevention, which focuses on keeping people out of prison and away from punishment by trying to stop them from committing crime in the first place. Situational crime prevention seeks to increase the risk of getting caught, not the severity of the punishment. In fact, situational crime prevention finds very little use for punitive legislation as a solution to crime because it is far too unspecific and far too removed from the situation in which the crime occurs to materially change the opportunity structure for a specific kind of criminal act. All the research evidence on deterrence suggests that when contemplating or committing a crime, offenders focus much more on minimising their chances of being caught than on reducing the severity of punishment if they are caught. The reason is simple: they have far more control over the former than the latter. Situational crime prevention is not in the business of blame nor of punishment. This is why it holds very little appeal for most conservatives, who believe that the only way to stop crime is to hold offenders responsible for their crimes and punish them severely.

It follows that 'three strikes' legislation has nothing to do with situational crime prevention, since the punishment occurs long after the crimes have been committed, making the idea of intervention moot. It might be argued that the deterrent effect of three-strikes legislation will prevent the commission of future crimes by the offender (or other offenders). The idea of prevention when used in this context of deterrent punishment means something completely different than its use in situational crime prevention. As the name implies, prevention in situational crime prevention is 'situationally' defined. Interventions are invoked in order to modify situations, which include actors and environments in addition to the particular offender. In other words, the three-strikes solution, as with all general deterrence, confounds the problem of crime with the problem of the offender. It is also a one-solution-fits-all approach, which, as we have said, is the opposite of situational crime prevention.

Second, zero tolerance law enforcement. This policy is a corruption of Wilson and Kelling's (1982) classic 'broken windows' theory, where the solution to a neighbourhood's crime problem is seen to lie in order maintenance – taking care of small incivilities and signs of disorder before more serious crime takes over. Exercising discretion about when and where to act is central to their notion. They did not advocate a general policy of zero tolerance and, of course, nor does situational crime prevention. The idea that one policy or solution fits all is quite contrary to the situational prevention, which argues for situation-specific solutions, and requires multiple and specifically directed interventions that are tailored to those situations.

Third, the politics of exclusion. Garland seems disturbed that some '20,000 gated communities have recently sprung up in the USA' (Garland, 2001: 162), and that middle-class citizens in urban settings take precautions, such as carrying little cash and driving instead of walking through streets thought to be dangerous. These security precautions he takes as evidence of an obsessive fear of crime among the middle classes. They are, he says, the prime movers of the politics of exclusion of late modern society. However, the precautions he identifies are not new or recent. Gated communities of various kinds have existed for hundreds of years and are hardly a product of late modernity. All large western cities with apartment buildings have long traditions of retaining porters or doorkeepers who control entry to the building. Gated communities are simply the reproduction of this security model in the suburbs. The idea or model of security is not new – it is simply adapted to different locations. So his claim that the access control exercised by these communities is a product of something recent is doubtful. Furthermore, his claim that 'over a short period of time...large numbers of people... [have adopted]... new and more defensive precautions as a matter of routine...' (Garland, 2000: 12) is accurate only to a point. And why should not people avoid becoming victims if there are sensible, common-sense things they can do about it?

In fact, Garland is painfully aware of this problem. He demonstrates thoroughly enough that the ideology of the welfare state has failed to bring about the desired changes in the social structure, which, most sociologists doggedly believe, once fixed will solve the problem of crime. The fact is that the sociology of the twentieth century continues to have great difficulty in accepting that the concept of class is in most cases an unhelpful abstraction. The identification of social class defies any consistent or precise definition. It varies according to whether it is thought of as an economic, cultural or social phenomenon. It forces individuals into categories at once vague and prejudicial. 'Lower-class neighbourhoods' assume that everyone in such a neighbourhood has particular attributes, or that all streets in that neighbourhood are insecure or unkempt. Similarly, the suburbs are stereotyped as being populated by middle-class families to whom particular (usually negative) attributes are ascribed. And, of course, the same negative ascriptions and motivations are applied to 'the rich'. Perhaps these gated or otherwise 'exclusive' communities are defining themselves as an exclusive class? The more accurate characterisation is to say that gated communities are simply the modern reflection of an ancient solution to human survival: to join together into a community for mutual benefit and protection. Humans have done this at least since they lived in caves and in primal groups. Situational crime prevention does not advocate gated communities because it does not need to. Rather, these solutions emerge in response to the human need for security. Situational crime prevention simply analyses such solutions and shows how and why they work, if they do.

Situational prevention and criminology

Situational crime prevention differs from most twentieth century criminology in at least two fundamental ways. First, as we argued in Chapter 1, it does not deal in abstractions. Thus when the approach identifies and describes opportunities or an opportunity structure in regard to a specific kind of crime, it does not mean 'opportunity' as used in the classic opportunity theory of American criminology (Cloward and Ohlin, 1960). Cloward and Ohlin referred to an abstract concept of 'blocked opportunities' and the supposed disposition of those whose conventional routes to success were blocked to turn to crime instead as a way of achieving their goals. No serious effort was made to assess the specific opportunities for particular crimes that presented themselves and in what settings, and, when an attempt was made to translate the theory's prescriptions into action through the Mobilisation for Youth project implemented throughout the USA in the 1960s, the opportunities provided were mostly in the form of youth clubs of various kinds. The assumption that all deprived youths were seeking 'success' and would 'turn to crime' to achieve it is a good example of a theory based on abstractions leading to a standardised, unworkable solution, and it is little surprise that the Mobilisation for Youth project proved to be a failure (Helfgot, 1981).

Second, we have shown in this book that situational prevention has ready application to the problems of a rapidly changing society, in this case e-commerce crime. Indeed, it fits this new class of crime almost like a glove. The rational choice and routine activity theories on which it is based convincingly explain the emergence and proliferation of crime on the Internet. They also help define the SCAREM properties of the computing environment that permit criminals to operate with impunity, and the CRAVED properties of information, which is the criminals' principal target. No such assistance in understanding these crimes would have been provided by traditional theories framed in terms of the sociological and psychological deprivations giving rise to criminal dispositions. Yet it is characteristic of the bias in the discipline that the few criminologists who have focused on crimes of the information age should have raised more alarm about the harmful consequences for crime of 'exclusion' from the Internet than about the huge new opportunities for crime that the Internet provides.

Part of the explanation, of course, is that the victims of this crime, especially of e-commerce crime, are businesses and corporations, which criminologists treat with disdain. A reading of the criminology textbooks reveals hardly any mention of business and its central role in capitalist society – even though capitalism provides the conditions for writing these books. For situational prevention theorists, on the other hand, business has a major role in crime (Gill, 1994; Felson and Clarke, 1997). Businesses are victims of vast amounts of crime (most of which is never officially recorded) and businesses make an important contribution to crime control through the security precautions they take. Of course, businesses also create substantial opportunities for crime through their products or practices, though they are rarely willing to acknowledge this or do anything about it when they are not the victims themselves (Clarke and Newman, 2002). Whether seen as victims, producers or controllers of crime, however, it is clear that businesses cannot be ignored if criminologists are to have any hope of understanding crime in the postmodern world.

While situational crime prevention may be helpful in explaining Internet crime, it is even more valuable in suggesting ways to control this crime. It provides a raft of opportunity-reducing techniques that with little adaptation allow both the ready classification of existing measures to prevent e-commerce crime and a methodology for identifying new, untried measures. It also provides a set of concepts – displacement, diffusion of benefits and criminal adaptation – that serves to alert e-commerce to the unintended outcomes of preventive measures – some good, some bad – that should be considered in deciding which action to take. In fact, making these decisions is so complex with so much riding on them that many e-businesses will need professional help from crime prevention specialists. These specialists will need to be familiar not only with the business environment, but with computing technology and situational prevention concepts. Training them is a job that departments of criminology could undertake, opening up career opportunities for their graduates to make a difference in the real world.

Conclusions

It is highly unlikely that modern society is hurtling towards a totalitarian system with control hidden behind every bush, building or social exchange, as seems to be envisaged by the critics of situational prevention and of late modern society in general. Totalitarian societies and democratic societies alike have much of this control embedded in them. The great difference is that in democratic societies the control is dispersed and distributed (as is economic exchange in open market economies, demonstrated by our review of the e-commerce environment in Chapter 2). Therefore, ultimate or total control in democracies is impossible. Total control requires a centrality of power that cannot exist in modern democracies since these operate according to free markets and distributed power structures. To imagine that situational prevention will change the political structure of a democracy and move it towards a totalitarian state is clearly absurd. Such influence over political and historical events that make or break nation-states lies far beyond the reach of situational prevention, particularly as it does not aspire to become an ideology unto itself.

It is incorrect to assume, as do critics of late modern society, that freedom is the opposite of control. Even Garland (2001: 197), who is usually very careful, seems to take this position when he refers to the 'dialectic' of freedom and control in late modern society. While we have suggested that there is indeed a tension between surveillance and privacy, we would argue that there is no special tension between their more abstract counterparts, freedom and control. Rather, they are simply twin consequences of the same process: the constant expansion in modern society of choices and opportunities, for citizens to enjoy and exploit the 'shock of the new'. It is clear that the motor vehicle opened up an enormous expanse of opportunities for individuals to go wherever they wanted, when they wanted and with whom they wanted. It also brought with it new laws and controls (speed limits and stop signs, for example) many of which make the exploitation of these new opportunities possible. Similarly, along with the new opportunities for control in democracies brought about by the information revolution – the databases, the tracking technologies, the records of individuals – the information society has provided citizens with much more freedom: more choices and open access to information on a scale far beyond that which occurred as a result of the invention of the printing press. In contrast to the introduction of the automobile, however, few laws and regulations have so far been introduced that impact directly on an individual's daily activities. The controls over daily activities have come, instead, from the business and security procedures necessary to make the exploitation of the opportunities provided by the technologies of the information society more and more efficient and beneficial for individual users, which of course includes businesses.

In sum, with more freedom comes more opportunity. And that logically means that there is more opportunity to commit crime along with any other form of behaviour. Given the one basic value of situational crime prevention – that it is good to reduce or prevent crime – it is to be expected that situational prevention will find many more applications as new opportunities for crime present themselves. In contrast, those criminological theories that remain fixated on the causes of crime and eschew the value of crime reduction – or at least relegate it to an insignificant place – will become less and less relevant to the information society. If there is any truth to the criticisms of situational crime prevention as a science of control, we respond that situational prevention is a servant, not of the 'culture of control' or totalitarianism but of democracy and open society.

Notes

1 The most obvious issue is the use of CCTV in a number of studies that purport to apply situational prevention techniques (von Hirsch, 2000). However, there is a general view by situational crime prevention critics that the overall approach is somehow advancing a broad clandestine or hidden surveillance throughout all of 'postmodern' society. The majority of the articles in the von Hirsch book, though restrained, appear to hold this view. The introductory chapter by Garland generally establishes this premise, which is expounded in more depth in his book *Culture of Control* (2001).

2 Though Staples subscribes to the idea of a panoptic society, in his latest work (Staples, 2000) he describes many situations of surveillance that reflect 'little brothers' or distributed, democratised kinds of surveillance that are not conducted by a central government but by local governments or private organisations.

3 Pundits abhor this eventuality, noting that the democratisation of knowledge produces superficiality (Postman, 1993).

4 In July, 2002, President Bush announced a remarkable plan to encourage utility workers and others in jobs that deal with the public to report suspicious activity. Staff (2002) 'Ridge denies program encourages Americans to spy on each other', *Wall Street Journal*, 17 July.

5 It is also, possibly, a characteristic that contributes to 'alienation', often complained of by critics of modern societies and described by David Riesman *et al.* (2001) in *The Lonely Crowd*.

6 It has been noted by Anderson (2001) that the first significant introduction of anonymity into communications occurred in 1840 when the postage stamp was introduced, thus affording anonymity of the sender. A similar history (accompanied by governmental concern) occurred in Europe when the telegraph was introduced (the government retained a monopoly on its use) and the telephone when automatic switchboards were introduced.

7 A recent *New York Times* article (Revkin, 2002) gives an account of ways to reduce anonymity of the mail currently being considered by the United States Postal Service, including the issuing of stamps with a unique barcode printed at purchase.

8 Get a fake ID and pay by credit card! http://www.phidentity.com/home.shtml for the UK; http://www.beatthebouncer.com/ provides fake drivers' licences and social security cards for the US.

9 However, the idea that government may hold sensitive information concerning individuals remains a highly charged political and cultural issue. Westin relates the attempt in 1966 of the US Bureau of Census to include in its census survey a question concerning religion, which Congress forbad (Westin, 1967).

10 Givens, Beth (2000) 'Written testimony for US Senate Judiciary Committee on Technology, Terrorism and Government Information, Senator John Kyl, chairman, July 12', http://www.privacyrights.org.

11 Rusch, Jonathan (2001) 'The Department of Justice's role in identity theft enforcement and prevention', Department of Justice, http://www.usdoj.gov/criminal.fraud/fedcase_idtheft.html.

12 National Consumers' League, http://www.nclnet.org/essentials/security.html.

13 Privacy Rights Clearinghouse, http://privacyrights.org. This organisation publishes many fact sheets on privacy rights and identity theft on the web. See also the Federal Trade Commission (FTC) identity theft hotline and data clearinghouse at http://www.comsumer.gov/idtheft. In the UK extensive advice to consumers concerning purchasing online and privacy rights is provided by the Office of Fair Trading at http://www.oft.gov.uk/html/consume/consume.htm.

14 Identity Theft and Assumption Deterrence Act as amended by Public Law 105-318, 112 Stat. 3007 (30 October 1998).

15 Saunders, Jurt M. and Zucker, Bruce (1999) *Counteracting Online Identity Fraud Under the Identity Theft and Assumption Deterrence Act*. Paper presented to the 14th BILETA conference 'Cyberspace 1999: Crime, Criminal Justice and the Internet', 29 March, College of Ripon and York, York, England.

16 For an excellent review of all the current options, see Anderson (2001). His conclusion is that iris scans are probably the most reliable with close to a zero rate of error.

17 There are scores of such services on the Internet. Just one example: Private Eye.com: https://www.yourownprivateeye.com/backgroundcheck.htm.

18 As Gary Marx (2001) notes: 'Modern technology offers a variety of ways of uncoupling verification from unique identity… Validity, authenticity, and eligibility can be determined without having to know a person's name or location.'

19 The technical details of smart cards were discussed in Chapter 6. As noted there, a vulnerability of smart cards to attack has been discovered. The technological arms race against fraudsters will no doubt continue.

20 Staff (2001) 'Privacy and security', *Global Finance*, January.

21 Staff (2002) 'List makers take control', *The Economist*, 20 September.

22 Prophet, Graham (2000) 'ISO is go', *EDN Europe*, June, vol. 45, no. 6, p. 26.

23 Reinhardt, Andy and Gross, Neil (2000) 'On beyond shoplifting prevention', *Business Week*, 2 October, no. 3701, p. 170.

24 Wood, Christina (1998) 'Tag it', *PC Magazine*, 12 February, p. 155.

25 *Ibid*.

26 Schmidt, Charlie (2001) 'Beyond the bar code', *Technology Review*, March, vol. 104, no. 2, pp. 80–2.

27 Staff (2002) 'Tiny Tags', *MIT Technology Review*, May.

28 Garfinkel, Simson (2002) 'An RFID bill of rights', *Technology Review*, October, p. 35.

29 Magid, Larry (2000) 'With home security products you can keep a watchful eye via net', *Los Angeles Times*.

30 Savetz, Kevin (2002) 'Lunchtime@kitchen-fridge.com', *Computer Shopper*, March, p. 32.

31 For an updated review of Linux embedded devices see http://linuxdevices.com.

32 Staff (2002) 'Something to watch over you', *The Economist*, 17 August, p. 61.

33 Rousseau's famous opening line to the *Social Contract*: 'Man is born free but everywhere he is in chains' (Rousseau, 1947: 1).

34 It is true that mobile phones do not indicate location, but technology is already available to make this possible.

35 As noted in the previous chapter, international organisations have been very active in regulating e-commerce, much of it directed to privacy rights. For example, in a global information society, national governments have difficulty in ignoring the directives and pressure issued not only by other governments, but also by international organisations of various kinds. For example, the European approach has been broader than the US. It restricts export of information about EU citizens to other countries that do not have the same standards of protection (such as the USA). In the European Safe Harbour Data-sharing Agreement (1 November 2001), the US Department of Commerce agreed to the EU's more stringent privacy requirements. This meant, among other things, that US Internet companies could risk losing access to European clients if they broke the agreement. This EU directive has been highly controversial, and its effect is yet to be seen. Two-thirds of the EU's countries have enshrined its principles into their own law (Staff, 2001, 'Privacy and security', *Global Finance*, January). The principles of the EU directive are:

- *Notice*. Individuals must be told what the information collected from them is to be used for.
- *Choice*. Individuals must be given a clear choice of not allowing their personal information to be used by third parties.

- *Security*. Organisations must make every effort to safeguard the data.
- *Access*. Individuals must be able to access their own information and amend it as needed.

The OECD has also been very active in developing guidelines for consumer protection and has campaigned to implement them in member countries (http://www.oecd.org/dsti/sti/it/consumer/prod/guidelines.htm). It has also been very active, in conjunction with the G8 countries, in enacting regulations and procedures for combating international organised crime and its activity on international electronic networks (Norman, Paul (2001) 'Policing "high tech" crime within the global context', in David S. Wall (ed.), *Crime and the Internet*. London: Routledge, chapter 12).

   In general, it may be said that the US, in contrast with European countries, adopts a market-oriented approach to regulation and control of privacy issues, whereas European countries depend more heavily on government intervention or influence. For international legislation see: UNCITRAL (2001) *Legal aspects of electronic commerce*, A/CN.9/WG.IV/WP.95, General Assembly, September; UNCITRAL (1999) *Report of the working group on electronic commerce. Draft uniform rules on electronic signatures*, A/CN.9/457, Vienna, February, UNCITRAL (1996) *Model law on electronic commerce with guide to enactment*, December, http://www.uncitral.org/english/texts/electcom/ml-ecomm.htm.

36 As we write, Juki-Net, a centralised, electronic national database of names, addresses and other personal information of all citizens in Japan has just commenced operation and received, surprisingly, some local opposition. Surveys revealed that 86 per cent of Japanese citizens said that they expected some personal information to leak from the system: Staff (2002) 'There's always someone looking at you – and people don't like it', *The Economist*, 10 August, p. 36.

37 For a balanced summary of arguments for and against national ID cards see Etzioni (1999).

38 An ideal scenario of airport security was recently outlined by Dan Tynan in *Popular Science* (September 2002), one that relied heavily on high-tech ID cards and RFIDs attached to luggage and cars.

39 It has already emerged in the information society that not having an identity may be a powerful defence against interrogation. Several of the Al Qaida terrorists did not have any identification which made it difficult to trace who they were, where they came from and who were their contacts, collaborators or relatives.

40 Staff (2002) 'Go on, watch me', *The Economist*, 17 August, p. 12.

41 Cummings, Jean (2002) 'Homeland plan roils agencies with fears of lost influence', *The Wall Street Journal*, Wednesday, 17 July. President Bush's speech outlined a plan to get the many government agencies working together in order to streamline homeland security and make much more information accessible to those agencies fighting terrorism. It has been met already with complaints from civil libertarians and from many of the bureaucracies that expect to lose power.

42 This is, of course, a characterisation of Marx that his supporters would abhor, especially because of the economic determinism in Marx's theory that excludes the possibility of individual choice in action.

43 Nor apparently its reviewers: the dust jacket to Garland's book carries a brief endorsement from Loic Waquant who urges criminologists to read the book because it '…convincingly demonstrates what Durkheim and Foucault postulated: that punishment is epicentral to the (trans)formation of modernity'.

References

Adams, Chris and Richard Hartley (2000) *The Chipping of Goods Initiative. Property Crime Reduction through the Use of Electronic Tagging Systems. A Strategic Plan.* London: Home Office Police Scientific Development Branch.

Ahuja, Vijay (1997) *Secure Commerce on the Internet.* New York: Academic Press.

Anderson, Ross (2001) *Security Engineering: A Guide to Dependable Distributed Systems.* New York: Wiley.

Arend, M. (1993) 'New card fraud weapons emerge', *ABA Banking Journal*, September, 85(9).

Ballard, M. (1994) 'Cheating at cards; smart cards', *Canadian Banker*, July, 101(4).

Bell, Daniel (1976) *The Coming of Post-industrial Society.* New York: Basic Books.

Bell, Josh, Ruben Gomez, Paul Hodge and Vikto Mayer-Schonerger (2001) 'An early scorecard: comparing electronic signatures legislation in the US and the European Union', *Computer Law and Security Report*, vol. 17, no. 6.

Bernstein, Terry, Anish B. Bhimani, Eugene Schultz and Carol A. Siegal (1996) *Internet Security for Business.* New York: Wiley.

Bury, L. (1999) 'Chips can be good for you', *Accountancy*, 123 (1269) 48.

Cavallo, A. and A. Drummond (1994) 'Evaluation of the Victorian random breath testing initiative', in D. South and A. Cavallo (eds), *Australasian Drink-Drive Conference 1993, Conference Proceedings.* Melbourne, Australia: Vicroads.

Chapman, Aub and Russell G. Smith (2001) 'Controlling financial services fraud', *Trends and Issues*, February, no. 189.

Chen, Kuo Lane, Huei Lee and Bradley W. Mayer (2001) 'The impact of security control on business to consumer electronic commerce', *Human Systems Management*, 20: 139–47.

Clark, K. (2000) 'In the war on fraud, a call for teamwork', *Chain Store Age*, 76(11).

Clarke, Ronald V. (1995) 'Situational crime prevention: achievements and challenges', in Michael Tonry and David Farrington (eds), *Building a Safer Society: Strategic Approaches to Crime Prevention. Crime and Justice: A Review of Research*, Vol. 19. Chicago: University of Chicago Press.

Clarke, Ronald V. (1997) *Situational Crime Prevention: Successful Case Studies* 2nd edn. New York: Harrow & Heston.

Clarke, Ronald V. (1999) *Hot Products. Understanding, Anticipating and Reducing the Demand for Stolen Goods*, Police Research Series Paper 98. London: Home Office.

Clarke, Ronald V. (2000) 'Situational crime prevention, criminology and social values', in Andrew von Hirsch, David Garland and Alison Wakefield (eds) *Ethical and Social Perspectives on Situational Crime Prevention*. Oxford: Hart Publishing.

Clarke, Ronald V. and Graeme R. Newman (2002a) *Modifying Hot Products*. London: Home Office.

Clarke, Ronald V. and Graeme R. Newman (2002b) *Secured Goods by Design: A Plan for Security Coding of Electronic Products*, Foresight Crime Prevention Panel, Jill Dando Institute of Crime Science, UCL, London: http://www.foresight.gov.uk/default1024.htm.

Clough, B. and P. Mungo (1992) *Approaching Zero: Data Crime and the Computer Underworld*. London: Faber & Faber.

Cloward, R. and Ohlin, L. (1960) *Delinquency and Opportunity: A Theory of Delinquent Gangs*. Glencoe, IL: Free Press.

Coderre, David (1999) 'Computer assisted techniques for fraud prevention', *CPA Journal*, August: 57–9.

Cohen, L. E. and Marcus Felson (1979) 'Social change and crime rate trends: a routine activity approach', *American Sociological Review*, 44: 588–608.

Colacecchi, M. (1993) 'Praise for AmEx's fraud control program', *Catalog Age*, November, 10 (11).

Cornish, D. B and Ronald V. Clarke (eds) (1986) *The Reasoning Criminal: Rational Choice Perspectives on Offending*. New York: Springer-Verlag.

Crockett, B. (1993) 'Visa tests anti-fraud technology', *American Banker*, 3 November.

Crowder, Nita (1997) 'Fraud detection techniques', *Computers and Auditing*, 54(2): 17–20.

Curry, Michael (1997) *Digital Places: Living with Geographic Information Systems*. London: Routledge.

Dandeker, Christopher (1990) *Power and Modernity: Bureaucracy and Discipline from 1700 to the Present Day*. New York: St. Martin's Press.

Davies, Simon G. (1997) 'Re-engineering the right to privacy: how privacy has been transformed from a right to a commodity', in Philip Agre and Marc Rotenberg (eds), *Technology and Privacy: The New Landscape*, Cambridge, MA: MIT Press.

DeCew, Judith Wagner (1997) *In Pursuit of Privacy: Law, Ethics, and the Rise of Technology*. New York: Cornell University Press.

Demery, P. (1998) 'An easy fix for fraud?', *Credit Card Management*, 11(2).

Denning, Dorothy E. and William E. Baugh Jr (2000) 'Hiding crimes in cyberspace', in Douglas Thomas and Brian Loader (eds), *Cybercrime*. London: Routledge.

Department of Trade and Industry, Foresight E-Crime Strategy Task Force (2001) *Strategy Framework*. London: Home Office.

D'Hont, S. (2000) *The Cutting Edge of RFID Technology and Applications for Manufacturing and Distribution*, Research paper, Texas Instruments TIRIS.

DiLonardo, Robert (1996) 'Defining and measuring the economic benefits of electronic article surveillance', *Security Journal*, 7:3–9.

DiLonardo, Robert (1997a) 'The incredible shrinking security tag: the latest on source tagging', *Security Technology and Design*, July.

DiLonardo, Robert (1997b) 'Source tagging – issues and answers', Unpublished paper, Robert DiLonardo Retail Consulting.

DiLonardo, Robert (1997c) 'Radio frequency identification technology: everything old is new again', *Security and Technology Design*, 4: 26–32.

DiLonardo, Robert (1998) 'Driving with and without a license', *Security Technology and Design*, June.

DiLonardo, Robert and Ronald V. Clarke (1996) 'Reducing the rewards of shoplifting: an evaluation of ink tags', *Security Journal*, 7: 11–14.

Drucker, Peter (2001) 'The next society', *The Economist*, 3 November.

Ekblom, P. (1988) 'Preventing post office robberies in London: effects and side effects', *Journal of Security Administration*, 11: 36–43.

Ekblom, Paul (2000) 'Future crime prevention – a mindset – a way of thinking systematically about causes of crime and solutions to crime problems', in Foresight (2000) *Turning the Corner*. London: Department of Trade and Industry, Crime Prevention Panel, DTI/Pub 5185/5k/12/00/NP, URN 00/136 CD Annex.

Ellison, Louise (2001) 'Cyberstalking: tackling harassment on the Internet', in David S. Wall (ed.), *Crime and the Internet*. London: Routledge, chapter 9.

Etzioni, Amitai (1999) 'Identity cards in America', *Society*, 36(5).

Felson, Marcus (2002) *Crime and Everyday Life*. Thousand Oaks, CA: Sage Publications.

Felson, Marcus and Ronald V. Clarke (1997) *Business and Crime Prevention*. Monsey, NY: Criminal Justice Press.

Financial Action Task Force (FATF) (2001) *Report on Money Laundering Typologies for 2000–2001*, 1 February, FATF XII, OECD.

Fitch, T. (1984) 'Fighting fraud; new technologies for the financial institution', *United States Banker*, March, Special Report.

Foucault, Michel (1995) *Discipline and Punish: The Birth of the Prison*. New York: Vintage.

Fukuyama, F. (1995) *Trust: The Social Virtues*. London: Hamish Hamilton.

Gambetta, D. (1988) *Trust: Making and Breaking the Cooperative Relations*. Oxford: Basil Blackwell.

Gandy, Oscar (1993) *The Panoptic Sort*. Boulder, CO: Westview Press.

Garfinkel, Simon (1997) *Web Security and Commerce*. New York: O'Reilly.

Garland, David (2000) 'Ideas, institutions and situational crime prevention', in Andrew von Hirsch, David Garland and Alison Wakefield (eds), *Ethical and Social Perspectives on Situational Crime Prevention*. Oxford: Hart Publishing.

Garland, David (2001) *The Culture of Control: Crime and Social Order in Contemporary Society.* Chicago: University of Chicago Press.

Giddens, A. (1990) *The Consequences of Modernity.* Oxford: Polity Press.

Gill, Martin (1994) *Crime at Work. Studies in Security and Crime Prevention.* Leicester: Perpetuity Press.

Gilling, David (1996) 'Problems with the problem-oriented approach', in Ross Homel (ed.), *The Politics and Practice of Situational Crime Prevention,* Crime Prevention Studies Vol. 5. Monsey, NY: Criminal Justice Press, pp. 9–24.

Goodman, Marc and Susan W. Brenner (2002) 'The emerging consensus on criminal conduct in cyberspace', *UCLA Journal of Law and Technology:* http://www.lawtechjournal.com/archives.php.

Grabosky, P. (2001) 'Computer crime: a criminological overview', *Forum on Crime and Society,* 1: 35–53.

Grabosky, Peter and Russell Smith (2001) 'Telecommunications fraud in the digital age: the convergence of technologies', in David S. Wall (ed.), *Crime and the Internet.* London: Routledge, chapter 3.

Grabosky, Peter, Russell Smith and Gillian Dempsey (2001) *Electronic Theft: Unlawful Acquisition in Cyberspace.* Cambridge: Cambridge University Press.

Grant, A., F. David and P. Grabosky (1997) 'Child pornography in the digital age', *Transnational Organized Crime,* 3(4): 171–88.

Hardie, Jeremy and Ben Hobbs (2002) *Companies Against Crime.* London: Home Office, IPPR Criminal Justice Forum.

Helfgot, Joseph H. (1981) *Professional Reforming: Mobilization for Youth and the Failure of Social Science.* Lexington, MA: Lexington Books.

Herbert, Daniel. (2001) 'Improve supply chain efficiencies through better management with RFID', *Material Handling Management,* February, 56(2).

Higgins, Amy and Sherri Noucky (2001) 'To catch a thief', *Machine Design,* 73(16).

Homel, Ross, Mary Hauritz, Gillian McIlwain, Richard Wortlet and Russell Carvolth (1997) 'Preventing drunkenness and violence around nightclubs in a tourist resort', in R.V. Clarke (ed.), *Situational Crime Prevention: Successful Case Studies,* 2nd edn. New York: Harrow & Heston, pp. 263–82.

Hope, Tim and Richard Sparks (2000) 'For a sociological theory of situations (or how useful is pragmatic criminology?)', in Andrew von Hirsch, David Garland and Alison Wakefield (eds), *Ethical and Social Perspectives on Situational Crime Prevention.* Oxford: Hart Publishing, chapter 10.

Hurley, Hanna (2001) 'Pocket sized security', *Telephony,* 240(18).

Iannacci, J. (1994) 'Leading the charge against credit card crime; innovations in credit card security features', *Security Management,* August, 38(8).

Ingraham, D. G. (1980) 'On charging computer crimes', *Computer Law Journal,* 2: 429.

Jeffery, C. R. (1971) *Crime Prevention Through Environmental Design.* Beverly Hills, CA: Sage.

Jerin, Robert and Beverly Dolinsky (2001) 'You've got mail! You don't want it: cyber-victimization and on-line dating', *Journal of Criminal Justice and Popular Culture,* 9(1): http://www.albany.edu/scj/jcjpc/.

Jones, Gareth and Mike Levi (2000) 'The value of identity and the need for authenticity. Research paper', in Foresight (2000) *Turning the Corner.* London: Department of Trade and Industry, Crime Prevention Panel, DTI/Pub 5185/5k/12/00/NP, URN 00/136 CD Annex.

Jones, Robert W. (2002) 'Taming the beast: an assessment of the fraud risk implications of the electronification of the US payments system', *Journal of Economic Crime Management,* 1(1).

Kalakota, Ravi and Marcia Robinson (1999) *E-Business: Roadmap for Success.* Reading, MA: Addison-Wesley.

Kalakota, Ravi and Andrew B. Whinston (1997) *Electronic Commerce: A Manager's Guide.* Reading, MA: Addison-Wesley.

Katz, Jack (1988) *Seductions of Crime: Moral and Sensual Attractions in Doing Evil.* New York: Basic Books.

Keeling, James E. (2001) 'Social engineering – for the good guys', 16 July, http://www.sans.org/infosecFAQ/policy/social_good.htm.

Key Note (1999) 'Home Shopping Report', January, UK: http://www.keynote.co.uk.

Key Note (2001) 'Home Shopping Report', January, UK: http://www.keynote.co.uk.

Key Note (2002) 'Home Shopping Report', January, UK: http://www.keynote.co.uk.

Kleinig, John (2000) 'The burdens of situational crime prevention: an ethical commentary', in Andrew von Hirsch, David Garland and Alison Wakefield (eds), *Ethical and Social Perspectives on Situational Crime Prevention.* Oxford: Hart Publishing, pp. 4–42.

Kutler, J. (2000) 'A lucky break-in?', *Institutional Investor,* 34(2) 22.

Laudon, Ken (1986) *The Dossier Society: Value Choices in the Design of National Information Systems.* New York: Columbia University Press.

Law Commission (1988) *Computer Misuse,* Working Paper No. 110. London: HMSO.

Law Commission of Canada (2002) *In Search of Security: The Roles of Public Police and Private Agencies: Discussion Paper,* Her Majesty the Queen in Right of Canada: http://www.lcc.gc.ca.

Laycock, Gloria and Nick Tilley (1995) 'Implementing crime prevention programmes', in M. Tonry and D. Farrington (eds), *Building a Safer Society, Crime and Justice: A Review of Research.* Chicago: University of Chicago Press.

Levi, M. (2000) *The Prevention of Plastic and Cheque Fraud: A Briefing Paper.* London: Home Office Research, Development and Statistics Directorate.

Levi, Michael (2001) 'Between risk and reality falls the shadow': evidence and urban legends in computer fraud', in David S. Wall (ed.), *Crime and the Internet*. London: Routledge, chapter 4.

Levi, M. and J. Handley (1998a) *Prevention of Plastic Card Fraud*, Crime Prevention Unit Paper 71. London: Home Office.

Levi, M. and J. Handley (1998b) *The Prevention of Plastic and Cheque Fraud Revisited*, Home Office Research Study 182. London: Home Office Research, Development and Statistics Directorate.

Levi, M., P. Bissell and T. Richardson (1991) *The Prevention of Cheque and Credit Card Fraud*. Crime Prevention Unit Paper No. 26. London: Home Office

Levy, Steven (1984) *Hackers: Heroes of the Computer Revolution*. New York: Bantam/Doubleday.

Lisker, J. (1994) 'Card of armor', *Security Management*, March, 38(3).

Lombardi, Rosie (1998) 'Shopping in cyberspace', *Camagazine*, April, 35–6.

Lyon, David (1994) *The Electronic Eye: The Rise of the Surveillance Society*. Cambridge: Polity Press.

Lyon, David and Elias Zureik (eds) (1996) *Computers, Surveillance and Privacy*. Minneapolis, MN: University of Minnesota Press.

McKinnon, Alan and Deepak Tallam (2002) *New Crime Threats from Ecommerce: Theft in the Home Delivery Channel*, Foresight Panel Crime Prevention Programme, UK Home Office Programme: http://www.foresight.gov.uk/default1024.htm.

McMillen, Jan and Peter Grabosky (1998) 'Internet gambling', *Trends and Issues in Criminal Justice* (Australian Institute of Criminology), no. 88, June.

Mann, Catherine L., Sue E. Eckert and Sarah Cleeland Knight (2000) *Global Electronic Commerce: A Policy Primer*. Washington, DC: Institute for International Economics.

Mann, David and Mike Sutton (1998) 'Netcrime', *British Journal of Criminology*, 38(2): 201–29.

Maremont, M. (1995) 'A magnetic mug shot on your credit card?', *Business Week*, 24 April, Science and Technology, p. 3421.

Marrinan, M. (1995) 'In the chips', *Bank Systems*, 32(5).

Marx, Gary T. (2001) 'Identity and anonymity: some conceptual distinctions and issues for research', in J. Caplan and J. Torpey (eds), *Documenting Individual Identity*. Princeton, NJ: Princeton University Press.

Marx, Karl. (1977) *Capital Vol. 1*, trans. Ben Fowkes. New York: Vintage.

Nader, Ralph (1966) *Unsafe at Anew york Speed*. New York: Pocket Books.

Nalla, Mahesh and Graeme Newman (1990) *A Primer in Private Security*. New York: Harrow & Heston.

Newman, Graeme R. (1997) 'Introduction: towards a theory of situational crime prevention', in Graeme Newman, Ronald V. Clarke and S. Giora Shoham (eds), *Rational Choice and Situational Crime Prevention*. Aldershot: Ashgate, pp. 1–24.

Newman, Graeme R. and Pietro Marongiu (1997) 'In Graeme Newman, Ronald V. Clarke and S. Giora Shoham (eds), *Rational Choice and Situational Crime Prevention*. Aldershot: Ashgate, pp. 115–62.

Newman, O. (1972) *Defensible Space: Crime Prevention Through Urban Design*. New York: Macmillan (published by Architectural Press, London, in 1973).

Newton, John, Det. Chief Insp. (1994) *Organised 'Plastic' Counterfeiting*. London: Home Office.

Nimmer, R. T. (1985) *The Law of Computer Technology*. New York: John Wiley.

Norman, Paul (2001) 'Policing "high tech" crime within the global context', in David S. Wall (ed.), *Crime and the Internet*. London: Routledge, chapter 12.

Nunno, Richard M. (2001) 'Electronic signatures: technology developments and legislative issues', *Government Information Quarterly*, vol. 17, no. 4.

Opp, Karl-Dieter (1997) ' "Limited rationality" and crime', in Graeme Newman, Ronald V. Clarke and S. Giora Shoham (eds), *Rational Choice and Situational Crime Prevention*. Aldershot: Ashgate, pp. 47–64.

O'Shaughnessy, John (1987) *Why People Buy*. New York: Oxford University Press.

Pamatatau, R. (1997) 'Visa sees smart cards as weapon against forgers', *NZ Infotech Weekly*, 6 October, News, National.

Plowden, William (1971) *The Motor Car and Politics 1896–1970*. London: Bodley Head,

Polding, L. (1996) 'Credit card fraud – the good news', *Credit Control,* 17(5).

Postman, N. (1993) *Technopoly: The Surrender of Culture to Technology*. New York: Vintage.

Poyner, Barry and Barry Webb (1997) 'Reducing theft from shopping bags in city centre markets', in Ronald V. Clarke (ed.), *Situational Crime Prevention: Successful Case Studies*, 2nd edn. New York: Harrow & Heston.

Prophet, Graham (2000) 'RFID and the smart label; bye-bye bar code?', *EDN Europe*, June, vol. 45, no. 6.

Rao, Bharat (1999) 'The Internet and the revolution in distribution: a cross-industry examination', *Technology in Society*, 21: 287–306.

Revkin, Andrew C. (2002) 'Can the corner mailbox be locked against terror?' *New York Times*, 10 September, F1 and F4.

Riesman, David, Nathan Glazer and Reuel Denney (2001) *The Lonely Crowd: A Study of the Changing American Character*. Hartford, CT: Yale University Press, abridged and revised edition.

Rousseau, Jean Jacques (1947) *The Social Contract and Discourse*. trans. and intro. G. D. H. Cole. London: Everyman's Library, J. M. Dent & Sons.

Rule, James (1973) *Private Lives, Public Surveillance*. London: Allan & Unwin.

Schieck, M. (1995) *Combating Fraud in Cable and Telecommunications*, ICC Communications Topics, No. 13. London: International Institute of Communications.

Schultz, E. Eugene and Thomas Longstaff (1998) 'Internet sniffer attacks', in Dorothy E. Denning and Peter J. Denning (eds), *Internet Besieged*. New York: Addison-Wesley, chapter 9.

Schwartz, Evan I. (2002/3) 'How you'll pay', *Technology Review*, December/January, pp. 50–7.

Shearing, Clifford D. and Phillip C. Stenning (1987) 'From Panopticon to Disney World: the development of discipline', in Shearing and Stenning (eds), *Private Policing*. Beverley Hills, CA: Sage.

Shearing, Clifford D. and Phillip Stenning (1997) 'From the Panopticon to Disneyworld: the development of discipline', in Ronald V. Clarke (ed.), *Situational Crime Prevention: Successful Case Studies, 2nd edn*. New York: Harrow & Heston, pp. 300–4.

Smith, Adam (1998) [1776] *An Inquiry into the Wealth of Nations*. London: Oxford.

Smith, Russell G. (1999) 'Identity-related economic crime: risks and countermeasures', *Trends and Issues* (Australian Institute of Criminology), September, no. 129.

Smith, Russell G. (2001) 'Cross-border economic crime: the agenda for reform', *Trends and Issues in Crime and Criminal Justice* (Australian Institute of Criminology), no. 202, April.

Smith, Russell G., Nicholas Wolanin and Glenn Worthington (forthcoming 2003) 'E-crime solutions and crime displacement', *Trends and Issues in Crime and Criminal Justice* (Australian Institute of Criminology).

Staples, Willam G. (1997) *The Culture of Surveillance: Discipline and Social Control in the United States*. New York: St. Martin's Press.

Staples, Willam G. (2000) *Everyday Surveillance: Vigilance and Visibility in Postmodern Life*.New York: Rowman & Littlefield.

Steel, J. (1995) 'Combating counterfeit credit cards: the technological challenge', *Credit World*, 83(5).

Stoll, C. (1989) *The Cuckoo's Egg*. New York: Doubleday.

Sutton, M. (1995) 'Supply by theft: does the market for stolen goods play a role in keeping crime figures high?', *British Journal of Criminology*, 35(3): 400–16.

Taylor, P.A. (2000) 'Hackers – cyberpunks or microserfs?', in Douglas Thomas and Brian Loader (eds), *Cyber Crime*. London: Routledge.

Taylor, Paul (2001) 'Hacktivism: in search of lost ethics?', in David S. Wall (ed.), *Crime and the Internet*. London: Routledge, chapter 5.

Thomsen, Roszel C. II and Antoinette D. Paytas (2001) 'US to EU! The United States amends its export controls of encryption, responding to recent developments in the European Union', *Computer Law and Security Report*, 17(1).

Underhill, Paco (2000) *Why We Buy*. New York: Touchstone.

United States General Accounting Office (1998) *Identity Fraud*. Briefing report to congressional requesters.

US Department of Justice (1999) *Cyberstalking: A New Challenge for Law Enforcement and Industry,* US DOJ at: http://www.usdoj.gov/criminal/cybercrime/cyberstalking.htm.

Verton, Dan (2002) *The Hacker Diaries.* New York: McGraw-Hill Osborne.

von Hirsch, Andrew (2000) 'The ethics of public television surveillance', in Andrew von Hirsch, David Garland and Alison Wakefield (eds), *Ethical and Social Perspectives on Situational Crime Prevention.* Oxford: Hart Publishing.

von Hirsch, Andrew, David Garland and Alison Wakefield (eds) (2000) *Ethical and Social Perspectives on Situational Crime Prevention.* Oxford: Hart Publishing.

Wall, David S. (2001) 'Maintaining order and law on the Internet', in David S. Wall (ed.), *Crime and the Internet.* London: Routledge.

Wasik, Martin (1991) *Crime and the Computer.* Oxford: Clarendon Press.

Westin, Alan F. (1967) *Privacy and Freedom.* New York: Atheneum.

Wilkins, Leslie T. (1997) 'Wartime operational research in Britain and situational crime prevention', in Graeme Newman, Ronald V. Clarke and S. Giora Shoham (eds), *Rational Choice and Situational Crime Prevention.* Aldershot: Ashgate, pp. 163–78.

Williams, F. (1988) 'The information society as a subject of study', in F. Williams (ed.), *Measuring the Information Society.* Beverly Hills, CA: Sage, pp. 13–15.

Williams, Phil (1997) 'Emerging issues: transnational crime and its control', in Graeme Newman (ed.), *Global Report on Crime and Justice.* New York: Oxford/UNCICP.

Willox Jr, Norman A., Thomas M. Regan and Cozen O'Connor (2002) 'Identity fraud: providing a solution', *Journal of Economic Crime Management,* Summer, 1(1).

Wilson, J. Q. and G. Kelling (1982) 'Broken windows: the police and neighbourhood safety', *Atlantic Monthly,* March, pp. 29–37.

Wortley, Richard (1996) 'Guilt, shame and situational crime prevention', in Ross Homel (ed.), *The Politics and Practice of Situational Crime Prevention,* Crime Prevention Studies Vol. 5. Monsey, NY: Criminal Justice Press, pp. 115–33.

Wortley, Richard (1997) 'Reconsidering the role of opportunity in situational crime prevention', in Graeme Newman, Ronald V. Clarke and S. Giora Shoham (eds), *Rational Choice and Situational Crime Prevention.* Aldershot: Ashgate, pp. 65–81.

Wortley, Richard (2002) *Situational Prison Control. Crime Prevention in Correctional Institutions.* Cambridge: Cambridge University Press.

Index